The Short Oxford History of

General Editor: Paul Langford

The British Isles: 1901–1951

Edited by Keith Robbins

AVAILABLE NOW

The Roman Era
edited by Peter Salway

The Twelfth and Thirteenth Centuries
edited by Barbara Harvey

The Sixteenth Century
edited by Patrick Collinson

The Eighteenth Century
edited by Paul Langford

The Nineteenth Century
edited by Colin Matthew

The British Isles: 1901–1951
edited by Keith Robbins

The British Isles since 1945
edited by Kathleen Burk

IN PREPARATION, VOLUMES COVERING

From the Romans to the Vikings
From the Vikings to the Normans
The Fourteenth and Fifteenth Centuries
The Seventeenth Century

Plate 1 The Canadian Prime Minister declared that Canada stood 'shoulder to shoulder with Britain and the other British Dominions in this quarrel'.

The Short Oxford History
of the British Isles

General Editor: Paul Langford

The British Isles

1901–1951

Edited by Keith Robbins

OXFORD
UNIVERSITY PRESS

OXFORD
UNIVERSITY PRESS

Great Clarendon Street, Oxford OX2 6DP

Oxford University Press is a department of the University of Oxford.
It furthers the University's objective of excellence in research, scholarship,
and education by publishing worldwide in

Oxford New York

Auckland Bangkok Buenos Aires Cape Town Chennai
Dar es Salaam Delhi Hong Kong Istanbul Karachi Kolkata
Kuala Lumpur Madrid Melbourne Mexico City Mumbai Nairobi
São Paulo Shanghai Singapore Taipei Tokyo Toronto

with an associated company in Berlin

Published in the United States
by Oxford University Press Inc., New York

British Library Cataloguing in Publication Data
Data available

Library of Congress Cataloging in Publication Data
Data applied for
ISBN 0–19–8731957 (hbk)
ISBN 0–19–8731965 (pbk)

10 9 8 7 6 5 4 3 2 1

Typeset in Minion
by RefineCatch Limited, Bungay, Suffolk
Printed in Great Britain by
T.J. International Ltd, Padstow, Cornwall

General Editor's Preface

It is a truism that historical writing is itself culturally determined, reflecting intellectual fashions, political preoccupations, and moral values at the time it is written. In the case of British history this has resulted in a great diversity of perspectives both on the content of what is narrated and the geopolitical framework in which it is placed. In recent times the process of redefinition has positively accelerated under the pressure of contemporary change. Some of it has come from within Britain during a period of recurrent racial tension in England and reviving nationalism in Scotland, Wales, and Northern Ireland. But much of it also comes from beyond. There has been a powerful surge of interest in the politics of national identity in response to the break-up of some of the world's great empires, both colonial and continental. The search for new sovereignties, not least in Europe itself, has contributed to a questioning of long-standing political boundaries. Such shifting of the tectonic plates of history is to be expected but for Britain especially, with what is perceived (not very accurately) to be a long period of relative stability lasting from the late seventeenth century to the mid-twentieth century, it has had a particular resonance.

Much controversy and still more confusion arise from the lack of clarity about the subject matter that figures in insular historiography. Historians of England are often accused of ignoring the history of Britain as a whole, while using the terms as if they are synonymous. Historians of Britain are similarly charged with taking Ireland's inclusion for granted without engaging directly with it. And for those who believe they are writing more specifically the history of Ireland, of Wales, or of Scotland, there is the unending tension between so-called metropolis and periphery, and the dilemmas offered by wider contexts, not only British and Irish but European and indeed extra-European. Some of these difficulties arise from the fluctuating fortunes and changing boundaries of the British state as organized from London. But even if the rulers of what is now called England had never taken an interest in dominion beyond its borders, the economic and cultural relationships between the various parts of the British Isles would still have generated many historiographical problems.

This series is based on the premise that whatever the complexities and ambiguities created by this state of affairs, it makes sense to offer an overview, conducted by leading scholars whose research is on the leading edge of their discipline. That overview extends to the whole of the British Isles. The expression is not uncontroversial, especially to many in Ireland, for whom the very word 'British' implies an unacceptable politics of dominion. Yet there is no other formulation that can encapsulate the shared experience of 'these islands', to use another term much employed in Ireland and increasingly heard in Britain, but rather unhelpful to other inhabitants of the planet.

In short we use the words 'British Isles' solely and simply as a geographical expression. No set agenda is implied. It would indeed be difficult to identify one that could stand scrutiny. What constitutes a concept such as 'British history' or 'four nations history', remains the subject of acute disagreement, and varies much depending on the period under discussion. The editors and contributors of this series have been asked only to convey the findings of the most authoritative scholarship, and to flavour them with their own interpretative originality and distinctiveness. In the process we hope to provide not only a stimulating digest of more than two thousand years of history, but also a sense of the intense vitality that continues to mark historical research into the past of all parts of Britain and Ireland.

Lincoln College   PAUL LANGFORD
Oxford

Contents

List of plates

List of maps

List of contributors

DAVID DUTTON, is Reader in History at the University of Liverpool and Visiting Professor in Humanities at Bolton Institute. His publications include *Anthony Eden: A Life and Reputation, British Politics since 1945: The Rise, Fall and Rebirth of Consensus*, and *Neville Chamberlain*.

W. R. GARSIDE, formerly Professor of Economic History at the University of Birmingham, is now Professor of History and Head of Department at the University of Otago, New Zealand. He has written extensively on government economic policy in twentieth-century Britain and is currently engaged on a comparative study of government/industry relations in Britain and Japan since 1945.

KEITH JEFFERY is Professor of Modern History at the University of Ulster. Among his books are: *The British Army and the Crisis of Empire, 1918–22, States of Emergency: British Governments and Strike-breaking since 1919* (with Peter Hennessy), *'An Irish Empire'? Aspects of Ireland and the British Empire, A Military History of Ireland* (with Thomas Bartlett), and *Ireland and the Great War*.

RODNEY LOWE is Professor of Contemporary History at the University of Bristol. He has published widely on British and comparative social history and policy. His major works include *Adjusting to Democracy, The Welfare State in Britain since 1945*, and *From Beveridge to Blair*.

SIÂN NICHOLAS is a Lecturer in Modern British History at the University of Wales Aberystwyth. Her research is in the field of British media history and national culture. She is the author of *The Echo of War: Home Front Propaganda and the Wartime BBC 1939–45*.

KEITH ROBBINS is Vice-Chancellor of the University of Wales Lampeter. He has published widely on modern British and International history. Pertinent to this volume are: *The Eclipse of a Great Power: Modern Britain 1870–1992, Politicians, Diplomacy and War in Modern British History, History, Religion and Identity in Modern Britain, Bibliography of British History 1914–1989*, and *Great Britain: Identities, Institutions and the Idea of Britishness*.

DUNCAN TANNER is Professor of History at the University of Wales Bangor. His publications include *Political Change and the Labour Party 1900–18* and two centenary histories of the Labour Party: *Labour's First Century* (edited with Pat Thane and Nick Tiratsoo) and *The Labour Party in Wales* (edited with Chris Williams and Deian Hopkin).

Plate 2 'Blessed are the ties that bind' —as they appeared in 1912.

Introduction: Halfway House— Isles and Empire over half a century

Keith Robbins

Signs of the times

Historians are always uneasy about the 'periods' with which they conventionally work. Why choose one set of dates rather than another to begin and end a particular book? It has often seemed convenient to take a century as a reasonable period within which to consider the development of one country. And, while such a practice remains common, some historians kick against the constraints which they feel are imposed by the mere passage of a century or half a century. They seek to escape from what they regard as arbitrary periodization dictated by the calendar and instead define their periods by allegedly more meaningful considerations and characteristics. For this reason, some 'centuries' have a habit of becoming 'long' centuries which extend forwards or backwards. Such 'long' centuries are then begun or ended by a specific event or events, cataclysmic or otherwise. The 'long nineteenth' is one such century in British history, and it is often thought to reach its 'real' conclusion by the catastrophe of the First World War. After that deluge, nothing could ever be the same again: an era had passed.

In this series, however, the nineteenth century ends in 1901, and the preceding volume was not allowed the luxury of a supposed 'logical' extension. However, this was no mere acquiescence in the thoughtless tyranny of the calendar. Arbitrary or not, the passage of a century is often a moment for taking stock. There is a seemingly irresistible tendency, manifest also at the beginning of the (millennial) twenty-first century, to use such a juncture as an occasion to ponder on the past and anticipate the future. 'The Victorian Era has definitely closed,' wrote Charles Masterman, journalist, politician, and social commentator, in the opening sentence to a volume entitled *The Heart of Empire* (1901). The forces which characterized that era had been expended and 'new problems were arising with a new age'. The fact that the death of Queen Victoria and of the nineteenth century so closely corresponded gave a certain public emphasis to change—but it was happening across the board anyway. Nature and time, as he put it, spared nothing, however customary, honoured, and secure. The volume which he edited had as its subtitle *Discussions of Problems of Modern City Life in England, with an essay on Imperialism*. Some critics condemned the linking of these two aspects of contemporary life. In a subsequent popular edition, however, Masterman was impenitent. There was no sharp delimitation of home and foreign affairs: the two were closely intertwined. The forces which made for unrest abroad were the same as stifled progress at home. The present could never take refuge behind the past.

That was all very well, surviving Victorians thought, but it was not clear that the present was an improvement on the past, and the future might be worse than the present. In 1908, A. J. Balfour, lately Prime Minister and now once again philosopher at large, thought that a lecture on 'Decadence' would be appropriately delivered at the University of Cambridge. 'What grounds', he asked, 'are there for supposing that we can escape the fate to which other races have had to submit?' His audience would have listened in vain for an answer that was either transparent or reassuring.

In the early 1900s plenty of other writers were prepared to ponder and speculate about the future. Some caught glimpses of 'new women' and thought that there was going to be a dramatic shift in gender roles and functions. Some sought to devise 'new theology' for a new century. Only rarely did it seem pertinent to such British commentators to suppose that they should focus narrowly, as they would have perceived it, upon 'the British Isles'. A 'British Isles', such as now exists at the beginning of the twenty-first century, understandably eluded the most ardent forecasters of 'things to come', whether considered from the standpoint of population, government, economy, or culture. Nevertheless, there was some sense that a crisis might be approaching in the relationship between the British Isles and those 'nations beyond the seas' that 'the British' (and more ambiguously the Irish) were busily building up within the British Empire. The outcome of such a crisis would determine whether, at some point, the British Isles would revert to being an internally complicated and somewhat fractious cluster of communities offshore from 'Europe' or whether they would still constitute the hub of an integrated global British enterprise: Project Greater Britain. Seeking to interpret *Some Signs of the Times* (1903), the then well-known Nonconformist preacher R. J. Campbell wondered whether 'our best are parting from us'. It was, he thought, a glorious thing that the country's young manhood would be carrying on the tradition of England overseas, but he was 'full of misgiving if our best leave us and our second best never try to rise'.

Ideals and realities

Whatever the future might hold, the fact was that the 'British Isles' of 1901 could not be disentangled from the world in whose development their people continued to play so large a part. The 'space' the British/ Irish occupied was far from being confined within insular limits. The study of geopolitics—examining the relationship between the geographical environment and national and international politics—took off in Europe and America in the early twentieth century. The most prominent British theoretician was Sir Halford Mackinder in *Britain and the British Seas* (1902), a title which itself gives the flavour of his concerns. Later, in *Democratic Ideals and Reality* (1919), Mackinder developed the concept that the three contiguous continents (Asia, Europe, and Africa) formed a 'world island', with America and Australia as lesser 'islands while the smaller Far Eastern islands were satellites. He identified a 'heartland' on the 'world island', and concluded that whoever ruled East Europe commanded the heartland, whoever ruled the heartland commanded the world island, and whoever ruled the world island commanded the world. Whether such theories now stand up is not the point. Their existence illustrated the extent to which there was a contemporary desire to place the islands in their global context. No history of the British Isles, short or long, it was argued, should neglect the constraints and opportunities provided by the seas in which they were placed. Nor could one ignore the extent to which they constituted, perhaps unpalatably, satellites of a continental 'mainland', even though their inhabitants only reluctantly, if at all, thought of themselves with Europe as their 'mainland'. It is this tension between 'democratic ideals' and 'reality', between the defence of 'the British Isles' and the preservation of the 'British Empire', between the unity of the British Isles and the accommodation of their diversity, between the demands and expectations of 'Britons' 'at home' and the problems of 'abroad', between optimism and pessimism about the future, and between social reform and imperial grandeur, which helps to give the first fifty years of the twentieth century some unity and coherence. These pressures were by no means entirely new, but as the decades passed they proved more and more difficult to reconcile.

Looking back from the early years of the twenty-first century, it is difficult to grasp the extent to which these confusing dualities still ran deep through almost every aspect of insular life. One might, indeed, almost ask whether it makes sense to think of a linear continuity between the British Isles as conceived in 1901 and the British Isles as conceived in 2001. At first sight, it might seem obvious that it is still 'the same country', but closer examination presents a rather more complicated picture. The British Empire, which loomed so large in 1901, is no more. It is likely, though one can never be sure, that historians of the first fifty years of the twenty-first century will be predominantly concerned with the two states (at least?) of the British Isles in the European Union and the fundamentally different context which that entails in comparison with the situation in 1901. If this does turn out to be the case, it is likely that the first half of the twentieth century will stand out as an age of awkward transition, brought to its close globally by independence in the Indian sub continent in 1947–50 and insularly by the confirmation of the Irish Republic. The British Empire would linger, in different parts of the world, for some decades after those years, but a fundamental step had been taken. Its implications for colonies elsewhere were unavoidable. The sun would set on the British Empire. The second half of the century, from such a perspective, consisted of a protracted, painful, and perhaps still unresolved adjustment to post-imperial reality coupled with the return to prominence of identity issues and their political implications within the British Isles themselves.

For most of the first fifty years, however, it was not self-evident that the great British Empire would and should come to an end. Winston Churchill had famously declared in 1942 that he had not become the King's First Minister in order to preside over the liquidation of the British Empire. Critics of Empire had become increasingly vocal since J. A. Hobson's *Imperialism* (1902) but their case had by no means triumphed, even though Donald Cowie, author of *An Empire Prepared* (1939) for the Right Book Club, lamented: 'London to-day is lousy with parasites who would theoretically have the British renounce their possessions, and who are to be found in practice to be the chief beneficiaries from these possessions.' Even in 1950, it could still be thought precipitate and perilous to effect such a 'renunciation'. Until that point, however, what the British Empire could and should mean was ambiguous territory for politicians and public alike. The period constituted an extended interlude during which it became clear that the high noon of Empire was over but during which its ultimate fate remained obscure. Now, although the distant trumpets of Empire can still be heard, their resonance diminishes with every passing decade. In these circumstances, it is not easy to cope with the first fifty years of the twentieth century in their relation both to the preceding century and to the twenty-first century.

A matter of balance

It is now hard for historians to agree on how best to deal with a country whose twentieth-century history has undergone such a profound transformation. Although contributors to this volume do not completely agree amongst themselves, and the same events are sometimes interpreted differently, there is general agreement that what gives the British Isles their distinct flavour during the decades under consideration is this sense of their being awkwardly and ambivalently poised between a high imperial and a post-imperial age. The emphasis placed in various sections on the 'British/Irish' issue within 'the British Isles' and on 'the British Isles' within 'the British Empire/ Commonwealth' sets this volume apart from the approaches adopted by two distinguished recent historians who have grappled with these issues. It is instructive to see how and why this is the case.

In his *A History of the Modern British Isles 1914–1999* (2000), Arthur Marwick seems almost to have forgotten that a British Empire existed. It merits no entry in his index, and there is only passing and almost incidental mention of its twentieth-century evolution. Of course, the author is in fact well aware that there was a British Empire, but he has evidently taken the view that at best it has only tangential significance as far as the 'British Isles' is concerned and need make no appearance in an account which is devoted to their post-1914 history. His volume, however, avowedly does address 'the British Isles' as a whole and make some assessment of the relationships between its constituent 'territories' of the United Kingdom, but in so doing strips them of that 'imperial destiny' which in the first fifty years arguably still served, to a greater or lesser degree, to subdue centrifugal forces. It is, however, not an account of the British Isles if that term is taken to involve an assessment of how the territories of the island of Ireland relate to each other and, separately, how they relate to Great Britain. Peter Clarke, on the other hand, in *Hope and Glory: Britain 1900–1990* (1996), with a perspective that remains substantially Anglocentric, despite some gestures outside England, does indeed give specific attention to issues concerning the development of the British Empire/British Commonwealth/Commonwealth—but within a framework which still suggests that a state called 'Britain' nonetheless carried on pretty much unchanged as a continuing entity until 1990. It has not done so thereafter, and that it has not done so should not come as a great surprise. The implication of this book is that 'the second fifty years' deal, increasingly as time goes on, with a United Kingdom/British Isles/'Isles' which emerges as a fundamentally different entity from what it had been in the first fifty years of the century. While it would be a mistake to fix too firmly on one particular date in this connection, it is around the fact of there being such a turning point at mid-century that this volume is structured. The transitions vary in completeness and velocity, as specific chapters show, but all reveal a period which witnessed the undermining of a bi-insular United Kingdom within the British Isles, and of a Greater Britain on the world stage.

Notwithstanding the rhetoric surrounding 'new century', however, and the sense which contemporaries had—whether they approved or not—that a new age of rampant hedonism was dawning as King and people sprung themselves gleefully from a Victorian straitjacket, there is no gainsaying that contemporaries also felt that this 'Edwardian' age, characterized in retrospect sometimes by images of glamour and sometimes of squalor, came to an end in 1914. Many accounts of modern British history have indeed either begun or ended in 1914. In his *English History 1914–1945* (1965), A. J. P. Taylor began his book by remarking that until August 1914 a sensible, law-abiding Englishman would hardly notice the existence of the state, beyond the post office and the policeman. He had no official number or identity card, could live where he liked and as he liked (just a touch of exaggeration here?), and could travel abroad without passport or permission. He was under no obligation to perform military service. Broadly speaking, the state acted only to help those who could not help themselves. All of this and more, Taylor suggested, was changed by the impact of the Great War. The state established a hold over its citizens which, though relaxed in peacetime, 'was never to be removed and which the Second World war was again to increase'. The history of the English state (as Taylor called it) and the English people merged for the first time.

Total war

In a variety of books over recent decades Arthur Marwick has also emphasized the centrality of the Great War. He concedes that there is room for legitimate debate about the precise effects of the Great War on virtually every aspect of British life, and perhaps also on the extent to which the changes that did take place were temporary or permanent in their impact. These are matters on which, in detail, historians do indeed differ. Marwick is surely right, however, to emphasize that 'without an understanding of the dimensions and nature of the Great War, there can be no complete understanding of Britain in the twentieth century'. The literature on that war is of course enormous. Few would doubt that it is appropriate to regard it as 'the first total war', even though that term can be variously interpreted. The upheaval transformed the lives of individuals and communities. There could be no complete return to the status quo ante. The British shared substantially in the experience of other European belligerent peoples. In cultural terms, Jay Winter has powerfully emphasized the European character of the war. 'Victory' or 'defeat' certainly created different subsequent climates for the countries concerned, but the path of collective slaughter was common. Victory had a taste of ashes, as he puts it. In forming a massive army from a small professional base the British conformed more than hitherto to a European 'norm'. Even so, there were important differences. Britain was not itself the site of battle. Although there were moments of anxiety about the maintenance of food supplies, the British people did not suffer the near-starvation which afflicted east-central Europe.

However, what the totality of the experience of the war meant for contemporaries defied their own capacity to explain—as it has defied subsequent historians. There was no single 'experience' which could be cashed in at a certain value but rather a multiplicity of experiences and emotions. How did one balance heroism and horror? Some men could not speak at all of what they had seen and done. There seemed often to be an unbridgeable gulf between those who had fought and their families at home. Whether the war created a comparable unbridgeable gulf between 'tradition' and 'the modern' has been the subject of continuing lively debate amongst literary scholars. Winter argues against the bifurcation of the cultural history of the war into 'high' and 'low', 'cultivated' and 'uncultivated'. The invocation of the dead constitutes, to his mind, an unmistakable sign of the commonality of European cultural life in this period. As is always the case, much depends in these debates upon the significance attached to these terms. For J. B. Priestley, First World War officer in France, successful interwar novelist and commentator, and Second World War prophet of better times, the Great War was *the* awful caesura. If it had not happened, or if it had been brought to an end 'before the worst took over from the best, the centre, not only in politics but in literature, might have held'. Others have pointed to the paradox, if that is what it is, that the greatest 'modernists' of the British Isles writing in the 1920s and 1930s—Yeats, Joyce, Eliot, Huxley, Lawrence—did not themselves participate in the war.

And, despite everything, the First World War, 'the war to end war', was followed by a Second. It was different both in character and in consequence, as subsequent chapters illustrate. Taken together, however, the two wars serve to demonstrate the extent to which what now stands out about 'the first fifty years' for the British Isles is the extent to which they were 'war-laden'. In a previous book, *The Eclipse of a Great Power: Modern Britain 1870–1975* (1983)—a second edition continued to 1992 (1994)—this author structured it into parts in such a way that one began in 1901 and ended in 1931 and the next began in 1931 and ended in 1956. This has led to some suggestion that no special significance is thereby attached to the two total wars. Insofar as my volume does not divide at 1914/18 or at 1939/45 the charge clearly has some substance. Now, however, at a greater distance in time, placing the two total wars in the middle of the two chronological divisions referred to may be thought to have greater logic than was originally apparent. The wars were indeed of great importance but neither came totally out of the blue. Between 1902 (when the South African war was concluded) and 1914 rumour of war was rife. The 'peace' of 1919 perhaps only had confident substance for a decade, and then with some fragility. Although naturally it is only in retrospect that historians can write as C. L. Mowat did of *Britain between the Wars, 1918–1940* (1955) or provide sections with that heading in works covering longer periods, the sense of these decades constituting a 'peace' that was precarious rather than permanent was never far away at the time. While it cannot be altogether claimed, when the Cold War was at its height, that peace was ensured, the expectations of the decades in Britain after the 1950s have been significantly different from those which obtained either before 1914 or before 1939. It is the case, in Korea and elsewhere, that Britain since 1951 has been involved in various conflicts, but their scale and the kind of national commitment they have entailed bear scant comparison with those of 'the first fifty years' when rumour of war and the reality of war was almost constant. As far as Britain was concerned, the twentieth did not turn out to be the century of total war but rather half a century—and it is the extent to which that has been the case which gives the first half its commonality of atmosphere and experience. In this connection, the possibility of nuclear war in the second half has further contributed in a major way to the demonization of war and a distancing of British society from values and beliefs which were held to be vital for national survival. It has progressively created a chasm between the two halves of the century which is not easily bridged.

Passing glory?

The point is poignantly made if we focus again on the figure of Winston Churchill, talismanic in war and the epitome of British defiance and resolution when all might have seemed lost. Geoffrey Best, his recent biographer, observes that 'glory' to Churchill's way of thinking was something which entire peoples could attain through shared achievement and self-assertion in the world. Historically, that meant by force of arms. The British people, however, are no longer comfortable in a war-accepting state of mind. Glory has had its day and there is embarrassment about the very concept of 'dying for your country' (the resolute Falklands campaign of 1982 caused only a momentary return to old heroic moulds). The question the biographer leaves open, however, is whether there is much of an improvement in not knowing whether there is anything in your country worth fighting for, whether you belong to this country or that, or even whether you belong to any distinctive country at all. If that is the condition of 2001, it was certainly not that of 1901 or of 1951.

Plate 3 Harold Nelson's design for the British Empire Exhibition stamp, embodying the confidence of an apparently secure imperial system. This was the first ever British commemorative stamp and was issued in two values, 1d. and 1½d., which between them would take a letter to any part of the Empire.

British Isles/British Empire: dual mandate/dual identity

Keith Jeffery

The Empire in the new century

'The dawn of the twentieth century finds us in possession of an Empire of which every Briton has cause to be proud,' wrote Clement Kinloch-Cooke in the February 1901 inaugural issue of the *Empire Review*. 'It extends to every quarter of the globe, embracing every kind of climate and producing every kind of commodity.' Kinloch-Cooke, imperial enthusiast and for twenty years a Conservative MP, edited the *Review* until his death in 1944. Seven years later the journal, briefly retitled the *Commonwealth and Empire Review*, went out of business, thus broadly reflecting the experience of the Empire itself. Yet the first fifty years of the twentieth century encompassed the apotheosis of the British Empire, the moment when it reached its zenith and was more unified, coherent, and powerful a world system than at any other time in its existence. But a summit is also a moment of decline, and the paradox of this half century is that the forces and developments which carried the empire to the peak of its power also contributed to its dissolution.

For Kinloch-Cooke, the opening of the new century was an

especially propitious moment for the founding of his new journal. Britons, both at home and in the colonies, he asserted, had in recent years neglected the 'imperial aspect'. But the Anglo-Boer War, which had broken out in 1899, had certainly concentrated minds. 'It has', he wrote, 'required a war to bring home to us the living reality of those places, great and small, painted red on the map of the universe.' Indeed, the map of the world with its great splashes of red was one of the most characteristic and iconic images of the British Empire at its apogee. At the turn of the twentieth century it was, truly, an Empire upon which 'the sun never set', and to most observers at home or abroad the British imperial edifice looked virtually indestructible.

The remarkable scale of the Empire was exemplified above all by the British possessions in south Asia, where 'the British Empire in India' extended over a territory larger than the entire continent of Europe, only excluding Russia, and comprised territory covering the modern states of Bangladesh, India, Myanmar (formerly Burma), and Pakistan. Around the Indian Ocean, Kenya (with Uganda inland), Somaliland in the Horn of Africa, Aden (South Yemen), Ceylon (Sri Lanka), the Malay States (Malaysia), and Singapore were all part of 'Greater Britain'. Substantial parts of West Africa, of which the largest was Nigeria, and east-central Africa, including today's Malawi, Zambia, and Zimbabwe, were British, as was Natal and the Cape Colony in southern Africa. While the Indian possessions included the largest population—an estimated 312 million people in 1900 (as against 41 million in the United Kingdom)—both Canada and Australia were larger in terms of area. But British North America (which included Newfoundland) and Australia, along with New Zealand, differed from other parts of the Empire in that their populations of white British settlers had come greatly to outnumber the indigenous non-white communities in each territory. This had an important influence on the way they were governed. The rest of the Empire included enclaves in South America, like British Guiana (Guyana), a particular concentration of dependencies in the Caribbean, and a motley collection of fortress colonies, coaling stations, and trading posts, including Gibraltar, St Helena, Fiji, the Falkland Islands, and Hong Kong.

Despite the apparent imperial coherence implied by the splashes of red on the world map, the Empire was governed in a bewildering range of different ways, though in practice this probably did not make very much difference to the average Briton's perception of it.

Imperial administration, however, was firmly underpinned by an assumption of white racial superiority: broadly speaking, the greater the white population the more responsible and democratic the government. Thus Canada, Newfoundland, and New Zealand were fully self-governing, as were the Australian states, which combined into the federal Commonwealth of Australia on 1 January 1901. In some respects these territories were politically more progressive than Britain. New Zealand, for example, gave women the vote in 1893, and Australia followed suit in 1902. Cape Colony and Natal, as well as a few other colonies, had responsible government, though participation in the political process was for the most part restricted to whites only. In India elected representatives of the indigenous population did not play any role until after reforms brought a very limited measure of internal self-government in 1919, while the colonies in tropical Africa and other places were ruled by governors, advisory councils, and colonial civil servants composed almost exclusively of white Britons from the 'Mother Country'. Also governed as colonies were some territories captured during the First World War—for example Palestine, Tanganyika (Tanzania), and German South West Africa (Namibia)—which were granted to Britain as 'mandates' under the League of Nations. That British colonial service administrators— district commissioners and the like—in many places acted impartially and, as they believed, in the best interests of the 'native' inhabitants of the Empire was no real substitute for democratic political structures and processes. Yet at the start of the twentieth century it was a situation regarded by most British people (if they thought about the matter at all) as the natural order of things, and it was only very sporadically challenged within the overseas Empire itself. Over the next fifty years these imperial power relationships, and the apparently imperturbable British assumptions underlying them, were fiercely challenged and fundamentally changed in a process which saw the transformation of the British Empire into the British Commonwealth.

The Boer War and its impact

Some of the forces underpinning that change became apparent in the Anglo-Boer War (1899–1902), arguably the last British war of imperial expansion, and a conflict which demonstrated both imperial weakness and imperial strength—a perhaps unexpected combination that was to recur during the first half of the twentieth century. Weakness was illustrated by the time and trouble required to conquer the two small Boer republics of the Transvaal and Orange Free State. It took over 400,000 troops and an estimated £200 million to defeat 50,000 Boer farmer-soldiers. The participation, however, of 28,000 troops from Canada, Australia, and New Zealand suggested that the mother country might not have to stand alone in any particular conflict, a point well taken by the British commander-in-chief, Lord Roberts. Roberts, a man with an eye on public opinion in Britain and across the Empire and well aware of the power and influence of the popular press, saw to it that detachments from each of the Dominions contributing to the war effort, as well as troops from the United Kingdom, were included in the column relieving Mafeking. When the town was liberated on 17 May 1900, after a siege of 217 days, the celebrations were so extraordinarily fervent and widespread that the term 'Mafficking' was coined to describe the extravagant and boisterous celebration of an event.

The outburst of imperialist popular enthusiasm on Mafeking Night (18 May), reflected the way in which modern technological developments were drawing the widely scattered parts of Britain's global Empire closer together than ever before. The news of the relief of Mafeking was telegraphed to Britain almost instantaneously, and was ideal headline fodder for the copy-hungry British mass circulation newspapers whose coverage amplified the drama and immediacy of the events in South Africa. Six British war correspondents were in Mafeking. Their reports, smuggled out during the siege, helped make the garrison commander, Colonel Robert Baden-Powell, an archetypal British imperial hero. Baden-Powell's own despatches certainly added to an image of insouciant, plucky derring-do. 'BP' went on to found the twin movements of Scouting and Guiding, just two (albeit the largest) among a number of youth organizations with a specifically patriotic and imperial purpose which flourished in the first half of the century. Baden-Powell's own agenda is clearly revealed in the title of the 1912 manual he wrote with his sister Agnes: *The Handbook for Girl Guides or How Girls can help build the Empire.* The wave of imperial enthusiasm stimulated by the Boer War, and articulated by enthusiasts like Kinloch-Cooke, fuelled hopes that even as Dominions like Canada and Australia developed autonomous identities, they might be drawn into an actively closer political relationship with the United Kingdom in some sort of imperial federation. The achievement of Australian unity, for example, far from advancing autonomy from Great Britain, seemed to offer a pattern for a wider and greater federation encompassing the whole empire and focusing a concentration of power greater than any previous global empire. Reporting on Australian developments, the *Melbourne Argus* grandiloquently asserted: 'No Emperor of the Old World, no Cæsar, no Alexander, could even imagine so wide a sovereign sway; no Czar, no American President, can hope for a realm so wide extended as that which a federated Great Britain will fuse into a whole.' At home the greatest proponent of imperial federation was Joseph Chamberlain, Colonial Secretary from 1895 to 1903. At the conference of prime ministers of self-governing Dominions and colonies held to coincide with the coronation of King Edward VII in 1902, Chamberlain raised the possibility of the colonies helping with imperial endeavours. Borrowing an image from Matthew Arnold, he described the United Kingdom as like some 'weary Titan' staggering under 'the too vast orb of its fate'. 'We have borne the burden for many years,' he said. 'We think it is time that our children should assist us to support it.'

But those children were not apparently much moved by Chamberlain's appeal. Only New Zealand, the 'most loyal Dominion' (and also one of the weakest), readily offered to share the burden of imperial defence. In the absence of Dominion support, and in the face of a growing challenge to Britain's imperial and other world wide interests from Great Powers such as France, Germany, Russia and the USA, the early years of the twentieth century saw a reassessment of Britain's strategic relationships, and a move away from the so-called 'splendid isolation' of the nineteenth century, whereby Britain had generally eschewed alliances with foreign states. The greatest challenge appeared to come from Germany, whose naval building programme offered a direct threat to Britain's vital maritime supremacy. The costs, however, of staying ahead of Germany while also matching, if not surpassing, the fleets of the other Great Powers were more than Britain, with or without imperial help, could bear. Thus British diplomats were given the task of solving a problem which the service chiefs and Treasury combined could not. The result was a strategic realignment in the first half-decade of the century which embodied agreements with Japan and France to secure British interests in East Asia and the Mediterranean, an understanding with Russia to ease the strain of competition in central Asia, and an assumption that Britain would not go to war against the USA. Notably absent was Germany, who emerged as Britain's greatest single rival. Despite Germany's own imperial interests, which posed some threat to British territories in Africa and the Pacific, if Britain were to go to war with Germany (as seemed increasingly probable), the most likely location for hostilities was in continental Europe.

Challenges of imperial defence

The tension between the expense of protecting Britain's imperial interests and the potentially even greater costs of 'home defence' against a European challenge was a theme which emerged strongly in the twentieth century. For the United Kingdom, the inescapable geopolitical reality was that, however pressing the threat to some distant part of the empire, the security of the mother country must come first. It followed that the defence of the far-flung empire must come second. The compelling (for British policy-makers) strategic logic underscoring this truth could not but dismay imperial decision-makers in Ottawa, Canberra, Wellington, or wherever, undermining their belief in the empire as a useful and protective world system and eroding their willingness to assist Britain when required.

Perhaps the best demonstration of the problems accompanying 'imperial defence' is to be found in the tortuous history of the Singapore naval base. Singapore, acquired by the British in the early nineteenth century, had by the beginning of the twentieth century become the eighth busiest port in the world, thriving on Britain's burgeoning eastern trade. Before the First World War the port had been modestly fortified, but a review of naval strategy after 1918 concluded that a main fleet base should be established on the island. The German challenge having been eliminated, Britain's main rivals in the Pacific were the USA and Japan, both significant naval powers. But Britain could not afford permanently to maintain in the East a fleet of sufficient strength to protect its regional interests against either rival. Thus a major base was needed, which could be defended until naval support arrived. Australia and New Zealand, naturally concerned for their own security, warmly supported the decision to develop Singapore, which was announced at the 1921 imperial conference. But actual work on the base was extremely slow, itself illustrating that combination of high-flown rhetoric with haphazard and imperfect action so characteristic of the twentieth-century British Empire. Economic constraints and political hesitations, especially among internationalist Labour leaders, who favoured 'collective security' and disarmament, held up any progress until 1928, when the contract for the main base works was let out. Empire financial contributions had already been promised from the Federated Malay States, Hong Kong, and New Zealand. Australia, however, having offered support in 1921, had subsequently earmarked the money for warships and had none now available for the base.

Though it was by no means complete, the Singapore base was formally opened in 1938. It included two enormous dry docks, each capable of accommodating the largest British battleships, and three airfields, along with 15-inch and 6-inch gun-sites across the island. By this stage, however, the 'Singapore strategy' upon which the base's very existence was predicated—that in time of war a major British naval force ('Main Fleet to Singapore') would be stationed at the base—was being undermined by developments in Europe. A revived German threat, combined with Mussolini's ambitions for Italy to dominate the Mediterranean, were threatening Britain's strategic security in Europe and narrowing the options available to the Royal Navy. Already in 1936 the British chiefs of staff had presciently concluded that 'the greater our commitments to Europe, the less will be our ability to secure our Empire and its communications'.

The Empire in the world wars

Despite the progressive degree of political autonomy granted to the Dominions (and marked formally by the Statute of Westminster in 1931), British defence planners in the years immediately before the outbreak of the Second World War continued largely to assume that the dominions would rally to Britain's side in times of peril. In the late 1920s the possibility of South Africa remaining neutral while the United Kingdom was at war briefly excited the Chief of the Naval Staff, who consulted the long-time Cabinet Secretary, Sir Maurice Hankey, on the matter. Hankey, sensibly appreciating the gulf between theory and practice, replied that the question of Dominion neutrality had been discussed before 1914. Although Canada and Australia had then stood out for the right to remain neutral, Hankey's recollection was that 'Mr Asquith privately held the view that it would be all right on the day, and that it was better not to force an issue on what he regarded as an academic question'.

While this tended to be Asquith's view on most issues, in this case he was absolutely correct, and the pattern of imperial assistance to the mother country established in the Boer War was repeated on an altogether greater scale in the World Wars of 1914–18 and 1939–45. On both occasions the Dominions and India rallied to the imperial war effort, though the timing, nature, and impact of their contributions, and that of the colonial territories, differed on each occasion and reflected changing political and social relationships within the empire. In August 1914 Sir Joseph Cook, Prime Minister of Australia, affirmed that 'when the Empire is at war, so is Australia', and in effect a declaration of war by the British government included all the imperial territories. Similar protestations of loyalty were made elsewhere. The Francophone leader of the opposition in Canada, Sir Wilfrid Laurier, proclaimed that 'all Canadians stand behind the mother country'. In India, one of the appointed Indian members of the Viceroy's Legislative Council declared that Indians were 'ready to meet any danger and render any sacrifices for the sake of the great and glorious Empire of which we are proud to call ourselves citizens'.

In 1939, while the Australian Prime Minister, Robert Menzies, again took the view that once Britain had declared war Australia was also at war, the response of other Dominion leaders reflected an assertion of varying degrees of independence from Great Britain. In Wellington the New Zealand premier took a few hours to consult his cabinet colleagues before war was declared. In both Canada and South Africa the decision was left to the legislature. Although both duly joined in, there was a very significant dissenting Afrikaner minority in South Africa. The most outstanding demonstration of imperial autonomy, however, was Eire—the twenty-six-county Irish Free State which had secured independence in 1921—which stayed neutral (though in effect benignly so) throughout the war. By contrast, India, despite having gained a measure of internal self-government, was committed to the imperial war effort by the Viceroy without consulting any Indian political leaders.

In both conflicts the Empire made a huge contribution to the war effort, exemplified by the numbers mobilized in the armed services (see Tables 1.1 and 1.2). In 1914–18 the Dominions and India provided 1.4 million each, constituting nearly one third of the Empire's total. The figures for the Second World War are even more striking. Some 2.7 million personnel from the Dominions, representing 22% of the empire total, and 2.4 million from India (20%) were mobilized between 1939 and 1945. The colonial Empire provided a comparatively small number (42,000) of service personnel in the First World War, and over half a million in the Second. But the mobilization of servicemen and women reflects only a part of the contribution made by the Empire in both conflicts. Great numbers of imperial subjects in both India and the colonies were enlisted—sometimes forcibly—into labour units both in battle zones and for war production at home. Up to 100,000 Indians served in such units behind the Western Front in 1914–18. In 1939–45 some 80,000 people were conscripted into war production work in Tanganyika, and a rather larger number of Nigerians were forced to work in tin mines to help replace imperial supplies cut off by the Japanese invasion of Malaya in December 1941.

The broad consequences of the Japanese conquests in 1941–2 confirmed that for Britain the most vital theatre of operations was always in Western Europe and the highest British priority was the defence of the United Kingdom itself. Dominion assistance directly helped with this. The Royal Canadian Navy, for example, was by the end of the war the chief provider of escorts for convoys on the vital supply link across the North Atlantic to the USA, the maintenance of which

Table 1.1 Military effort of Empire/Commonwealth in the 1914–1918 War

	Total mobilized	Killed or died of wounds	Wounded	Missing and POWs [a]
Australia	412,953	58,460	152,100	164
Canada	628,964	56,119	149,733	306
India	1,440,437	47,746	65,126	871
New Zealand	128,525	16,132	40,749	5
South Africa	228,907	7,241	11,444	33
United Kingdom	5,704,416	662,083	1,644,786	140,312
Others	42,000	3,336	3,504	366
TOTAL	8,586,202	851,117	2,067,442	142,057

[a] Prisoners repatriated not shown.

Source: Cook and Paxton, *Commonwealth Political Facts* (London 1979), p. 207. Reproduced by permission of Palgrave Macmillan.

Table 1.2 Military effort of the Commonwealth in the 1939–1945 War

	Total mobilized	Killed	Wounded	Missing	Prisoners of war
Australia	992,545	31,395	65,000	2,475	22,885
Canada	1,086,343	42,042	54,414	2,866	9,051
India	2,394,000	24,338	64,354	11,754	79,489
New Zealand	214,700	11,625	15,749	2,129	7,218
South Africa	410,056	12,080	14,363	–	15,044
United Kingdom	6,515,000	357,116	369,267	46,079	178,332
Others	504,250	7,716	7,386	14,393	8,265
TOTAL	12,116,894	486,312	590,533	79,696	320,284

Source: see Table 1.1.

ensured that the British Empire ended up on the winning side in both World Wars. Dominion personnel also significantly strengthened the Royal Air Force in the United Kingdom. But the situation of Singapore, other British possessions in South and East Asia, and the antipodean Dominions, starkly revealed the strategic realities of the time. With France collapsing in June 1940 London told Canberra and Wellington that sufficient forces would not be available to counter a Japanese advance: 'In the circumstances envisaged, it is most improbable that we could send adequate reinforcements to the Far East.' So much for the 'Main Fleet to Singapore' promise embedded in the building of the base. In the mean time British Empire forces were active in the Mediterranean and Middle Eastern theatres, fighting Italians in North Africa and securing imperial communications through the Suez Canal and the Red Sea. There were few enough resources left to protect Singapore, which fell to the Japanese in February 1942. It was, wrote Churchill in his war memoirs, 'the worst disaster and largest capitulation in British history'. It also marked the start of a strategic realignment for Australia and New Zealand, away from Britain and towards their fellow Pacific power, the United States.

The World Wars, which demonstrated such an impressive mobilization of imperial power, also provided the opportunity for imperial-minded politicians to shin up the greasy pole of politics at home. In 1914–18 ardent imperialists like Curzon and Milner, along with the South African General Smuts, served in the 'Imperial War Cabinet' under Lloyd George, himself more of an imperialist than is sometimes recognized. Winston Churchill's political career was dramatically revived by the Second World War. Having excluded himself from high political office after 1929 largely through his opposition to constitutional reform in India, in September 1939 he was brought into the cabinet. On becoming Prime Minister in May 1940 he at once defined the war in specifically imperial terms, telling Parliament that without 'victory' there would be 'no survival for the British Empire, no survival at all for all that the British Empire has stood for'. For Churchill and others, moreover, the victorious outcome of both wars could be held to vindicate their imperialist rhetoric. At the 1921 imperial conference Lloyd George asserted that the war had 'demonstrated—I might say revealed—that the British Empire was not an abstraction but a living force to be reckoned with'. Yet when it came to codifying that 'living force', the Dominions, and even India, were reluctant to commit themselves to much in the way of formal arrangements. At the same conference W. F. Massey, the Ulster-born Prime Minister of New Zealand, told his colleagues that there was 'a far stronger power in the British Empire to-day than any words that might be placed on paper, either printed or written—that is, the sentiments of the British people . . . right through the Empire . . . You cannot go beyond sentiment.' Here, perhaps, we have a clue to the extraordinary resilience of the British Empire in the first half of the twentieth century. Although Massey was not entirely correct in his analysis, since much of the overseas Empire did gain clear practical benefits from the British link (for example, in economic and security terms), certainly for the 'white' Dominions, and to a certain extent for the rest of the Empire too, the whole system was reinforced by powerful but intangible factors such as sentiment, culture, kinship, and shared 'British' values.

Mobilizing popular imperialism at home and abroad

One imperial enthusiast who sought to promote these forces was Reginald Brabazon, twelfth Earl of Meath, who proposed that the birthday of Queen Victoria, 24 May, should be set aside as an annual imperial celebration. In 1903 he founded the Empire Day Movement (motto: 'One King, One Flag, One Navy'), which campaigned with considerable success to have the anniversary marked in schools throughout the Empire. The movement succeeded in getting 24 May established as a public holiday in Australia, Canada, India, New Zealand, and South Africa, though never in the United Kingdom, reflecting the fact that in terms of popular support and emotion the Empire always meant more to Britons overseas than it did to the British population at home. In 1905 6,000 schools in all parts of the Empire were said to have participated in Empire Day ceremonies; by 1922 this had risen to 80,000. Indeed, the movement's vigour in the interwar years reflected the apparently paradoxical way in which popular engagement with the Empire seemed to increase while politically and constitutionally it was drifting apart. Another paradox lay in the extent to which at the same time modern technology—railways, steamships, telegraph cables, wireless, aeroplanes, and so on—was helping to draw distant parts of the Empire—itself a classically old-fashioned form of political organization—closer together than ever before.

The combination of modernity and tradition is well illustrated by the largely twentieth-century phenomenon of the royal tour. One popular commentator, W. Eden Hooper, remarked that the year 1901 possessed 'peculiar significance in the history of the British Empire' through its combination of the end of Queen Victoria's 'glorious reign', the inauguration of the Commonwealth of Australia, the 'great struggle in South Africa for British supremacy', and the 'Great Colonial Tour' of the Duke and Duchess of Cornwall and York (later King George V and Queen Mary). Although primarily arranged for the heir to the throne to preside at the opening of the first Australian federal parliament, since the intention was also to thank the Australian colonies for their assistance in the Boer War, New Zealand and Canada had a case for visiting as well. Thus the basis was laid for a 45,000-mile journey which took the royal party to every Dominion, together with Malta, Aden, Ceylon, Singapore, and Mauritius. Indicating a sharp appreciation of the importance of publicity, four journalists were accredited to the royal party. One of these favoured reporters, E. F. Knight of the *Morning Post*, asserted that the tour had 'been of estimable service to the British Empire', and had challenged 'that cynicism, that strange indifference to Imperial interests' which was so prevalent in Britain. The tour had 'so brought Englishmen and colonials together that this miserable selfish state of feeling at home has, it is to be hoped, been made impossible for the future'. The Duke of Cornwall himself appeared to concur with this optimistic opinion. In December 1901, a month after returning from his eight-month tour, he told a dinner at the Guildhall in London that wherever he had gone he had found 'unmistakable evidences of a consciousness of strength, a consciousness of a true and living membership in the Empire, and a consciousness of power and readiness to share the burdens and responsibilities of that membership'.

In 1905–6, the Duke (now Prince of Wales) visited India, and in 1911–12, as King George V, on his own initiative returned to the subcontinent for a Coronation Durbar (Court) to mark his succession as

Emperor of India, a title invented only as recently as 1877. Although the installation of Queen Victoria as Empress of India is credited with helping to revitalize the British monarchy at a time when its popularity had somewhat declined, it is debatable how significant this grandiose title was to Britons at home. If they inspected the coins in their pocket they would find 'IND IMP' (India Imperator/Emperor of India) among the abbreviated royal titles listed thereon, and the royal cipher 'GRI' (Georgius Rex Imperator) confirmed that both George V and his son, George VI, carried the style 'king-emperor'. Although the British had effectively ruled India since the end of the eighteenth century, the 'Indian Empire'—the greatest of all British imperial conceits—lasted only seventy years. Yet while it existed, from 1877 to the achievement of independence for India and Pakistan in 1947, it marked Britain out as both a major Asiatic power and (although the great majority of the population were Hindu), with 62 million Muslims, as the greatest Islamic power in the world.

Religious considerations affected the arrangements for the 1911 durbar, and demonstrate some of the difficulties raised when the ceremonial trappings of the British Empire encountered its multicultural reality. The original idea was for King George to place a crown on his own head at the climax of the ceremony, but this was vetoed by the Archbishop of Canterbury. Arguing that a coronation was a religious and not a political act, and that the sacramental nature of the coronation in London could not be repeated, he said that King George had no right to crown himself. The Indian administration's concern for Hindu and Muslim susceptibilities, moreover, meant that a Christian ceremony was out of the question. In the end a secular event of considerable pageantry—of a sort the British became particularly adept at in the twentieth century—was organized to mark the King-Emperor's visit to his greatest possession. On the day of the durbar (12 December 1911) the king appeared wearing a crown specially made for the event in an artificial amphitheatre containing 100,000 spectators, 35,000 soldiers, and a massed band of 1,600. It was, reported The Times, 'surely the most majestic assemblage ever seen in the East'. And so it remains, symbolizing the high point of the British Empire in India. No subsequent visit was made by a reigning king-emperor. When King George's eldest son, the Prince of Wales (later King Edward VIII), toured India in 1921–2 he was met with widespread protests and a boycott by Indian nationalists.

In other parts of the Empire, however, the glamorous and dashing crown prince represented the integrative power of the monarchy. From 1919 onwards he embarked on a series of tours, taking in not just India and the Dominions, but many parts of the colonial Empire in Africa and elsewhere. Much of the impetus for these travels came from George V, a man clearly determined to preserve and even amplify the position of the British Crown Imperial. George V's second son, the Duke of York, also played an imperial role when he represented his father at the inauguration of the new Australian parliament house in Canberra in 1927. After he succeeded to the throne (as George VI) in 1936, he embarked on what was intended to be a series of tours taking in all the major parts of the empire. Although a visit to India was put off (partly for Indian domestic political reasons), in 1939 he became the first reigning British monarch to visit Canada. Marking the importance of publicity for these events, the royal train across North America was accompanied by fifty-eight press correspondents and twelve photographers. 'Never before', wrote Reuters representative Gordon Young, 'had an independent Dominion welcomed its reigning monarch at its seat of Government.' The whole tour was felt 'to be the outward visible sign of an Empire's unity', an act giving 'fresh significance to that fine phrase of the Statute of Westminster which refers to the British Crown as "the symbol of the free association of the members of the British Commonwealth of Nations"'. The Second World War interrupted the King's planned series of imperial progresses, but in 1947 he visited South Africa, as well as northern and southern Rhodesia (now Zambia and Zimbabwe). Ill health prevented a further tour to Australia and New Zealand, but by then the pattern of the reigning monarch systematically visiting Britain's Dominions and colonies (taken up with even greater intensity by George VI's successor, Queen Elizabeth II) had been firmly established, a practice facilitated by the latest forms of transport—aeroplanes replacing steamships—and brought to the widest possible audience by the most modern forms of mass communications—the cabled reports of the Duke of Cornwall's 1901 tour being superseded by radio broadcasts and newsreel films in the 1930s and 1940s.

Imperial circuses: Empire exhibitions and ephemera

The nearest the British themselves got to the sort of specifically imperial celebration associated with royal tours was in a series of Empire exhibitions, which drew on a precedent of festivities marking the golden and diamond jubilees of Queen Victoria in 1887 and 1897. During the decade and a half running up to the outbreak of the First World War there was a particular concentration of shows, pageants, and spectacles with imperial connotations. London Exhibitions Limited made a commercial success of events at Olympia, Earl's Court, and its own 'Great White City and Stadium', constructed in 1907. There were also officially sponsored exhibitions, such as the Sydenham Crystal Palace Coronation Festival of Empire in 1911 which was intended 'to demonstrate to the somewhat casual, often times unobservant British public the real significance of our great self-governing Dominions, to make us familiar with their products, their ever-increasing resources, their illimitable possibilities'. The displays included three-quarter scale models of all the Dominion parliament buildings and an 'All-Red Tour' on a miniature railway taking visitors from Newfoundland to South Africa, past such exhibits as a Jamaican sugar plantation, a 'typical Indian bazaar' and a 'quaint Maori village' from New Zealand. These events were not confined to the capital: shows were held in Wolverhampton and Cork in 1902, Bradford in 1904, and Dublin in 1907. There were empire exhibitions in Glasgow in both 1901 and 1911. Among the exotic displays at the latter was an 'equatorial colony' complete with 'West African natives'.

The greatest of all the imperial exhibitions was that held in the London suburb of Wembley in 1924–5. On a 220-acre site and with a £12 million budget, buildings were erected representing each of the major Empire territories. The Indian pavilion, for example, was designed to incorporate features from the Taj Mahal, and West Africa was represented with a mud-walled town, supposedly based on the northern Nigerian city of Kano. There were Palaces of Engineering, Industries, Arts and Beauty, a forty-acre fun fair (perhaps the most popular part of the whole exhibition), the (then) largest sports stadium in the world, and numerous displays calculated to demonstrate the staggering range of imperial products and achievements. These included a model coal mine and a statue of the Prince of Wales constructed out of Canadian butter. A spectacular Pageant of Empire was staged in the stadium, involving some 12,000 performers, 1,000 doves, 730 camels, 500 donkeys, 300 horses, 72 monkeys, 3 bears, and a macaw. The scenes depicted included 'The English Fleet in the Mediterranean', 'The Early Days of India', and 'The Pageant of Newfoundland'. There was also a torchlight military tattoo, a scout and guide jamboree, and mass concerts featuring exclusively British music. Although the exhibition drew in large numbers of visitors— 17 million in 1924 and 9 million the following year—it is difficult to estimate whether the event had any enduring impact on British public opinion, beyond perhaps reinforcing an impression of the apparent power and evident permanence of the Empire.

Fifty years after visiting the exhibition, Eric Pasold, an immigrant recently arrived from eastern Europe, still powerfully recalled 'the nostalgic picture of this mightiest of all empires as displayed at Wembley'. The sheer extent of the Empire unforgettably impressed him, as it must have countless numbers of other visitors. 'Nigerians in their colourful robes, cowboys from Calgary, dusky East African beauties, Indians, Malays, Chinamen, Australians, New Zealanders and Fiji islanders in an endless variety of human types' were all 'members of one great empire, united under one king and flag, linked by the English language, financed by sterling, ruled by British justice and protected by the Royal Navy. How proud they must feel, I thought, and how I envied them.' But the event also attracted a fair amount of satirical comment. A WGTW (Won't Go To Wembley) Society was formed and sophisticates sneered at its populism. 'I've brought you here to see the wonders of the Empire,' remarks one character in Noel Coward's *This Happy Breed*, 'and all you want to do is go to the Dodgems.' More significant criticism came from a body representing mainly West African black students based in London who complained that Africans (used for example in living tableaux of 'native' life and occupations) were held up to ridicule. Thus, amid the rather self-satisfied celebration of the actual and potential benefits of the Empire, there were a few dissenting voices, indicating perhaps that the results of British education might not always, nor necessarily, strengthen the Empire, at least as it was conventionally manifested at Wembley in 1924–5.

The empire exhibition spawned all manner of ephemera and bric-a-brac, such as pencil cases, ashtrays, matchboxes, branded soaps and toffees, biscuit tins, and paperweights in the lion figure used as the exhibition symbol. The Post Office participated with its first ever commemorative stamp, another demonstration of that late-flowering British imperial sentiment of the first half of the twentieth century. The design, specifically commissioned to be 'symbolic of the British Empire', bore the king's effigy, and a lion (which became known as the 'Wembley Lion') on the background of a rising sun. (That the sun might equally have been setting naturally did not occur to anyone at the time.) Slogan postmarks to advertise the exhibition were used both at home and throughout the Empire, which the Post Office claimed was 'the biggest postal advertising campaign ever undertaken by any postal authority for any single purpose'. The Empire Exhibition stamp issue had been warmly approved by King George V, himself a keen philatelist, and ten years later he further welcomed a special stamp issue to mark the silver jubilee of his reign. The occasion of the jubilee was celebrated with the very first coordinated issue of stamps (250 in all) throughout the Empire. A common design, featuring Windsor Castle, was used for the forty-four crown colonies and Newfoundland. It is perhaps worth remarking that it took until 1935 for there to be any common postage stamp of any sort for the dependent British Empire. The 1935 issue, moreover, was the first of only six common Empire stamp issues over an eighteen-year period, culminating with the coronation of Queen Elizabeth II in 1953. From the philatelic evidence, therefore, itself indicative of underlying cultural attitudes, it might be argued that the notion of the Empire as a coherent world system was at its most pervasive between 1935 and 1953.

Four of these common imperial issues—the 1935 silver jubilee, the coronations of George VI (1937) and Elizabeth II, and the silver wedding of George VI and Queen Elizabeth (1948)—celebrated royal occasions, emphasizing the extent to which the British royal family were a central, emblematic component of imperial unity. George V was the last British monarch who played an unambiguously imperial role throughout his reign, although even he could tire of this. In the early 1930s, when the king was recuperating from a severe illness, Lord Lee, then Vice-President of the Gaumont-British Picture Corporation, was asked if he could provide some films to lift the

King's spirits. On enquiring about suitable subject matter, Lee was told that 'above all, he did not want to be shown descriptive films about his Empire, of which he said he "heard and saw quite enough in other ways"'. In public, however, the situation was quite different, illustrated by his last words, 'How is the Empire?', as reported by *The Times* of 21 January 1936. Again, a more human alternative, 'Bugger Bognor' (on being told he could convalesce at the Sussex seaside town), marks the difference between public virtue and private preference.

One imperial development with which the monarch was intimately concerned was the creation in 1917 of a new British order of chivalry, the Most Excellent Order of the British Empire. With George V's enthusiastic support, the innovation was deliberately conceived to provide a morale-boosting reward for war service. Indeed, the original idea was to have a more democratic system of awards than had hitherto been the case, making awards available to women and persons denied existing British honours by virtue of their low social status. In November 1918 Lord Crawford defended the large number of recipients of the order as being 'humble people who had been, and were, doing great work for the country'. From the start the order was designed to cover the whole Empire, with half the annual honours after 1922 reserved for the Dominions, colonies, and other territories. Canada, however, effectively opted out after 1919, and South Africa after 1925, though both allowed some awards for service in the Second World War. With independence in the late 1940s, Britain's south Asian possessions ceased to make recommendations. In the United Kingdom, however, the order has gone from strength to strength. Retaining its original motto, 'For God and the Empire', at the turn of the twenty-first century, when that Empire had become defunct, the order's title was left as virtually the only remaining official usage of the term 'British Empire'.

George V's role as the personification of imperial unity was powerfully reinforced by the new medium of wireless broadcasting. The opening of the Wembley exhibition by the king on St George's Day, 23 April 1924, provided the occasion for the newly established British Broadcasting Company to set up its very first major outside broadcast. Empire Day programmes became a major annual event, with contributions from the empire being included from the 1930s. In December 1932 the BBC Empire Service was inaugurated with a specific brief to broadcast programmes to the Empire, and that year the first royal Christmas Day speech was made by George V, inaugurating an extremely robust British Christmas tradition. Concerts of 'Empire music' were frequently broadcast, naturally featuring works by Sir Edward Elgar, the quintessential English imperial composer. He wrote an 'Imperial March' for the Wembley exhibition and at the opening ceremony conducted 'Land of Hope and Glory', words by A. C. Benson originally set in 1902, which had become a sort of unofficial imperial anthem.

Imperial bread: economics and Empire

Despite the cultural delights (both high and low) served up at Wembley, the central message of the exhibition remained the commercial potential of the empire. This had always been a core belief for imperial enthusiasts, and from 1926 to 1933 it was given vigorous propaganda support by the Empire Marketing Board (EMB) whose role was to promote the empire for the economic advantage of Britain and its overseas possessions. Using the most modern advertising techniques, the EMB produced a stream of material including books, pamphlets, posters, information packs for schools, broadcasts, and films. In 1933 it was calculated that the board had distributed some ten million leaflets and pamphlets with titles such as *A Book of Empire Dinners* and *Why Should We Buy from the Empire?* The EMB ran a nationwide series of public lectures, and projected a vision of 'complementary economies' where the Empire would broadly provide raw materials while Britain supplied manufactured goods. Punchy slogans emphasized economic development—'Jungles to-day are gold mines tomorrow'—and clever advertisements showed what housewives could do to help. 'Have an Empire Xmas Pudding' exhorted one in 1926. Canadian flour, Australian or South African raisins, English or Scottish beef suet, Indian pudding spice, and Jamaican rum would 'make as delicious a plum pudding as you have ever tasted. And you will enjoy it all the more', continued the text, 'if you remember that, by using Empire fruit to make it, you give a helping hand to the thousands of British settlers Overseas—most of them ex-Servicemen and their families—by whom that fruit is grown.'

The creation of the EMB reflected a number of similar imperial initiatives aimed at economic cooperation within the Empire. These attempts were not really prompted by exclusively imperial considerations, despite the declarations of imperial visionaries such as Lord Beaverbrook, the Canadian-born owner of the *Daily Express*, or Leopold Amery, Colonial Secretary 1924–9. The 'imperial' schemes entertained by successive British governments in the 1920s and 1930s were at best merely stratagems of enlightened self-interest, designed to help bolster the British economy during a period of first strain and then deep international recession. As with Britain's strategic imperatives, the pattern of its economic interest did not always fit comfortably within any purely imperial world system. Imperial markets, even though they were more than twice as important in 1938 as they had been in 1913, never constituted even half of Britain's total exports. In 1913 80% of Britain's imports were from foreign countries; in 1938 the figure was still 61%. As for Empire imports from Britain, in 1938 these amounted to only one third of total imports (some 10% less than in 1914), and in 1937 foreign countries purchased more than half of all the Empire's exports. Up to the Second World War, foreign markets were consistently more important for Britain than imperial ones. The crucial point, however, is that following the First World War, as Britain was finding it harder to compete in the markets of industrialized countries, the Empire seemed to offer an attractive, perhaps economically less demanding alternative.

The main consideration in officially sponsored imperial economic ventures was the domestic situation in Britain, where high levels of unemployment wonderfully concentrated the minds of decision-makers. Subsidized emigration was regarded by some as a panacea, and between 1919 and 1931 various overseas settlement agencies assisted nearly 600,000 migrants to imperial destinations. By 1932, however, more people were migrating into the United Kingdom from the Empire than vice versa. Unemployment in the Dominions had its impact too. Imperial preferences, however, were the greatest red herring in the imperial sphere. Some system of preferences could work well if 'complementary economies' actually existed within the Empire. But the Dominions (and India) were developing manufacturing industries of their own and building tariff walls to protect them. The impact of the world economic slump after 1929 nevertheless brought Britain and the Dominions together to an imperial economic conference in Ottawa in 1932. Neville Chamberlain, the Chancellor of the Exchequer, was perhaps ambitious to fulfil his father's dream of Empire free trade. Great Britain would be the workshop of the Empire, if no longer of the world, while the grateful Dominions would supply the mother country with food and raw materials. But the Ottawa conference was a failure. The Dominions, themselves devastated by the Depression, were as keen to protect their own industries as to benefit their farmers and primary producers. Britain, on the other hand, would not impose food taxes to favour imperial producers at the expense of the British consumer. Empire free trade was not (and had never been) feasible because it was not in the common interest of the various countries of the Empire.

The practical economic benefits of the Empire was a theme quite explicitly developed in the Glasgow Empire Exhibition of 1938. On a 175-acre site there were 'over 100 palaces and pavilions', including one 'built by the Empire Tea Market Expansion Bureau' representing 'all the great tea-producing regions of the Empire'. The event attracted twelve million visitors and contained all the usual features, combining pleasure ('the biggest dodg'em track in the world'), curiosity (a Zulu village and an Indian temple), and instruction (in one display 'an ordinary piece of blind-cord is traced to Tanganyika sisal, a hairbrush to Falkland Islands whalebone'). But it was also clear that this exhibition was as much concerned with stimulating Scottish employment and promoting local depressed industries like engineering, shipbuilding, and shipping as it was with presenting the Empire to the world. As it turned out, Glasgow was the last great Empire exhibition. The world-shattering events of the next few years, while accommodating a demonstration of collective imperial effort and power, also released forces which gravely undermined the very concept of Empire itself.

Imperial commonwealth: democracy and Empire

The ideological mobilization which accompanied and sustained the British war effort reflected the view that the Second World War was a crusade on behalf of freedom and democracy against the uniquely evil forces of fascism. But ideology was a double-edged weapon, and the espousal of clearly democratic war aims could undermine the basis of Empire. The 'Atlantic Charter', agreed by Winston Churchill and the United States President Franklin Roosevelt in August 1941 as a general statement of policy, included an affirmation of the 'rights of all peoples to choose the form of government under which they will live'. Churchill dismissed the notion that there could be any contradiction between this and the practical reality of British imperial rule, and assured Parliament that 'British policy towards the colonies was covered by declarations in harmony with the Atlantic Charter'. In *The British Way and Purpose*, a 1944 pamphlet prepared by the Directorate of Army Education to explain current affairs and British war aims, the Empire was itself described as a guarantor of freedom. Because it was collectively strong it gave 'each of the countries in it a sense of security', and it provided 'personal freedom' by giving 'each man and woman freedom from the "aggression" of any neighbours against his life or his belongings'. The Empire, moreover, gave 'the dependent country a chance of winning its full freedom as a nation within the shelter of the British Empire', a formulation in which the understanding of 'full freedom' perhaps left something to be desired.

For the Dominions, despite (and perhaps because of) their enormous contributions to the war effort, the experience of the Second World War largely confirmed their political independence from Britain. Ironically, in some cases the formal achievement of autonomy was actually linked to wartime mobilization. Australia, for example, only adopted the Statute of Westminster in 1942 in order to remove legal impediments to 'the more effectual prosecution of the war in which his Majesty the King is engaged'. But elsewhere in the empire the linking of Empire and freedom was less readily appreciated. In March 1940 the President of the Indian National Congress declared that 'India cannot endure the prospect of Nazism and Fascism, but she is even more tired of British imperialism'. Although in 1942 Britain offered India 'Dominion status' after the war, the 'Quit India' movement of the same year presented the greatest challenge to British rule since the Indian Uprising of 1857. The actual mobilization of imperial soldiers raised political expectations among many. In July 1946 a group of demobilized soldiers in Tanganyika told the colonial authorities that they had been 'fighting for our own freedom and not for the imperial purposes'. A rally of ex-soldiers in Accra (Ghana) in

1948 which was followed by widespread disturbances was blamed on the fact that 'by reason of their contacts with other peoples including Europeans [the ex-servicemen] had developed a political and national consciousness'.

The exploitation of imperial resources, with increased economic activity and state intervention, had a social and political impact overseas, just as it did at home. The radicalization of the British electorate, which contributed to the landslide Labour victory in the 1945 general election, was echoed by political stirrings across the Empire and a general increase in nationalist demands for at least a share in government. This was most advanced, and most difficult to resist, in south Asia, where independence eventually came in a great rush in the postwar years: India (partitioned into India and Pakistan) and Burma in 1947, Ceylon in 1948. Initially a Dominion (with the British monarch remaining as head of state), in 1950 India became a fully independent republic, while remaining within what the Statute of Westminster had called the 'British Commonwealth of Nations', but which was increasingly known simply as the 'Commonwealth'. The transition from 'Empire' to 'Commonwealth', which had been gathering pace throughout the first half of the twentieth century, marked a fundamental change in the relationship between Britain and its overseas possessions. The term 'Commonwealth', much favoured by the white South African leader Jan Christian Smuts, provided a halfway house between a fully functioning Empire, clearly subordinate to the United Kingdom, and complete political autonomy for all of its constituent parts. The transition was also a symptom of Britain's changing status as a Great Power. It might be said that the history of the British Empire was the history of Britain's economic and political predominance in the world, while the history of the Commonwealth is that of Britain's relative decline in global terms. From the early years of the century this decline meant that the British had to seek allies to help secure their position in the world. The foreign agreements secured before 1914 have already been noted, but the experience of both World Wars confirmed that Britain was increasingly unable to act unilaterally in world affairs, and above all confirmed the importance of friendship with the United States. The emergence of the Commonwealth demonstrated the extent to which Britain's imperial territories—or at least the Dominions—were also themselves assuming the status of allies. In a sense 'Commonwealth' was a concept meaning that foreign countries were becoming more important to Britain than the Empire and, conversely, that the more politically autonomous parts of the Empire were becoming more like foreign countries in their relationships with the former mother country.

While the Dominions and India were drifting politically away from the United Kingdom, during and immediately after the Second World War the colonial Empire enjoyed something of a resurgence. 'Constructive imperialism' was championed by enthusiasts in the Colonial Office and elsewhere, enjoining the merits of government-subsidized development and welfare schemes, which would enhance economic efficiency and productivity, improve living standards, and (it was hoped) reduce social and political unrest in the colonies. Politicians began to talk in terms of 'trusteeship' when speaking of the Empire, stressing equal relationships and common economic and social benefits. A Colonial Development and Welfare Act in 1940 was one manifestation of this new commitment, though it was not of much practical use. The most extravagant example of this policy was the over-ambitious East African groundnuts scheme, planned after the Second World War to bring large-scale economic development to Tanganyika while helping to supply Britain's urgent need for vegetable oils. Hastily planned and ineptly executed, the scheme was a calamitous failure and was effectively abandoned in 1951, having cost the British taxpayer some £50 million.

Sport, sterling, and 'sigint'

In cultural terms there was not much of a divergence between Britain and the Dominions in the late 1940s. If anything, the contrary was true. Kinship links were strengthened by a marked postwar increase in British emigration to the existing white settler societies. Between 1946 and 1949 130,000 Britons went to Canada and 138,000 to Australasia, three or four times the average numbers departing in the 1930s. Many more people emigrated to South Africa, which had not hitherto been a very popular destination, and considerable numbers also went to southern Rhodesia. More significant for Britain, perhaps, was the start of inward migration from the non-white empire. In June

1948 the troopship *Empire Windrush* arrived in London with some 500 immigrants from Jamaica, the first of a great wave of postwar migration from the Caribbean to the United Kingdom. In some respects intra-imperial relationships seemed quite unchanged after 1945. The first postwar British Empire Games were held in Auckland in 1950. The games had been inaugurated in Hamilton, Ontario, in 1930 by loyalist Canadians looking for an alternative to the increasingly American-dominated Olympics. Only in 1954 was the name changed to the British Empire and Commonwealth Games, and not until 1970 was 'Empire' finally dropped from the title. For many, sporting contests provided the most tangible link with the overseas empire. The visits of cricket teams from South Africa, Australia, New Zealand, and the West Indies in successive years from 1947 was a reassuring confirmation of the enduring importance of those links, though the victory of the West Indies in their series was possibly less comforting.

The enormous economic cost of the Second World War had a direct impact on Britain's relations with the wider world. Not only did it leave Britain heavily indebted to the United States but the pressures of the conflict concentrated the fairly loose prewar sterling bloc into a closely integrated monetary association which survived for two decades after 1945. The pressing need to repay the American debt put a premium on any dollar-earning exports (such as rubber or tin from Malaya) that the Empire could produce, and the sterling area, which encompassed all of the Empire and Commonwealth except Canada, provided a greater level of economic coherence to the Empire/Commonwealth than it had ever previously enjoyed. But the organization depended on the underlying strength of the British economy for its successful operation, and only survived so long as that requirement was met. Britain's postwar indebtedness, however, was not confined to America. Reflecting the growth of nationalist feeling in India, Britain agreed in 1939 to pay the costs of employing Indian forces outside the frontiers of India—that is to say for imperial, rather than purely Indian, purposes. By 1945 the British had run up a huge debt with India of over £1,300 million, for the use of the Indian armed services in such places as North Africa and even Burma.

In the late 1940s Britain still had very extensive extra-European commitments. The colonial Empire in the tropics in Africa,

South-East Asia, and the Caribbean was largely intact, and while eventual independence was envisaged for most territories, few imagined that this would come as quickly as it did. Although Palestine was abandoned in 1948, there were still British defence installations 'East of Suez', in South Arabia and the Gulf, as well as Hong Kong, Malaya, and Singapore. In part these existed to protect British investments and secure its vital supplies of oil, but they were also part of the defence of the 'free world' against the threat of Communist revolution. British and Commonwealth troops served in the Korean War (1950–3) alongside US forces fighting against communist North Korea and its ally China. In the bipolar conditions of the Cold War, Britain's extensive overseas possessions provided valuable strategic capital for the American-led Western Alliance. Yet Britain's most important strategic commitment after 1945 lay not in the Empire at all, but as part of the Atlantic Alliance, underpinned by the North Atlantic Treaty Organization (NATO), which Britain, the United States, Canada, and the major Western European states established in April 1949. There was, however, a lingering imperial legacy which reinforced Britain's role within the Western Alliance. In 1947 Britain, the United States, Canada, Australia, and New Zealand signed the UKUSA agreement, by which the five countries agreed to share signals intelligence-gathering ('sigint') facilities. With this highly secret and highly significant arrangement Britain, the superpower of the late nineteenth century was able in part to keep up with the superpower of the twentieth century.

The end of Empire

Britain in 1950 was no longer the great imperial power it had been in 1900, but it remained a power with imperial trappings and more than residual imperial responsibilities. Although in strategic terms it was firmly committed to an Atlantic and continental European defence alliance, it was to be another twenty years before that orientation was translated into membership of the European Economic Community (later the European Union). The Empire, which loomed so large in both high policy-making and popular culture, seemed virtually to have faded away. There were no great Empire exhibitions after 1945.

The best that could be managed was a series of travelling shows organized by the Central Office of Information in connection with a 'Colonial Month' in 1949. The great celebration designed to restore national morale in 1951 was, significantly, the Festival of *Britain*. There were no pavilions for separate Empire or Commonwealth territories, though the keen-eyed visitor to the Dome of Discovery would find 'Commonwealth agriculture', 'Minerals of the Commonwealth' and, in a general display of modern communications, 'Commonwealth links'. As the official guidebook noted, the South Bank Exhibition and the nationwide festival as a whole were explicitly designed to 'add up to one united act of national reassessment, and one corporate reaffirmation of faith in the nation's future'. It was evident, moreover, that 'the nation's future' had no imperial dimension.

Of all the British overseas possessions, India was always the most imperial and the most important. Its loss in 1947 marked the single most significant stage in the 'end of Empire' for Britain. In 1902 the Assistant Director of Military Operations at the War Office, Colonel W. R. Robertson, wrote that 'in fighting for India, England will be fighting for her imperial existence'. In the mid-1940s, despite having successfully defended the subcontinent against the Japanese, the British let their great possession slip away with astonishing rapidity. At the end of the year of Indian independence, J. C. Smuts remarked that 'the Roman Empire took five hundred years to die. Here we count a similar process almost by months.' Mordantly reflecting on the same events, and on the end of empires, the imperial historian John Gallagher observed that 'there was nothing spectacular about the end of the affair'. While the last of the Byzantine emperors had died fighting on the walls of Constantinople in 1453, in February 1952, as reported by *The Times*, the last King-Emperor, George VI, 'passed peacefully away in his sleep' at his country house of Sandringham.

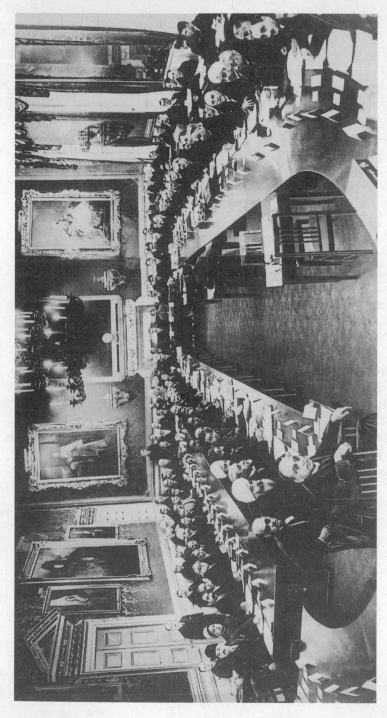

Plate 4 The 1931 Round Table Conference was to prove only one of the many attempts to determine the future of India round tables of varying sizes and complexities.

Electing the governors/the governance of the elect

Duncan Tanner

Writing in 1942, Lord Wedgwood of Barlaston claimed that 'British parliamentary government is better than any other method of government, better than any other variety of democracy, and better now than it ever was in the past'. He was not the first to proclaim the superiority of the 'Westminster model' to both its north American and European 'competitors'. However, unlike many of his predecessors Wedgwood was concerned that Britain had not exported this apparently unmatchable system to its imperial possessions. This chapter examines Wedgwood's distinction between the British and imperial process of democratic change. Whilst the former rested on the consent of the governed, the latter evidently did not. Yet there is also a common thread that winds through this necessarily selective examination of British and imperial politics. The system of electing the governors may have varied; but a key concern was always to keep power in the hands of a ruling elect. At 'home' the elect was the new class of professional politicians. Within the Empire it was the old class of British mandarins, and those moderate allies who would help them

I should like to thank the editor and Dr Nicholas Owen of The Queen's College Oxford for their perceptive comments on an earlier draft.

manage the emergence of democracy. Politicians at home and abroad felt that the public needed to be guided and educated, and that this should be done through the wise office of (benevolent) public servants.

The structure of British politics before 1914

The British political system was moulded in the decades preceding the First World War. A substantial extension of the franchise and redistribution of parliamentary boundaries in 1884–5 created a mass (male) electorate. Most of these voters were householders aged 30 or more. Nonetheless, some politicians were concerned about their capacity to make rational political judgements. The power of those with a 'stake in the country' was preserved to create a bulwark against democracy. Property owners and those with university degrees could vote more than once.

Nonetheless, this only diluted the democratic process. Prominent politicians and academics still felt that the effectiveness of the 'Westminster model' was endangered by mass democracy. The evolution of politics in the United States, where a mass electorate had put vulgar demagogues into positions of power, had sounded a warning. The pattern of politics in continental Europe was hardly better. Informed European observers described parties degenerating into bureaucratic machines, dominated by a central ruling clique which was able to manipulate both its own party and public opinion.

Events within Britain fed these fears. Traditionalists regarded Gladstone's 'moral' campaigning as artfully hypocritical. Subsequent events were even more threatening. By 1908 David Lloyd George and others had developed a radical and populist form of Liberalism. Many felt his incitement of class hostility was blind to all morality (since Lloyd George was uncontrolled by his party leader, who was often blind drunk). The Liberal government of 1906–10, wrote Lord Robert Cecil, whose family had helped rule Britain for centuries, was a government of 'cardsharpers . . . no longer fit for the society of gentlemen'. The Liberal party was now dominated by members of the middle classes—and by professional politicians with a capacity for sharp sentences and self-publicity. The Conservatives were especially upset. Lloyd George was 'the little Welsh attorney' (in their eyes three insults in one). However, his style of politics helped the Liberals to win elections in 1906 and 1910. Traditionalists needed a response that went beyond condemnation.

Faced with such changes, the Conservative Party reluctantly elevated those members of their party who possessed similar skills. Yet Lord Randolph Churchill (Winston's father)—who led the way in the 1880s—was barely tolerated. He was 'thoroughly untrustworthy', commented the Earl of Dudley, 'scarcely a gentleman and probably more or less mad'. By 1900 a new champion had appeared, Joseph Chamberlain, a Birmingham manufacturer and an ex-Liberal. He too was resented. 'Damn these Chamberlains,' wrote Lord Derby, himself a skilled political manipulator. 'They are the curse of the party and the country.' The content and style of Chamberlain's politics was bad enough. His cultural habits (poor wine and food which was 'expensive, ostentatious, middle-class and uneatable') were another indication of how the party—and politics—had gone to the dogs.

Pushed by the need to win mass support, the composition of the party elites began to change. By 1910, the proportion of Tory and Liberal MPs from landed backgrounds had fallen to 26% and 7% respectively. Such people were still well represented on the front benches (we should not assume that 'landed' MPs were all bone-headed squires) but preferment was increasingly difficult. Fortunately for them, there were other areas where gentlemen amateurs could give service without soiling their hands in the mire of popular politics—especially the House of Lords and the Empire. The former was used to resist the rising tide of liberal democracy between 1906 and 1914. The most dramatic instance was in 1909–11, when the Tory majority in the Lords initially rejected the Liberals' budget. The January 1910 election—fought as a conflict between the 'peers and the people'—went the people's way. Although the diehards in the Lords tried to resist the consequences of a second Liberal election victory in December 1910, their capacity to delay legislation was subsequently reduced to just twelve months. In the aftermath of the 1911 Parliament Act the Liberals introduced further reforming legislation, including a proposed extension of the franchise to men (with the option of extending this to women), the disestablishment of the Church in Wales, and—greatest of sins in the Lords' eyes—a Home Rule Bill for Ireland. The structure of the united, Anglican, patriarchal kingdom was under threat. In response, some Conservatives advocated use of the referendum on key issues or suggested adopting proportional representation, believing this would help prevent 'demagogues' from abusing their political power.

Conservatives who tried to compete with the Liberals frequently proclaimed the importance of Britain's links with its Empire. There were good reasons to think this might be popular. In 1900 the Conservatives had triumphed in an election dominated by Britain's success in the Boer War. Coming not long after Queen Victoria's Diamond Jubilee, when the Empire had displayed its 'unity' for all to see, this seemed to confirm the Conservatives as orchestrators of national grandeur and success. Throughout the period 1900–14 the Conservatives attempted to recapture this success. In leading this crusade, Joseph Chamberlain drew support from a wide variety of people within the party. He envisaged a huge imperial trading bloc, able to compete with Germany and the USA and protected and united behind tariff barriers. Chamberlain even suggested reforming the House of Lords to include representatives of the Empire.

Whilst this programme appealed to educated imperialists, Chamberlain also recognized the need for broader support. Hence he stressed tariffs as a means of keeping out 'foreign' goods and securing employment in Britain. He claimed tariff revenues would fund social reforms for the British electorate. The mass electorate had to be mobilized if conservative values and traditions were to survive.

The tariff campaign was defeated because it proposed introducing taxes on imported food. Here was a material problem which even Chamberlain could not obscure. After three election defeats, the Conservatives chose a new leader (Bonar Law) and a 'new' issue on which to fight (Ireland). Conservatives saw Home Rule for Ireland as the first stage in the dissolution of both the UK and the Empire. Many, including Bonar Law, were appalled by this prospect. Some lent tacit support to Irish Protestants who were threatening armed resistance. A few peers even started to arm their tenants and friends, ready to defend the Union. More constructively, other leading Conservatives raised alternatives to Home Rule. This included support for a federal Britain, with Ireland (along with Wales and Scotland) having a devolved assembly. As always, what was to happen to England in such a scheme was problematic—even the restoration of the Anglo-Saxon heptarchy had its advocates. This was known as 'Home Rule all round'. Conservatives hoped it might preserve the United Kingdom and lead to the creation of an Imperial parliament by removing items of 'parochial' interest to the devolved assemblies.

For traditionalists there was one further threat on the horizon: socialism. It is important to draw a distinction here between the idea of socialism and the challenge of the new Labour party. The latter drew support from Tory working men as well as from Liberals and was thus an obstacle to a Tory revival. However, Labour's support was limited and localized. It was 'socialism' as an ideology of intervention and social justice, as an assault on the rights of property and the assumed superiority of traditional rulers, which was a danger. The Conservatives feared anything that arrayed the owners of property against those who had none. Thus the growth of industrial unrest after 1911 was a threat because it might expose this social divide, not because there was any serious 'revolutionary' danger. The Liberals sought to manage such conflict, using state legislation to set minimum wages in some industries and negotiating with unions in others. They were generally successful. Mass democracy was advancing, leading to a new kind of politics. The Liberals were in the ascendant; the Tories were in shock.

All this was turned upside down by the First World War. The Liberal and Labour parties both split over Britain's participation. Whilst the majority supported it, vociferous minorities felt the conflict was unnecessary, the product of an arms race, secret alliances, and the encouragement of a xenophobic nationalism by a traditional ruling elite and the popular press. Amongst Labour's leaders, Ramsay MacDonald and Philip Snowden resigned rather than support British intervention. By contrast, the Conservatives exhibited an unambiguous patriotism. Moreover, Britain received committed support from its colonies. Empire and nation were to the fore. Liberty and democracy were pushed to the rear. When militant Irish home rulers engaged in an armed uprising in 1916 and some Liberals opposed conscription as an invasion of liberty, the public backed the Conservatives' strong stress on national needs. The mass electorate was no longer the opponent of traditionalist values, but its champion.

The First World War and its aftermath

War also altered the domestic political structure. A coalition government was formed in 1915. Party conflict during wartime seemed absurd. In 1916, following the Liberals' apparent failure to run the war efficiently, the Conservatives joined a new coalition government under Lloyd George. The Liberal leader, H. H. Asquith, was forced to resign, his reputation in tatters, his supporters embittered by the orchestrated and populist press campaign that led to his downfall. Lloyd George formed a high-powered 'inner cabinet' to get things done. Censorship was tightened and some individual rights were curtailed under the Defence of the Realm Act. Trade union rights were diluted or suspended.

As the war ended it became clear that those who had fought for peace, but had no vote under the prewar system, had now to be involved in constructing the victory. Thus in 1918 all men over 21 were given the vote. As it was politically difficult to continue excluding women—to do so would have divided the country and the coalition government—politicians effected a compromise. Women over 30 were enfranchised, provided they owned property or were married to a householder. This kept men in a majority and pacified opponents of change, who felt younger women would be politically irresponsible. Similar changes took place in other European countries (although some, like France, still withheld the vote from women). All the old doubts about the dangers of mass democracy—temporarily forgotten when the people became partisan traditionalists during the war—now re-emerged. Indeed, for members of the British establishment they were intensified. The small but symbolically significant Easter Rising in Ireland proved an inspiration to nationalist movements across the British Empire, as did the declarations of US President Woodrow Wilson in favour of national self-determination and the Bolshevik uprising in 1917. Traditional values—at home and in the Empire—were in danger. Popular opinion—at home and abroad—re-emerged as a threat to the traditional governing elite.

Where democratic systems existed, opponents of Britain's imperial position were able to express their desire for change at the ballot box. Thus in Ireland Sinn Fein, the militant nationalists, won a landslide victory in the 1918 elections. Their MPs boycotted Westminster and established an independent Irish assembly (the Dáil) in Dublin. By September 1919 the Dáil and Sinn Fein had been proscribed by the British government, in a climate of increased violence and civil disorder. The Government of Ireland Bill which followed failed to satisfy Irish demands. It excluded Ulster from the new Irish state and retained some powers in British hands. War ensued—initially against the British. However, some Irish nationalists eventually accepted the exclusion of Ulster and a treaty with Britain. The pro-treaty party (Cumann na nGaedheal, later Fine Gael) was attacked by the anti-treaty party (Fianna Fáil) led by Éamon de Valéra. Civil war ensued.

The Irish situation had some impact, both on British attitudes and on nationalist opinion within the Empire. 'If we lose Ireland,' claimed Field Marshal Sir Henry Wilson, an Anglo-Irishman, 'we have lost the Empire.' There was similar unrest in India, Egypt, Persia, and Palestine, at a time when Britain's military obligations in Europe weakened its capacity to resist in the Empire. Those opposed to Britain were assumed, in some cases correctly, to be copying the Irish example. Churchill wrote of the demands made by Egyptian nationalists: 'If we leave out the word "Egypt" . . . and substitute the word "Ireland", it would with very small omissions make perfectly good sense and would constitute a complete acceptance of Mr de Valéra's demands.'

British rulers often responded with military might. In Ireland an irregular force nicknamed the 'Black and Tans' was given a counter-revolutionary remit. They used vicious methods. The same methods (sometimes the same people) were used in Palestine and Iraq. Military resistance continued to have its advocates into the 1920s and 1930s. During 1930, for example, whilst the Labour leader Ramsay MacDonald was organizing peaceful discussions on the future of India, he was offered a different strategy by the Earl of Inchcape: 'we have pandered to native agitators in a way that has given them the idea that the more trouble they make the more chance there is of getting rid of the British from the country. The only way to govern an Asiatic country is by a benevolent dictatorship.' He suggested a few extra divisions of fresh troops, with the instruction to give no quarter.

If a section of the British establishment felt its world was under attack in the Empire, events at home made them even less secure. Fearing moral degeneration and class conflict, prewar radical

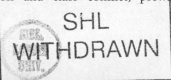

conservatives like Lord Milner and Lord Willoughby de Broke formed the British Workers' League and the National Party to maintain the 'spirit' of wartime patriotism. They and others wished to continue with a coalition government initially seen as a temporary wartime measure. The old political divisions, they argued, were no longer significant. There were newer dangers—Bolshevism, the disintegration of Empire, the devaluation of patriotism, honour, and religion, the erection of class hatred and envy as the focal point of politics. Industrial unrest in 1919 fuelled this sense of crisis. The answer was a coalition government to avoid splits within the forces of order and a strengthening of the House of Lords, so that lapses of public taste (such as the election of a Labour government) could be controlled. As Lloyd George stated in 1921, 'it was not enough to give that Second Chamber power, it must also be given authority, without which it would be as matchwood in a serious crisis'.

Restructuring postwar politics: electing the governors

The coalition government collapsed in 1922. Party differences and ambitions were too strong. As importantly, those who wished to resist the tide of democracy became less influential than those (evident even before 1914) who felt that the new democracy could be 'managed'. This shift back towards the 'management' of opinion helped structure the nature of postwar British politics. There was a parallel development within imperial politics.

During the coalition years, Conservative party leaders painted a picture of a country divided between 'the people' on the one hand and the selfish and bullying forces of organized labour on the other. They used the popular press and other means to try and mould public opinion. The new mass electorate—even the much-feared women voters—were increasingly seen as an important, but fickle, source of Conservative support. This approach proved remarkably successful. The collapse of the coalition government in 1922 led to an election which the Conservatives won handsomely. Labour made headway (at the Liberals' expense) and became the main anti-Tory party with around 30% of the vote. Perhaps becoming a little overconfident, in

1923 the Conservatives again supported the introduction of tariff
barriers, repeating the policy commitment which in the Edwardian
period had led to electoral disaster. Once again the party sank beneath
the weight of its self-imposed burden. Labour became the second
largest party (after the Conservatives). With Liberal support, it
formed a minority government in January 1924.

The first Labour government lasted less than a year. In December
1924 the Tories achieved a landslide victory. Labour increased its vote
to 33%; but the Tories obtained a massive 47%, as the Liberal vote
collapsed. Many of the Liberals' forty MPs were elected with tacit
Conservative support. A two-party system had been established.
There was a clear—and secure—government majority and a clear
opposition, at a time when European democratic models were producing unstable coalitions. Nonetheless, the British system was hardly
'democratic'. In 1923 the Liberals and Tories had returned fewer MPs
than their electoral support merited. In 1924 it was Labour's turn to
feel aggrieved. Despite polling 2.5% more than in 1923 and gaining a
million new votes, it returned forty fewer MPs.

The British 'first past the post' system continued to determine the
outcome of elections. The Liberals' effected an electoral revival in
1929. Despite polling 23.5% of the vote, they returned just fifty-nine
MPs. With 37.8% of the vote—much less than twice the Liberal
total—Labour elected nearly five times as many MPs and became the
single largest party. The Tories, with just 69,000 fewer votes than
Labour, returned thirty-seven fewer MPs. Labour formed its second
minority government, again with Liberal support.

The geographical distribution of political support had a clear
impact on British elections. The concentration of the coal, steel, cotton textile, shipbuilding, and engineering industries in parts of Wales,
Scotland, Lancashire, and the north-east of England, created a pha-
lanx of solidly working-class seats which tended to return Labour
MPs. The Conservatives likewise had a solid core of support in the
south of the country, including both rural areas and affluent suburban seats. This created the *impression* of class polarization, though
in reality many working-class men and women voted Liberal or Tory.
Working-class seats in Liverpool, Birmingham, Bristol, and Ports-
mouth returned Liberals or Conservatives for much of the 1920s, as
did industrial centres such as Walsall, Stockton, South Shields, and
Chatham. Labour only managed to broaden its appeal in 1929, when

it captured around seventy seats—largely in London and the west Midlands—for the first time. Whilst the expansion of municipal housing estates in these areas was creating a new type of largely working-class constituency, the party's success rested on its capacity to alter its image to fit the needs of these and other groups.

All British parties attempted to portray themselves not as the party of a class but as the party of the 'people'. The Conservatives were particularly successful. They presented themselves as above 'sectional' interest, as the party of moral values, the family, stability, and order. They were especially adept at attracting support from women, and most had few doubts about extending the vote to women under 30 (the 'flappers') through the 1928 Equal Franchise Act. Whilst party leaders did not dominate their party's image as they do today, the Conservative leaders attracted growing attention from a developing mass media, using this to good effect between 1924 and 1929 and again in the 1930s.

Baldwin's attempt to tame the electorate and harness it to the cause of traditional values was more about presentation than substance. In well-publicized speeches he claimed to be an 'ordinary man', a 'plain man', a 'common man'—and 'an Englishman'. He sought to mobilize the 'sober element', the 'responsible element'. He attacked 'vulgar wealth' and indulgent privilege. He proclaimed the importance of 'English sanity'. Britain—and its Empire—were great representations of what that sanity could achieve. Those who wished to abandon those achievements were enemies of all the 'common people'. Socialism was an alien import, the product of an intelligentsia ('a very ugly word for a very ugly thing') which sought to impose itself on the common sense of the majority. Although Baldwin spoke much of 'England', the Conservatives were a 'national' party. In 1924, for example, they won a quarter of all seats in Wales and half the seats in Scotland.

Historians regularly claim that Baldwin promoted tolerance within his own party, notably restraining colleagues from passing stronger anti-trade union legislation after the General Strike. However, the Conservatives also constructed (inaccurate) depictions of Labour as a threat to the country. Thus Labour was 'Bolshevist', the handmaiden of the Soviet Union. In 1924 the Conservatives promoted fictitious newspaper stories which claimed the USSR was fomenting industrial and political discontent within Britain (the Zinoviev letter episode). In 1931, they claimed that Labour would confiscate savings from Post

Office accounts if elected. The Conservatives utilized popular psychology, the press, radio, and later newsreels to put over their message. Party election agents were told that their business was to 'sell Conservatism to the public'—and not to forget that they had 'the best of wares to offer'. In the 1930s film presented new opportunities. Baldwin and Neville Chamberlain mastered the art of the 'fireside chat', speaking informally to camera and directly to the individual viewer.

Labour was equally keen to demonstrate it was not a 'class' party. Its 1918 constitution set the tone, claiming it was the party of the workers 'by hand and by brain'. Arthur Henderson, one of the most significant influences on Labour's organizational structure and strategy, encouraged local parties to recruit new middle-class and women members, rather than rely on the male trade unionists who were such a significant element already. He established policy advisory committees to draw upon Labour's new intellectual recruits and supported the adoption of ex-Liberals as parliamentary candidates in order to demonstrate that Labour was a 'safe' anti-Tory force. He also fought hard to prevent party radicals from associating with Communists, so that Labour's moderate image was not undermined from within. He ensured that the Communists' attempt to affiliate to the Labour party was rejected, and tried to ensure that individual Communists were expelled. Labour members who continued to cooperate with Communist groups were disciplined and brought into line.

The party's leader, Ramsay MacDonald, was even more committed to this approach. MacDonald was determined to show that Labour was 'fit to govern'. In office during 1924, he proceeded cautiously. He was unhappy about industrial action and was especially cautious about the 1926 General Strike. Labour developed a programme of reforms designed to create well-paid work within a strong economy, with opportunities for all and an end to class distinction. In *Labour and the Nation*, the party's programme for the 1929 election, socialism was portrayed as neither a utopian creed nor a 'blind revolt against poverty and oppression'. Socialism had already brought about better public services within local government. Now it was inspiring Labour to organize the resources of the community 'with a single eye to securing for all its members the largest possible measure of economic welfare and personal freedom'. British political stability was based in part on accepting but trying to manage democracy. It drew on a commitment to moderation and on a political system that reinforced the strength of the dominant party. These circumstances did not prevail elsewhere.

The imperial dimension

Attempts by large parties to capture the centre ground were unusual within Europe. In continental Europe the development of radical Nationalist/Fascist groups on the right and Socialist/Communist parties on the left was polarizing politics. The centre ground was taken by a series of smaller parties representing sectional groups— especially rural voters and professionals—and parties with a strong regional or religious identity. Politics was more polarized, democracy much weaker. Politics in Ireland threatened to follow this lead. In Northern Ireland, 'confessional' politics was the norm; indeed, mainland British parties stood aside whilst 'Irish' parties were left to fight on 'Irish' lines. The largely Protestant Unionist party dominated the devolved Ulster parliament. Their treatment of Catholics, manipulation of electoral boundaries for political gain, and creation of a Unionist police force scarcely caused a ripple in domestic British politics. The Unionists drew support from Protestant voters irrespective of their class background and generally won ten of the twelve Westminster seats. The smaller nationalist community at times elected two MPs. In southern Ireland too the 'national question' dominated. The 1921 'articles of agreement' created an 'Irish Free State', which had Dominion status within the still British Commonwealth. This meant that Irish leaders swore an oath of allegiance to the British crown and allowed the British government some say in matters of defence. The pro-treaty party Fine Gael was initially dominant. However, the anti-treaty Fianna Fáil gradually gained strength, forming a government in 1932. As in Britain, neither was a 'class' party in the real sense. Fine Gael initially drew more support from the wealthier elements, but could not have been elected by this constituency alone. However, the parallel with Britain should not be pushed too far. In Ireland, minor parties representing specific groups fared quite well. Labour was largely a rural workers' party, whilst the farmer's party (which gained 12% of the vote in 1923) represented the larger farming interests. This was closer to a 'European' than a

'British' pattern of politics. In the 1930s, Fine Gael even had a charismatic proto-fascist leader, Eoin O'Duffy, who had his own paramilitary faction.

The pattern of democratic change within the British Empire was different again. Although countries like New Zealand and Australia developed similar party political structures to Britain, within the Empire itself Britain declined to replicate the 'Westminster model', or to create a Western democratic system. To some extent this is understandable. The Empire contained a vast array of different countries, with different histories, patterns of administration, and populations. Some countries contained politically active white settlers, with no desire for democratic change. Others were uneasy and artificial amalgamations of different tribes or religious/ethnic groups, where a 'Westminster model' was unlikely to work. British governments were unwilling to try and devise a single approach. Frequently independent-minded local British officials were also unlikely to accept anything which ignored local circumstances. An apocryphal story records the response of one district official in India to an order from his superior in Britain: 'Your letter . . . which is before me, will shortly be behind me in another capacity.'

British politicians claimed it would be irresponsible to introduce democratic systems into countries with no democratic traditions. In 'black Africa' this reflected a crude set of racial ideas about the incapacity of black peoples to govern with reason and fairness. Even in India there was no attempt to establish a gradual process of democratization, culminating in independence. The Morley–Minto reforms of 1909 aimed at bringing more Indians into reformed governing councils, but this was meant to reconcile the conservative and weightier elements within Indian society to British rule rather than establish a political structure which would lead to self-government in the near future. The Indian reforms enfranchised interests, not people, as in eighteenth-century not twentieth-century Britain. There were separate elections for different communal groups, reserved seats on local bodies for particular ethnic groups, large numbers of nominated representatives, and protected rights for the autocratic Indian princes within their own 'kingdoms'. The franchise for all elections was very narrow indeed. Even by 1914, the municipal electorate in Bombay constituted 1% of the city's population, or around 11,500 voters. Nonetheless, those who wished to resist all change were less significant that those who wished to create a more liberal system, preserving British rule by involving some local elements and devolving some powers. A sense of civic consciousness was deemed desirable. Reforms designed to move in this direction attracted some support within Britain, but less in India. However, the British in India were neither uniformly racist in their attitudes nor unconcerned with the future of a country many loved and cherished. If successive viceroys and many British residents saw educated Indians as unfit to govern their own country, it was in part a consequence of paternalistic attitudes, and a concern with the perceived reluctance of 'educated Indians' to display a sense of civic consciousness.

The Morley–Minto reforms stimulated political alliances between different groups within provinces, and between 'national' politicians (anxious to secure or retain a seat in the Delhi legislature) and provincial groups. This escalated existing changes. An indigenous urban political culture had been developed in the late nineteenth century (paralleling developments in Britain) with civic groups, women's associations, social service leagues, and other such bodies all seeking to expand their independent role. However, the (dominant) Indian National Congress and minority Muslim League were not allowed to play anything like the same democratic role as parties in Britain (although the latter was cultivated since it might oppose the creation of a separate Indian state, dominated by the Hindus). Parties thus increasingly made their case through other means. Over the next thirty years, Indian parties continued to develop on religious and nationalist lines, with Hindus, Muslims, and Sikhs all eventually seeking their own separate and independent states. Parties did not adopt the same role in the Empire as they did in the UK.

The rise of separatist nationalism across the Empire concerned British leaders during the war, but became a major worry thereafter. In India Gandhi's policy of non-cooperation with British authority in 1921–2 led to major disruption and violence, at a time when Britain's military resources were stretched to breaking point by similar problems elsewhere. These developments coincided with a substantial shift in British administrative policy. Although the 1919 Government of India Act was not a retreat from Empire, its liberalizing influences were hidden by a tougher rhetoric, aimed at appeasing Tory diehards. The British Secretary of State for India, Edwin Montagu, described accusations that this was a retreat from Empire as 'a complete fallacy'.

Lloyd George made similar noises. 'We are now masters in India', he wrote, 'and we should let it be understood that we intend to remain so.'

The 1919 Act reflected the Montagu–Chelmsford report of 1918 (Chelmsford was the Indian viceroy). This proposed devolution of legislative and financial powers from the centre to nine provincial assemblies. Indians were to dominate here and in the Delhi Legislative Council, elements of which were to be elected on a broader (but still restricted) franchise. Nonetheless, the viceroy's Legislative Council was only an advisory body. This system of 'dyarchy' differed substantially from the constitutional position in Britain. Nor was it very democratic. Within the provinces, British-appointed provincial governors retained control over law and order and taxation. At national level, financial and banking policy was under British control, since British interests—revenue and stability—had to be secured. Political censorship was retained.

If in Britain those who wished to resist democracy gave way to those who wished to manage it, the pressure to resist democratic change in India was stronger. For an older generation of British imperialists, the 1919 Act represented the end of unquestioned British domination, even though imperial politicians hoped it would create new alliances with Indian princes and landowners, divide the nationalists, and preserve British control. Once again, they had to be placated. Whilst a review of the 1919 Act was promised, Montagu told the House of Commons in 1922 that any further democratic 'advance' would be dependent on Indian 'good conduct' and cooperation with the imperial mission. Subsequent changes were within these parameters. The 1924 Lee Commission, which investigated the role of the all-powerful Indian civil service, recommended more 'Indianization', not to lay the foundations of a new state but to preserve British rule through good governance. Nor were further franchise reforms part of an attempt to develop a participatory sense of citizenship. In Bombay, changes in the municipal franchise and electoral laws allowed women to sit as councillors and extended participation. However, the franchise still excluded most ordinary workers. Anti-strike legislation helped turn many trade unionists against the state, and trade union leaders who were coopted onto committees lost support to the Communists as a result. Britain institutionalized a system of patronage, not democracy, and this pushed people towards extremist

groups. British rule did not create racial politics (although it helped
it along). In many respects, Britain wished to design an 'Indian' version of Britain's 'stable' system. However, what resulted was rather
different and much less effective.

The governance of the elect?

The quality of governance is much dependent on the quality of the
governors. Did the British system of domestic and imperial governance produce 'the governance of the elect'? In Britain politics was
becoming a serious—and at times seriously boring—business even
before 1914. The future Marquis of Londonderry complained of an
eight-hour day spent in the House of Commons, desperately trying
(and failing) to 'take an interest'. Lord Ernest Hamilton MP gave up
the fight, amusing himself by racing his brother along the Commons
terrace on bicycles borrowed from the dining room waiters. Party
leaders were not amused. Politics was becoming less a gentleman's
game, more a profession practised by those with interest and ability.

By contrast, the Empire could be a haven for the gentleman amateur, whose curriculum vitae stressed social rank rather than political
aptitude. A few examples will illustrate the point. The senior British
official in Dublin prior to the civil war, Sir Maurice Headlam, had
failed the entrance examination for the Indian civil service. He took
the Dublin post because he was a keen fisherman. Imperial posts were
well rewarded and involved a lifestyle that few in Britain could afford.
In the 1920s the Viceroy of India was paid more than the President of
the USA (and three times more than ministers in the British government). Posts as governors were also well rewarded. Once India had an
Empress, social decorum demanded that representatives of the monarch held elevated social positions. Of course, there was also substantial personal expenditure on the pomp and splendour that many felt
necessary to impress the Indians (and which some, like Curzon,
found particularly enjoyable). As a result, as one jaundiced professional administrator commented, the top colonial jobs went to
people 'selected rather for the coronets they have inherited than for
any distinction they have gained'. Whilst there were occasional self-
made men and newly ennobled peers amongst colonial governors

(notably the Marquis of Reading, Viceroy of India 1921–6) the vast majority of such people were drawn from the British aristocracy. It was only below this level, or in areas where political sensitivity was needed, that professional elites drawn from upper-middle-class families were beginning to emerge (as they were in Britain).

At the same time, where posts were ceremonial, and were located in countries where agriculture was economically important, the landed aristocracy might be well qualified for their tasks. Some leading imperial figures had long-standing family connections with the Empire and an accumulated understanding of its cultures. A few were from the political top drawer. However, others were political discards, hardly equipped for the political problems they were to face. Viscount Chelmsford, Viceroy of India from 1916 to 1921, was 'little more than a nonentity'. He was serving as a captain in the Territorial Army when he received the call to office. Lord Willingdon, once Governor of Bombay and Viceroy of India during the second Labour government, had been an undistinguished back bench Liberal MP. Labour's first choice for the post had been less 'aristocratic', but even more obscure

Was the 'governing elect' in Britain that different? It was, of course, less aristocratic by the later 1920s. As in the Empire, Parliament contained many loyal journeymen, alongside overconfident and opinionated individualists, whose idiotic pet schemes caused their leaders endless embarrassment. The idle, the inefficient, and the inebriates were all there, in good numbers. However, such people seldom got past junior office (drunkards were an exception to the rule: to exclude them would have seriously depleted the front bench). The 'professionalization' of politics had produced a new kind of leader. There were no 'party schools', in the tradition of the German socialists, but successful politicians were increasingly expected to play an informed role in developing policy or in presenting the party's programme. As a result, a training in law or economics became increasingly common amongst the nation's leaders, on both sides of the House of Commons.

This development was much less pronounced within the Labour Party, since its first generation of leaders consisted in the main of self-educated men from working-class backgrounds. Yet even here the position was changing. The party had always contained an academic element—Fabians like Sidney Webb, academics like G. D. H. Cole and ex-Tory patricians, like the (non-practising) barrister Clem Attlee. It was strengthened in the 1920s and 1930s by recruits from other political organizations. This included former Liberal MPs, such as Charles Trevelyan (Labour Education Minister in 1924 and 1929) and William Wedgwood Benn (Secretary of State for India in 1929). It also included former Tories, recruited for their administrative or professional expertise, notably Lord Parmoor (Lord President of the Council in both Labour governments) and his son, Stafford Cripps, perhaps the outstanding barrister of his generation. Within the Tory party, the landed gentry continued to be well represented, but it generally needed more than this to gain a place at the Cabinet table. Baldwin's cabinet contained sharp lawyers, like Lord Birkenhead, and professional politicians from political families, notably Austen and Neville Chamberlain. By the early 1930s more than two-thirds of MPs had received a university education.

The professionalization of politics was matched by growing professionalization within the supporting political machines. Both parties created research departments (although neither with much enthusiasm). Labour's policy advisory committees were an important vehicle for academic recruits, notably from Oxford University and the London School of Economics, both of which supplied Labour with copious advice on economics and international relations. The process was taken still further in the 1930s with the advent of groups such as the New Fabian Research Bureau.

Nonetheless, governments and governors relied heavily for advice on the permanent 'governing class', the senior civil servants. The British civil service grew considerably across this period. The three branches of the colonial civil service were even larger and even more influential. Within Britain, senior civil servants were drawn almost exclusively from Oxford and Cambridge universities and the main public schools. Around three-quarters of the Indian civil service was drawn from public schools and Oxbridge, and largely from upper-middle-class backgrounds. Once in the service, recruits learnt a particular code and ethos. They were responsible as much to higher civil servants as to their political masters, and were promoted by seniority and by their peers, not by the politicians. Here was a real governing class, administering the Empire with efficiency and commitment and on agreed lines, and sustaining the ever-increasing activities of the domestic British state.

Yet the civil service was not trained to be creative nor expected to be political. The impact of the so-called 'Treasury view' on economic policy-making between the wars nicely illustrates the conservative impact of the civil service. Whilst the Treasury's approach to economic policy may have been more flexible and pragmatic than historians once recognized, it was still rooted in economic orthodoxy. Its most dramatic influence was in 1931, when the Labour Chancellor of the Exchequer, Philip Snowden, was strongly advised to balance the budget through cuts in expenditure (including a 20% cut in unemployment benefit) and to stay on the gold standard. Snowden's rigid adherence to this view helped split the Labour party, leading to the formation of a National government and to Labour's massive defeat in the 1931 election. The same policies were followed across the Empire, and through the same influences. Indeed, the development of a central bank in India and the creation of the sterling area reinforced and institutionalized this economic view. Of course, some politicians (like Philip Snowden) shared these views and needed no prompting. But the civil service could make it difficult to be innovative.

The role of the civil service in the Empire was even more significant, in part because of the sheer distance from London. Indian district officers governed huge areas, generally dispensing not just law and order, but justice. The problems were often further up the hierarchy. For an older generation of civil servants their 'gentlemanly role' included a sense of honour, public service—and often a strong sense of racial superiority and 'Christian duty'. For Sir Arthur Hirtzel, the most important India Office official in the 1920s, this meant passionate support for Britain's imperial role: 'the race to which he belongs', he wrote, 'is the noblest, and the citizenship and ideal for which it stands are the highest—are, in fact, so high that all the world must needs accept them.' Similar views were held by the financial ministers to the Council of India and by many others in senior positions. The influences which this elect group brought to bear were generally conservative, but were always well-informed. This made them very difficult to ignore.

Historians have suggested that there was little difference between Labour and Conservative policies on many issues between the two wars, partially because of these influences but also because all parties sought to woo the centre ground. However, the extent of this consensus should not be exaggerated. The differences between British parties were not as pronounced as the differences between parties in continental Europe, but they were not insignificant. They were also masked by Labour's policies in office. Elements within the Labour party felt a consensus had been artificially constructed, because in office party leaders and civil servants had undermined Labour's true radicalism, and because Labour's own experts had been ignored. They became increasingly concerned to draw up programmes for office that reflected the views of a *Labour* elect, which should in time become a new *governing* elect.

In both 1924 and 1929, Labour leaders ensured that many of the party's radical experts were excluded from Cabinet office. Long-standing opponents of Foreign Office values, such as E. D. Morel and Norman Angell, were passed over in 1924. Labour's vociferous Indian expert, Josiah Wedgwood, whose ideas terrified the Conservative Secretary of State for India in the early 1920s, was given a minor domestic role and kept away from imperial affairs. In 1929, Ramsay MacDonald appointed the ageing Lord Passfield (Sidney Webb) to the Colonial Office. Initially he advanced the civil servants' pro-Arab line over Jewish settlement in Palestine, ignoring the party's advice. He allowed the Conservative-dominated East Africa Select Committee to bury Labour's White Paper on native policy, which had been designed to challenge the dominant role of white settlers. Later, he felt he was being bullied into taking a different line. Oddly, in Ceylon, Labour established a new political system between 1929 and 1931, abolishing an electoral system which embraced just 4% of the population and introducing a system which enfranchised all men and women over the age of 21. But this was an exception. Labour's policy of granting Dominion status (gradually) fell (more rapidly) by the wayside. The conservatism of the leadership irritated Labour's small but expert group of imperial policy advisers, which included academics like Harold Laski and Philip Noel-Baker (both of the London School of Economics) and those with practical experience of the Indian subcontinent, such as Leonard Woolf and Major David Graham Pole.

There were similar problems over domestic policy. In 1929 Labour's Education Minister, Charles Trevelyan, reflecting the views of the party's own educational experts, argued that the school leaving age should be raised to 16 and education allowances paid to help working-class children stay in school. He resigned when MacDonald and Snowden, apparently reflecting the 'Treasury view', withdrew their support. Snowden and MacDonald's 'capitulation' to the Treasury over public expenditure cuts in 1931 was the final straw for those who believed that a traditional 'governing elect' had 'tamed' the party. Such claims were unfair. The economic crisis made it difficult to implement many of Labour's bolder plans, as did opposition from the Liberals and Tories (although Snowden at least needed little persuading). Nonetheless, Labour's commitment to developing the influence of its own 'governing elect' was substantially enhanced by the events of 1929–31.

After the 1931 split, the need to prepare and then implement radical policies dominated Labour politics. However, such concerns were academic. Facing combined opposition from the Liberal and Conservative parties, Labour gained just 31% of the vote in 1931 and returned a mere fifty-two MPs. The National Liberal and National Labour parties, with just 5.2% of the vote, returned forty-eight MPs. This reflected Conservative attempts to create a 'national' alliance, and again demonstrated the absurdities of the British electoral system. The National government had a huge majority. Its supporters saw it as the saviour of the nation and the Empire. It would stand against Bolshevism and anarchy and preserve Britain's standing in the world. As with the coalition government in 1918, this was proclaimed as a victory for the people over political sectarianism, as a victory for 'democracy' over 'politics'. In reality, the government was almost immune to public opinion. Ironically, far from this being a check on reform, the National government effected a series of progressive changes in both domestic and imperial policy.

The National government and the Empire

The parallels with the earlier coalition government are especially strong so far as imperial issues are concerned. In 1931–2, as in 1919–20, the government faced demands for change from within both Ireland and the Empire. The 1931 Statute of Westminster put the Dominions on the road to independence. A Fianna Fáil electoral victory in 1932 raised the possibility that Eire would leave the Commonwealth. Nationalist unrest within the Empire was growing. Politicians again perceived a crisis. Willingdon, the new Viceroy, welcomed the National government as an opportunity to solve 'our Indian problem on non-party lines'. Hoare, the new Secretary of State for India, made it clear that he wanted nothing 'in the nature of a surrender on the lines of the Irish Treaty'. However, he too recognized that concessions had to be made.

The position was complex. The 1930 Simon Commission report, which reviewed the 1919 Government of India Act, raised the possibility of an Indian federation. However, the exclusion of Indians from the Simon Commission's discussions caused such resentment that the contents of the report were overshadowed and ignored. Lord Irwin (Viceroy 1926–31) established further talks, the Round Table conferences, to which Indian leaders were invited. Irwin supported greater Indian representation within the viceroy's central executive in order to retain India within the Empire. When the National government rejected this proposal, there were further disturbances in India. As a result Gandhi and 36,000 other leaders were arrested early in 1932.

Debates over India dominated British politics between 1932 and 1935. There were nearly 2,000 speeches in parliament on this topic alone. If Labour undermined the 'consensus' by renewing its support for Dominion status, Tory backbenchers shattered it by resisting any concessions. The government's chief opponent was Winston Churchill, who had resigned from the Shadow Cabinet in 1931 when Baldwin accepted the idea of a 'federal' solution for India. Churchill and his eighty allies launched a lengthy war against the proposal. The Government of India Bill was finally passed in August 1935. Although the federal aspects discussed in 1930–1 were still in the bill, this aspect never really got going. Events in India had shown such ideas to be unworkable. However, the powers of provincial assemblies were increased and the franchise extended. The role of Indians within the national legislative council was expanded. Despite diehard blustering, this was no retreat from Empire. As Lord Linlithgow, Viceroy from 1936 put it, the 1935 act was framed as a way of 'maintaining British influence in India. It is no part of our policy . . . to expedite in India constitutional changes for their own sake.'

Over time the National government became progressively more liberal in domestic and imperial policy. On the domestic front there was a new education act, legislation to support maternity care, and interventionist policies in agriculture, along with other social legislation. Within the Empire, advice given to the Indian civil service in 1937 put the change neatly: 'The civilian who used to serve by ruling, must learn to rule by serving.' The Colonial Office recognized that indirect rule in 'black Africa' had neither contained social change nor delivered economic success. It developed a new emphasis, promoting better land management and agricultural improvements. These changes eventually resulted in the 1940 Colonial Development and Welfare Act. The new aim was not independence, but better governance.

There were other factors promoting change. In order to secure India's financial position (so that it could pay for its own administration and defence) tariffs had been introduced. This developed Indian industry at the expense of British exports, making the 'loss' of India less economically and politically difficult. Similarly, changes in Irish politics made the prospects of changes there less threatening. The new 1937 constitution did not declare Ireland a republic, since this would have made reunification with northern Ireland in the future an impossibility. Moreover, by comparison to the proto-fascist leader of Fine Gael, Eoin O'Duffy, de Valéra was a statesman, who presented himself as a 'national' leader. Having gained the acceptance of the Irish business class, he was fast heading for the centre ground and dissociating himself from his radical past. The IRA had been banned in 1936. Support for marriage, Catholicism, the family, and conventional morality made Ireland an unlikely model for rebellious British territories. De Valéra's relationship with Germany during the Second World War, and Eire's separate stance during the conflict, were a source of irritation—but an irritant reduced once Fine Gael's electoral domination of Irish politics was ended in 1948. The new 1949 Treaty of Ireland Act created difficulties for the Irish and British governments, not because it proclaimed Ireland a republic with no allegiance to the crown, but because backbench Labour MPs objected to the exclusion of Northern Ireland. These voices were ignored. Northern Ireland was seen by some as an aberrant and embarrassing 'backwater', which provided unwanted evidence of the way that 'primitive' instincts could deflect politics from its 'true' course.

The National government and electoral politics

The governments of 1931–40 were a huge political success. The National government won the 1935 election convincingly, its 53% of the vote producing a massive 429 seats. Electoral pacts with National Liberals helped it to win more than half the seats in Scotland and nearly a third of those in Wales. Its claim to be a responsible and non-partisan body, protecting the welfare and stability of the nation at home and abroad and avoiding war if possible, was attractive to voters across Britain. Labour, by contrast, with more votes than ever before, returned just 154 MPs (far fewer than in 1929). Nonetheless, it had made significant progress. A new and practical programme had been constructed. It captured the London County Council for the first time in 1934, extending its hold in 1937. Thereafter progress was limited. Rearmament provided employment in depressed areas, reinforcing the National government's claim to be the party of the nation. This claim was well expressed through carefully managed newsreels, radio broadcasts, and the popular press. The government made good use of George V's jubilee in 1935, and skilfully managed the subsequent abdication crisis without denting its public standing. Whilst the Labour Left felt the National government was insufficiently concerned with the rise of international fascism, or with the ravaging effects of unemployment, such criticism only aroused social-ist passions—it did not undermine the National government's dominance.

The policies pursued by the National government help to explain why fascism made little headway in Britain, despite Mosley's charis-matic leadership of the British Union of Fascists. The poor never became destitute. The lower middle class never saw their livelihoods disappear. There was no widespread collapse into lawlessness, no mob violence on the streets. Social observers felt that in Britain mass unemployment had created mass apathy and disillusionment with the political process. They were concerned that long-term and youth unemployment, rural depopulation and the growth of new towns characterized by individualistic lifestyles would undermine civic and public consciousness. Concern was also expressed about the way that mass culture and the Americanization of popular entertainment had 'dulled' the popular mind. Voluntary groups were formed to try and rebuild the sense of citizenship that underpins a successful liberal democracy. If democracy had been tamed, taming it had created its own problems.

The Second World War and its aftermath: assessing Labour's record

War changed both the structure of party politics and political attitudes to the people. Following Chamberlain's removal as Prime Minister in 1940, Labour was drawn into Churchill's new Cabinet. Attlee became Deputy Prime Minister. Party politics was suspended. Individual rights and liberties were curtailed. Conscription was introduced. Governments faced huge logistical and practical problems. Politicians became technocratic organizers of 'solutions'. 'Planning', the buzzword of the 1930s, became an imperative need. Direct intervention by the state became a feature of all aspects of policy, from manpower planning through to purchasing and distribution of goods. Although all parties could accept this, Labour was more comfortable with such ideas. In the 1945 election campaign it argued that these controls should continue after the war whilst the government reconstructed Britain, attacking poverty and want in the process. For the first time, circumstances favoured Labour. The party could not be termed unpatriotic (as it had been in 1918) because of its wartime role. In fact, Labour appeared 'above party', to be 'national' in its interests and demeanour—like the coalition government of 1918–22 and the National government in the 1930s.

If war restored the people's faith in the Labour party, it also restored Labour's faith in the people. The sacrifices made, the collective endeavour and 'Blitz spirit', seemed to suggest that the people and Labour were at one in their support for collective solutions to collective problems. King George VI and his queen conspicuously showed public spirit, visiting the bomb-damaged areas of London in a display of British resolve. This helped restore the image of the monarchy, after the problems presented by the abdication crisis in 1936. In that year King Edward VIII had been cornered into abdicating when it had been made plain to him by Baldwin that he could not remain on the throne and marry an American divorcee, Mrs Wallis Simpson. He was succeeded by his brother, George VI, but it appeared momentarily that the institution of monarchy was in some doubt. In 1945, Labour and the monarchy were both served by stressing national unity. In the 1945 election, Labour offered a practical but idealistic programme of short-term material improvements, supported by a longer-term vision which it hoped an electorate of caring and active citizens would embrace.

The electorate certainly voted for Labour in large numbers. The party won a landslide victory in 1945 with 49% of the vote. Labour obtained 393 seats, compared to just 189 for the Conservatives. In traditionally Labour seats, the party's candidates were returned with huge majorities. Shocked Labour candidates in seemingly unwinnable Tory areas were also elected. The new Parliamentary Labour Party was brimful of talent. Nor was Labour unprepared for office. Textbooks invariably reiterate the claim that on entering office Labour found its file on nationalization contained just two pamphlets (one of them in Welsh). In fact, the broad lines of policy had been thrashed out across the 1930s, in policy committees that have received little attention from historians. Many of those engaged in this process now entered office. Attlee himself had participated in discussions in several areas of policy. Morrison at Transport had established a model for public services when head of the London County Council. The back benches were full of a new generation, reared on the economic problems and international crisis of the 1930s and determined to attack their underlying causes. This was truly a government of the elect.

In office, Labour faced huge difficulties. Its priority was reconstructing the economy and rehousing the people. It made significant progress with these problems, whilst also implementing a series of other reforms, especially the introduction of a National Health Service. Labour also wished to encourage popular participation, to create a 'real' democracy rather than the apathetic democracy of the 1930s. The 1948 Representation of the People Act abolished the second vote which some property owners and all university graduates had enjoyed since 1918, introduced universal suffrage in municipal elections, and made provision for a redistribution of parliamentary boundaries. Labour sought to restore powers to local government, and to ensure public involvement in the replanning of the Blitz-damaged cities. At the same time, however, its desire to ensure efficient and effective public services and economic growth led to an emphasis on centralized state planning and regulation. Thus Labour rejected the idea for a decentralized national health service, as advocated by the Socialist Medical Association, and rejected the introduction of a Secretary of State for Wales, a devolved Welsh assembly or even regional governance (an idea that had gained support during the war). Attlee, like most Labour leaders, saw nationalism as a corrosive and irrational force, with its roots in social and economic injustice. He claimed that devolution would not solve the economic problems of Wales, and argued that Welsh voters would be happier if British policies addressed their economic difficulties. A decade earlier, he had noted the economic causes behind nationalist sentiment in India—adding pragmatically that it would take a 'giant's hand' to address those problems, and concluding that this 'could not be an alien hand'. As in Attlee's view Indian nationalists were not especially 'progressive', he remained sceptical about nationalism as a political force and about India's prospects. Self-determination for India was the only 'solution', but that did not make it a 'solution' which should be applied elsewhere, and especially not within Britain.

Labour did not assume that every colony should receive independence during its spell in office. Advocates of immediate decolonization, like the venerable Fenner Brockway, mainstay of almost every anti-imperialist movement in Britain in the period from 1900 to 1951, were more than matched by tough-minded imperialists like the Foreign Secretary, Ernest Bevin. Bevin stressed British strategic interests, US opinion, and the needs of the British economy. In the Far East (where Labour clung to its colonies) such concerns determined policy. Nonetheless, it would be a mistake to see Labour's policy as little different from that of the Conservative party. The Fabian Colonial Bureau (FCB) had been established in 1940 to promote economic development plans for the colonies. Under Arthur Creech Jones, the FCB drew a sharp distinction between countries ripe for independence (such as India) and countries 'such as the East and Central African territories' which were not. It had constructive plans for both. More dramatic action could be difficult. In Palestine, even Fenner Brockway recognized that immediate British withdrawal would not lead to a peaceful settlement, that the 'indigenous peoples', left to their own devices and free of the yoke of imperialism, would not necessarily act as good citizens.

There was some progress. Creech Jones became Colonial Secretary in 1946. Ably supported by John Parker and Andrew Cohen, the Colonial Office injected substantial amounts of money into development projects through the Overseas Food Corporation and Colonial Development Corporation, whilst also attempting to create viable and independent countries with working constitutions. There were unheralded successes, achieved against considerable odds in Nigeria and the Gold Coast, but there were also failures. Labour was still pragmatically unwilling to create difficulties in countries dominated by white settlers (Parker was sacked for doing so). The result of Labour's conflicting ideas on policy in Palestine was a disastrous lack of any clear direction and a focus on maintaining law and order.

In India and Palestine, circumstances—including the cost of maintaining law and order—now favoured British withdrawal. However, it did not make it inevitable. Attlee and Cripps had continued to seek a settlement during the war, albeit largely before 1942 and motivated by the desire to keep the Congress party engaged in the war against Japan. Even this was against Churchill's wishes. 'Hands off the Empire is our maxim,' Churchill had claimed in 1944, 'and it must not be weakened or smirched to please any sob-stuff merchants at home or foreigners of any hue.' Bevin was also unhappy about the division of the country, including the creation of a Muslim state (Pakistan) which would be separated into East and West Pakistan by the mass of India. Britain had tried to use Muslim fears about Hindu domination as a bulwark against calls for independence—but the tactic had evidently failed. Attlee demanded practical action. As he bluntly put it to Bevin, 'If you disagree with what is proposed you must offer a practical alternative. I fail to find one in your letter.'

It was perhaps this 'Fabian' instinct—a tendency to prioritize good collectivist governance by a determined 'elect', and to advocate practical but passionless solutions to problems—that caused Labour's electoral downfall in 1951. A narrow victory at the 1950 election (315 seats to 298 for the Tories) was followed by defeat in 1951 (when, despite out-polling their rivals, Labour returned seven fewer MPs). Although some in the 'Celtic fringe' felt neglected by the metropolitan centralization of power, it was in the south and amongst women voters that Labour support's collapsed. Labour had been so intent on 'solving' problems that it had stopped listening to a section of the democracy. State regulation and rationing—belt-tightening 'good governance', justified as worthwhile in the interests of longer-term developments—was not what people wanted after ten years of sacrifice. Britain had experienced the 'governance of the (collectivist) elect'—its reaction was to elect a different set of governors, more attuned to their individual aspirations.

The democratic system created in Britain across the early part of the twentieth century had weaknesses and critics. The electoral system regularly produced bizarre results. Some of these results were exaggerated by pacts between elements of the ruling elite, anxious to escape from the consequences of Britain's competitive democracy. Between 1918 and 1922—and again between 1931 and 1945—coalitions were produced and maintained when a way of life, in Britain and in the Empire, was threatened by what politicians saw as 'irrational' forces. If democracy was a danger at home, it was a real threat in the Empire. Putting the Empire at the mercy of 'foreigners' was deemed distinctly undesirable. Of course, democratization could not be resisted: it had to be contained and managed. Labour shared some of these concerns about a mass democracy. Yet many Labour politicians and activists also idealized the people, whether at home or overseas, believing they could become active and moral citizens. The people, by contrast, seldom idealized politicians or embraced their ideological aims, often supporting those who appeared 'above' party. In 1951 a Labour 'governing elect' grown distant from these ordinary desires was rejected at the polls. However, a new era was dawning. The British political elite contained a rising generation of professional politicians, whose political interests and values were honed by the domestic, European, and imperial crises of the 1930s. They had a rather different agenda. They would also turn gradually to the new tools of the political class—to the media, opinion polls, and psephology—to try to manage and mould opinion and to construct the electorate's ideas on both domestic and imperial policy.

Plate 5 'Welcome Home My Boy'.

The British Way and Purpose

Keith Robbins

British genius

The initials B.W.P. first appeared in the British Army's crop of cryptic abbreviations in the autumn of 1942. The Army Council had given general approval to the allotment, throughout the months November 1942–February 1943, of three hours per week from training or working time to education. To help the miscellaneous instructors who were assembled for this awesome task, a series of four monthly booklets were produced which would help soldiers to understand what was at stake in the war. The series was extended and debate began. A consolidated edition was published in 1944. The Army Bureau of Current Affairs had been created in August 1941 so that soldiers, in a modern democracy, could understand what came to be referred to as 'the British Way and Purpose'.

Also in 1942, the University of Cambridge, through its Press, was equally active in addressing *Current Problems* under the editorship of Sir Ernest Barker, who held the first Chair of Political Science. Written at a rather different level, a steady succession of volumes tried to get to the heart of the British matter. What did Britain 'stand for' in the middle of a Second World War in less than half a century? The authors ranged very widely in search of an answer; education, strategy, law, culture, ideology. What had happened to Britain in four decades and why? Where was the country going? What did the future hold? There was no easy answer to these questions. For Barker himself, in another book also published in 1942, 'Britain' did not possess a simple uniformity. Britain was not one, but many. Even so, the many were nonetheless one. This metaphysical reconciliation had a great attraction for writers who tried to explain both for their fellow citizens and the world at large just what 'Britain and the British People' stood for at this apparently critical juncture. Although the moment of maximum danger for Britain had perhaps passed, there was still vast uncertainty about the future. When so much was apparently changing there was a need to reassess and then reaffirm what it was that gave Britain its peculiar character and place in the world.

Publications of this kind, however, do not tell the full story. There was a feeling, in private at least, that the first half of the twentieth century was witnessing the end of 'Project Britain' as it had existed globally since at least the eighteenth century. 'It looks to me', wrote Cuthbert Headlam 'mid-Victorian' MP (as he described himself), in his diary in March 1942, 'as if G.B. might really sink into being a mere island in the North Sea, or become one of the members of a sort of pan-American group, if the Americans will take us on.' He thought it possible, however, that the Americans would prefer to cut adrift altogether from Europe and leave Britain out of the picture. If Britain were to join some European federation, 'we should only be a very insignificant portion of it—and if we stayed out of it, we should be at its mercy'. The future, he thought, certainly did not look very alluring for the British. He could not conceive, however, that they would pass entirely out of the picture and become of no account. He hoped, not altogether sanguinely, that there was still vitality in the British way.

It is not surprising that war once again provoked this fresh bout of introspection. As the American anthropologist Margaret Mead noted in the summer of 1942, 'in wartime people begin to think again in terms which had fallen into disrepute in the last quarter of a century, in terms of national character'. What were the peculiar patterns of strength and weakness exhibited by particular peoples? In peacetime this might be a matter for academic discussion, but in a last-ditch war these patterns would constitute the imponderables that could determine the outcome. In 1943 Mead came to Britain and did her bit to relate American troops to 'the British Community' and vice versa. She wrote in the belief that it was only by peoples developing their separate genius as they cooperated more and more with each other that a well-ordered world society of peoples could emerge.

It was not easy to encapsulate the separate genius of the British, though that was not for want of trying on the part of many authors. Of course, trade in superficial stereotypes had been active for centuries, but what was now being sought went deeper. There was a widely felt need to find a convincing 'location' of Britain after nearly half a century of ideological and institutional turmoil. That period had seen—in many European countries—the overthrow of monarchy, the separation of Church and state, the arrival of fascism and communism as powerful and strongly supported ideologies, the death of parliamentary government and the arrival of dictatorship, and even, in some cases, bitter and bloody civil war. Since these developments did not occur in Great Britain, it could appear that it was an exceptionally fortunate country that had found a way of adapting its institutions and structures without violence and without succumbing to the illusory utopianism to be found elsewhere—a model from which the world had much to learn. Put another way, however, this possibly blissful immunity from the upheavals which were taking place elsewhere might suggest rather an ossifying society unwilling to be challenged in its self-satisfied insularity by new movements and new ideas. In 1937, writing to a Canadian friend, Sir Michael Sadler, Master of University College, Oxford, thought that young minds were learning much from seeing what was happening elsewhere. But to be a young German or young Italian (unless highly individualized and critical) was more self-transcending than, for the time being, it was to be a young Englishman or Scot (unless you were a strong communist or fascist). 'The last thing I want', he concluded, 'is that we should fall into the Falsehood of the Extreme. But the time of waiting and watching and balancing is hard to bear, a little dispiriting and not invigorating for most people.' British 'exceptionalism', the pursuit of a possibly enervating balance over the first four decades of the century, therefore either offered 'lessons' for reconstruction and recovery for others to emulate in the post-Second War world, particularly other European countries, or suggested that Britain was a country of complacent immobility, locked in a self-regarding obsession and deluding itself into believing in the potentially universal appeal and significance of its core values and institutions. There was, therefore, some urgency to try to say, once again, what it was that Britain really 'stood for'.

The diversity of the kingdom

Many writers, however, found virtue in their inability to give precise answers to this question. Barker was one who readily conceded that the country's unity in diversity, or more exactly its mixture of unity and diversity, was something that puzzled and indeed baffled the inquirer and the statistician. Sometimes social formations and institutions covered 'the whole of the British nation' but sometimes they belonged only to one of the nationalities which made up that nation, and in yet other instances there were ethnic mixtures and overlapping identities about which it was impossible to speak with precision. This diversity could be administratively irksome and intel-lectually irritating in its infuriating fuzziness, but it was nevertheless predominantly seen as a defining strength. It reflected the complex pattern of relationships across the British Isles as they had evolved over centuries.

What this untidy legacy also brought with it, however, was a polit-ical inability, perhaps an intellectual unwillingness or even a psycho-logical incapacity, to consider what the British nation actually was. In his *Human Nature in Politics*, first published in 1908, the political scientist Graham Wallas noted: 'We have not even a name, with any emotional association, for the United Kingdom itself.' The national anthem seemed to him a peculiarly flat and uninspiring specimen of eighteenth-century opera libretto and opera music. The only per-sonification of his nation which an artisan in Oldham or Middles-brough could recognize was the picture of John Bull, a fat, brutal, Englishman invented in the early eighteenth century. Only the Union Jack, though as destitute of beauty as a patchwork quilt, was fairly satisfactory. 'The United Kingdom of Great Britain and Ireland together with its Colonies and Dependencies' did indeed not trip easily off the tongue as a description of a state. The Liberal electoral victory of 1906, however, brought the 'Irish question' back on the United Kingdom political agenda and again forced contemporaries, rather unwillingly, to ask themselves how much or how little unity a 'United Kingdom' required if it was to be a viable political enterprise.

Ireland's ambivalent status as a part of the United Kingdom was again apparent. Viewed from one perspective, Ireland was distinct from the other national constituents of the Kingdom in that it was a 'British colony', though one of a rather peculiar kind even in a rather peculiar British Empire. Viewed from another perspective, however, there was no reason in principle why, with appropriate arrangements, it could not play its full and equal part in a 'British' polity which was in any event only homogeneous—ethnically, culturally, and religiously—up to a certain point. In increasingly dramatic circumstances, politicians and people both in Britain and Ireland were forced to address the extent to which 'the United Kingdom of Great Britain and Ireland' was viable politically, however much there might be a kind of unity in the complex cultural/geographical entity commonly referred to as 'the British Isles'. The old questions about the meaning and practicability of 'Home Rule' returned to the political agenda. Moreover, the prospect of Home Rule in Ireland itself deepened rifts within that island not only between its 'North' and 'South' or between Protestants and Catholics. To reduce the issue to such simple antitheses of course disguises the divisions within all Irish 'communities' about the nature of their identity and the kind of relationship that should exist between Ireland and 'Great Britain'. To an Englishman like George Wyndham, briefly Irish Chief Secretary at the turn of the century, it was still possible to see 'the whole lot' of the Irish as being fully incorporated in the 'British' imperial enterprise: Unionist, Nationalist, Celt, Norman, Elizabethan, Cromwellian, Williamite, agriculturalist and industrialist, educationalist and folklorist.

Wyndham claimed that this was not simply a dream, but it turned out to be so. There were moments in the years immediately before 1914 when it appeared that there might be civil war in Ireland and, further, that the emotions aroused might spill over into Great Britain and lead to violence there too. Looking at these developments, observers from the European mainland did not invariably conclude that the United Kingdom was inherently tranquil and immune from the kind of ethnic and cultural disputes occurring elsewhere in Europe, for example in Austria-Hungary.

The call of duty

It was true, however, that unlike the Russian, Austro-Hungarian, and Ottoman empires, the United Kingdom state that had entered the European war in 1914 survived its conclusion—though in the event only for a short time. At one level, the mobilization of all the communities of the British Isles could be said to be a triumph for insular 'Britishness'. During the war the domestic British scene was not without social and economic tension, but there was no marked conflict between England, Scotland, and Wales as such. The 'Revolt on the Clyde', or the unrest in South Wales, were expressions of local grievances in their industrial communities rather than 'national' confrontations. It was, however, a little galling for those inhabitants of the United Kingdom who lived outside the borders of England to find that it was 'England' which was at war, though this was not a novel experience for them. It was of course the case that the mainland European powers could not cope with the concept of 'Britain' and obstinately continued to refer to 'England'. It is not surprising, therefore, to find the Foreign Secretary, Sir Edward Grey, noting in June 1914 (a trifle optimistically?) that the German government was in a peaceful mood and 'very anxious to be on good terms with England'.

The willingness of Scots to fight for this 'England' was manifest. Few joined the holidaying revolutionary socialist John Maclean in drawing the slogan 'Grey is a liar' on such walls as he could find. David Kirkwood, another Scot who also hated war, recorded later that he was 'too proud of the battles of the past to stand aside and see Scotland conquered'. That many of those emblematic battles of the past had been against England was neither here nor there in the present crisis. At the very least, in the eyes of prominent public figures, the war would demonstrate the essential unity of a nation otherwise apt to be divided in August between football spectators and frequenters of grouse moors, the former being more numerous. Figures should be treated a little carefully, but it is normally claimed that no part of the British Empire reacted more patriotically than Scotland—and suffered more heavily. Apparently, there was anxiety to join the fray before its speedy conclusion would deprive volunteers of their opportunity. Myth and legend surrounded the Scottish soldier, distinctively dressed and deafening his colleagues by the skirling of the pipes, once again punching beyond his weight in the Union cause. And, in the end, in the person of Sir Douglas Haig, it was a Scotsman who on the actual field of battle arguably won the war for Britain, albeit one corrupted by Clifton College and Oxford University. Scotland's contribution, however, remained that of a nation within a nation. As 'Ian Hay' expressed it in 1931 in 'the book of the Scottish National War memorial', as a small country Scotland was 'small enough to be acutely conscious of herself as a whole'. That was why, at the time of his writing 'Scotland alone among the nations has erected a National War Memorial commemorating in detail the service of every unit of her Arms, and the name of every one of her hundred thousand dead'.

The British Prime Minister who, in another sense, 'won the war' was a Welshman, a Welsh-speaking Welshman. As such, Lloyd George was the first of his countrymen to hold this position. He had come to power in 1916 in a political coup in the extraordinary circumstances of war. Whether a Welshman would have been likely to reach 10 Downing Street in ordinary circumstances is a matter for speculation—he has certainly had no successor. In 1914, he had used 'small nation' rhetoric to good effect with his fellow countrymen. Surely, he surmised, Welsh hearts were moved by the fate of Belgium. It was, like Wales, a small nation, 'a poor little neighbour whose home was broken into by a hulking bully', and it needed to be rescued. It is clear that Lloyd George did not suppose that Wales itself was the victim of its neighbour's bullying. However, nineteenth-century Welsh Nonconformity had developed the notion that Wales was peculiarly addicted to peace. In the circumstances of 1914, however, if true, it no longer seemed appropriate. The Bishop of Llandaff was adamant that 'we' could not as a nation stand by 'in our seagirt isle' and see the weak trampled on by a cruel and relentless horde. Whether the nation was Welsh or British is not clear—but the Great War was evidently not the moment to bother with such a nicety. And Wales did respond in ample numbers with volunteers, initially at least, anxious to dispel the notion that Wales was not a military nation. Lloyd George was instrumental in creating the 38th (Welsh) Division, in which volunteers from Wales would have their language and Nonconformity respected. It was an astute move. Kitchener, detecting a tendency to wildness and insubordination in Welsh regiments, was not enthusiastic. The only senior Welsh-speaking officer in the British Army was appointed to command the division. And, when the war was over, it was a piece of Scottish conceit for 'Ian Hay' to suppose that Scotland alone had erected a National War Memorial. The Welsh National War Memorial was unveiled in Cathays Park, Cardiff, in June 1928 by the Prince of Wales. The three entrances to the 'shrine' were draped with the Union Jack, the White Ensign, and the flag of the Royal Air Force. The Welsh Dragon did not make an appearance. There was a sense in which in and through the war Wales had 'come of age' in a British context, even if, by its conclusion and in the immediate aftermath of the war, Lloyd George's own reputation in Wales itself was tarnished. The memorial in his own constituency, Caernarfon, unusually, did boast a dragon but it was draped with both the Welsh and Union flags (the Union Jack could not accommodate a dragon amidst its many crosses), and at the unveiling ceremony both anthems, 'God Save the King' and 'Land of my Fathers', were seamlessly sung by the assembled bilingual company.

The war, therefore, did not destroy 'Great Britain', though the memorializing of it provided testimony to the extent to which its national communities had recognition. In Whitehall, in the heart of London, close to the centre of official and parliamentary British life, what had originally been conceived as a temporary centrepiece for a victorious march past of the allied victorious armies became permanent. It had an enduring life as the British war memorial, though nothing formally indicated that it was a war memorial. The Cenotaph was quite extraordinary. It has been noted that it did not have the slightest mark of contemporary patriotic, romantic, or Christian symbolism. What this indicates can be speculated upon. One comment, however, might be that whatever the war had really been fought for and what it meant for 'Britain' could not be conveyed in words. At the very heart of what was still the greatest empire in the world was a pure white agnosticism. And as for the English, they had no 'national war memorial' at all.

Ireland: the parting of the ways

Even if Great Britain was intact at the end of the war, and arguably even strengthened, domestic events during its course undermined the prospects for 'Great Britain and Ireland' as a single state. In August 1914 it was by no means a foregone conclusion that this would turn out to be the case. The following month the Irish Home Rule Bill reached the statute book, though with the proviso that it would only come into effect at the close of hostilities and then with a possible special arrangement for Ulster. John Redmond, leader of the Home Rule Party, expressed support for the war and even urged his followers to volunteer. What better demonstration could there be that Home Rule posed no threat to the security of Great Britain? Opponents would thus be wrong-footed both in the north of Ireland and in Britain? However, he was not successful in obtaining a formation analogous to the Welsh for the Irish National Volunteers. Other contrary strategies were canvassed, though, all in some degree variants on the theme that England's difficulty was Ireland's opportunity. Various groupings, whose ambitions went beyond mere Home Rule, sometimes far beyond it, manoeuvred for position. On the other hand, in the early months of the war, the level of enlistments suggested a significant belief in a 'common cause'. Thereafter, however, volunteers fell away and the mood began to change. It is difficult to come to a balanced judgement about the extent of enthusiasm for the war before 1916. That Ireland was recognized as 'different' can be seen from the recognition that if conscription were introduced in Great Britain it should not apply in Ireland. Even so, in some British quarters the degree of voluntary contribution suggested that a new spirit was abroad. It is also the case that there were significant provincial variations. Predictably, Ulster supplied a disproportionate number of volunteers. Moreover, it was without difficulty that the Ulster Volunteer Force was incorporated as a distinctive Ulster division of the British Army. It was a fighting force which was 'one with Britain heart and soul'. Its terrible heroism on the first day of the battle of the Somme—1 July 1916—suggested, at least to the *Tyrone Constitution*, that the whole United Kingdom was singing with the glory that Ulstermen had won anew. That the Battle of the

Boyne had also occurred on 1 July (1690) did not go unnoticed at the time.

Singing, though, was not conspicuous throughout the whole of Ireland at this time. The Easter Rising in Dublin in 1916 was a dramatic attempt at revolution. It changed the whole context of debate, but produced no uniformity of initial response as sections of Irish opinion tried to understand and interpret what had happened. Was it the work of crazy poets, deluded Germanophiles, or absurd separatists (if these were separate categories)? The manner in which the Rising was dealt with, even when its occurrence in the middle of a war is acknowledged, suggested an imperial reflex at work and an insensitivity to the likely consequences. Opinions hardened as the executions and arrests followed and swiftly rendered obsolete the compromises that might have allowed a united Home Rule Ireland to emerge whenever the war came to an end. Lloyd George made one further effort to bring the parties together, but failed. Éamon de Valéra, released from internment in 1917, was the rising star in Ireland. When the war did come to an end, Sinn Fein had eclipsed and supplanted the Home Rule Party in Southern Ireland, as the general election result of December 1918 decisively demonstrated. Sinn Fein's agenda demonstrated how much had changed in a short time. Two possible outcomes in 1914 now seemed far-fetched: North–South accommodation in Ireland and a freshly forged but reconfigured British–Irish nation-state. In September 1914, writing to Bonar Law, Winston Churchill had speculated about how 'a new world' might be dawning in the relationships within the United Kingdom. Ulstermen could never be coerced if they had gone to the front to 'serve the country', but equally Englishmen could never again regard Irishmen as traitors if they 'shed their blood willingly and generously with our own men'. In supposing that what he called the old flags of the Victorian era could be hung up, however, he had made a mistake. The bitter struggles of the immediate postwar years made it evident that the United Kingdom of Great Britain and Ireland had no future. The price of settlement, however, was partition and the establishment of the Irish Free State in 1922 on the analogy of a dominion within the British Commonwealth. This step was naturally a moment of great political significance in British–Irish relations. It ended the political union of the British Isles that had been in existence since 1801.

Inevitably, however, there still appeared to be unfinished business.

As the ensuing civil war in the Free State showed, firm republicans regarded it as an inadequate substitute for what they really wanted. And a deeper problem could not be avoided as the new state searched for administrative and constitutional structures for itself. Was 'Irishness' necessarily the antithesis of 'Britishness', or had the past, particularly the past of the previous hundred years, left an indelible legacy even at the point of rejection? It was an obvious question in the sphere of language and culture where, for some, 'de-Anglicization' seemed a feasible strategy. In many other respects, however, as Professor Lee has observed, it was difficult for administrators and politicians not to be impressed by the British model and British conventions. Post-1919 Britain still appeared the greatest power in the world, and its governmental patterns must surely be those to be substantially emulated. Irishmen were not inclined to seek guidance from, for example, the new Baltic states—small agricultural creations like their own. Thus, paradoxically perhaps, the Irish Free State was still more 'British' than had at one stage seemed likely and more 'British' than seemed proper to those who sought severer separation. However, also paradoxically, partition enabled the new state to be created without the simultaneous and potentially greater task of creating a nation out of the inhabitants of all the island of Ireland—to contend with and potentially destabilize the new state. The extent to which the Irish Free State, in its successive constitutions, could then be a self-consciously 'Catholic' state facilitated its consolidation but simultaneously made it seem increasingly 'foreign' to other Irishmen who embraced Britishness with a fervour which looked as though it would embarrass the British of Britain.

Equally, there were question marks against the nature of the new devolved government established in Northern Ireland. Was it a Protestant statelet for Protestant people? Was it viable? The outcome in Ireland as a whole had all the hallmarks of a compromise and perhaps one of dubious durability. It could not be said to have been reached without force, or the threat of force, being employed during the preceding struggles, either by the British government and its agencies or by 'loyal' or 'republican' volunteer forces. It did not add lustre to the 'British Way'. In this respect, British–Irish politics between 1910 and 1925 had more in common with the relationships between dominant and subordinate elements within divided and disintegrating 'multinational' states on the European mainland than British governments either realized or liked to admit.

It was not the case, however, that truncation led to clarity with regard to nationality. Northern Ireland was not part of Great Britain, but its people were British subjects. A majority of them could live comfortably with a British/Irish identity, stressing the one element or the other as circumstances or feelings dictated. It was not clear that the British of Great Britain regarded them as British. In practice, it came to seem that the existence of a devolved government in Belfast kept the affairs of the province 'out of sight, out of mind' as far as mainland Britain was concerned. Even so, simply because the redefined state was the United Kingdom of Great Britain and Northern Ireland, there remained an element of Irishness (albeit strongly Scots Irish) in Britishness. While Irish people, through the successive phases of the Free State, might define themselves against a British (or at least English) 'other', the British state could not define itself against an Irish 'other'. Despite these and other overhanging ambiguities and tensions, the supposed settlement of the 'Irish question' removed any impetus to seek a more comprehensive, pan-insular reordering of institutions and government.

That 'settlement' was in fact only the beginning of a protracted and still prickly period of adjustment between a new, small, and remarkably resilient state and a Britain which was not merely substantially the larger of the two states of 'the British Isles' but which still saw itself, in some sense, as the voice of global 'Greater Britain'. It was inevitable, therefore, that the leadership of the Irish Free State were prominent in those interwar inter-imperial discussions which produced a new Commonwealth, though one which was still 'British'. It was in this context, however, that the place occupied by the Free State was still distinctive. Desmond Fitzgerald, the External Affairs Minister, noted in 1926 that his country, 'being an ancient kingdom with a great past', could not acquiesce in a state of things which could be tolerated by 'direct offspring' of Great Britain. It was right for the states of the Commonwealth to cling together for their mutual interest but that had to be absolutely detached from any form of control over the dominions by the British Parliament. When he became President of the Executive Council of the Free State in 1932, however, de Valéra had no interest in clinging together. His country did not attend the Imperial Conference of 1937. The new constitution of that year was emphatically autochthonous, i.e. home-grown. Even so, 'Ireland' had not formally left the Commonwealth, though the concept of 'External Association' virtually amounted to the same thing. It was sometimes supposed that this illogicality was a necessity because departure would consolidate partition. Ireland remained neutral during the Second World War and this stance, though domestically inescapable, served further to emphasize that Dublin was not interested in the defence of the British Way. By the same token, the conflict enabled the Northern Ireland government to assert its British loyalty. It was in these circumstances that in April 1949 Ireland not only declared itself a Republic but left the Commonwealth. In June, the Ireland Act passed at Westminster affirmed that in no event would Northern Ireland or any part of it cease to be part of the United Kingdom without the consent of the parliament of Northern Ireland. Taken together, it appeared that these actions brought both clarity and rigidity in the structures which would prevail in 'the Isles' henceforth. Yet there still remained 'anomalies'—that Britain continued to treat Irish immigrants as Commonwealth citizens and offered a special relationship to the Irish economy—which perhaps indicated that when bitterness and intransigence abated, the seemingly ineluctable emphasis on separation which had marked the first fifty years of the century might give way, in new contexts, to more subtle understandings of the totality of relationships between and within the islands.

Residual consolidation

There had been a brief period in the years before 1914 when some minds had supposed that differences within Ireland, and between Ireland and Britain, might be best reconciled by what was referred to as 'Home Rule All Round'. There might be two devolved governments in Ireland, one in Wales, one in Scotland, and one in England (or a number in a regionalized England). They would all operate with substantial levels of autonomy beneath what was then still referred to as the 'Imperial Parliament' at Westminster. There were substantial difficulties with these proposals in their various forms, not least the 'English question', but it was because they appeared to offer a breakthrough in Ireland that they had really been put forward. There had indeed been groups in both Wales and Scotland which had advocated 'Home Rule'—a somewhat imprecise term—but they had not generated sufficient support to take this cause forward on their own. The notion of 'Federal Britain', with clearly articulated and legally enshrined levels of decision-making, now largely disappeared from view. Indeed, notwithstanding the widespread federalism now established in the overseas 'British' Dominions and indeed some lingering hopes that the British Empire might be 'federated', federalism as such came to be thought unBritish. There was no call to equip the Britain which now endured with the fancy and probably unstable constitutional arrangements being established by states both new and old in postwar Europe.

And so it remained for the rest of the first fifty years of the century. Although nationalist parties emerged in both Scotland and Wales, their impact on the functioning of the British state was minimal, as indeed it was in Scotland and Wales themselves. In part this was because those involved in their activities fell out not infrequently on the precise nature of their objectives and the means by which they might be achieved. Although identified as objectives in some quarters, the achievement of the right of Scottish sailors to wear the kilt or success in appointing ambassadors who could speak Gaelic did not resonate strongly in a context in which Scotland suffered severe industrial and social difficulties. There was to be a mood which suggested that Scotland was a 'dying' country whose problems could be only marginally remedied by some degree of political devolution. Rhetoric about the glories of the British way did not resonate so readily in Scotland but equally did not precipitate a major demand for separation. In Wales, likewise, industrial and social problems were to prove acute. The strong cultural and linguistic emphasis in the embryonic nationalist movement restricted its capacity to attract a large following in these circumstances. However, it was also a climate that engendered some scepticism about the intrinsic merits of the British Way. As in Scotland, there were some conversions to and flirtation with a fascism/corporatism or a communism/syndicalism that had an explicitly European flavour. There were also attempts (though their importance should not be exaggerated) by intellectuals, sometimes converts to Catholicism, to place Wales/Scotland 'in a European context' rather than to see their identities as subordinate variants of a 'British Way' under the hegemony of an England which showed little disposition to seek such a context for itself.

Putting the British case

People who wrote about these weighty matters were apt to be historians. At last in Cambridge, Lord Acton meditated a great Cambridge Modern History, the first volume of which was published in the year of his death, 1902. Another Cambridge historian, F. W. Maitland, paid tribute to 'a master of contemporary history, quite such an impartial judge of modern England, so European, so supranational, so catholic, so wise, so Olympian, so serene'. Acton, for example, wanted the History to include an account of the Battle of Waterloo which would satisfy French and English, Germans and Dutch. Acton was indeed a rather unBritish Briton. Less Olympian historians sometimes wondered whether such a degree of detachment and supranationality was either possible or desirable. British historians had a particular and inescapable perspective on British history. If anybody could discern its intrinsic character and significance for the present, they could. History as an academic discipline had been expanding rapidly. There was scarcely a university (in a system which was itself expanding) that did not have a chair of history. Political history was its dominant concern. The Historical Association, founded in 1906, brought practitioners, teachers, and the wider public in contact with each other. A decade later, its new journal published an article which recognized the value of American and European history but stressed that it was necessary to keep in mind 'the history of England as a whole and the English nation from the early times, the development of the British Constitution and the character of British nationality'. The transition from history of the English nation to the character of British nationality was apparently seamless. Another contributor in fact pointed out how little knowledge of the British Islands as a whole students possessed. They were 'so absorbed in the history of England that they had a very limited acquaintance even with that of Scotland and Ireland'. Other writers argued that one should not suppose that the British character should be restricted to its manifestation in the British Isles: 'Greater Britain', A. F. Pollard argued, 'is the completion and perfecting of Great Britain, and in Greater Britain Great Britain is realizing and expressing itself.' Historians, however, should not be mere national propagandists. They should see themselves as exponents of 'enlightened patriotism'. British historians served the best interests of their country if they tried only to serve the interests of truth. Such disinterestedness could even be held itself to be an oddly British characteristic. In the circumstances of 1914–18, however, to have such aspirations was something of a counsel of perfection.

Historians and political scientists, whether or not they were enticed into the Foreign Office (where some of the best-known names of the next generation busied themselves in the Historical Section producing no less than 174 handbooks, allegedly very useful, to prepare for peace) or served in capacities which were more or less explicitly propagandist, had no doubt that the outcome of the war would be momentous for 'our whole British civilization' as G. M. Trevelyan put it. Oxford dons, among whom a younger Ernest Barker was prominent, swiftly set out in September 1914 to give *Great Britain's Case*. Germany's obsession with power and militarism was blamed. It was assumed that the firm link between Englishness and law, which they identified, did not apply in the case of Germany. A steady stream of Oxford Pamphlets followed, and although the Clarendon Press wished to distance itself from the notion that they constituted propaganda, that is not entirely the impression which they convey. A formidable war of words developed in which the difference between German and British historians in their nationalist enthusiasm was a matter of degree.

In his capacity as a wartime President of the new British Academy (1902) devoted, amongst other disciplines, to historical study, the venerable James Bryce tried to sum up a lifetime's reflection on what his country 'stood for' in the world of states. The people of Great Britain, from his perspective, constituted a nation that included three nationalities—English, Scotch, and Welsh (he was by background himself an Ulster-Scot). Meditating on the principle of nationality, he implied that to be a nation with nationalities was a very sensible situation. Recent experience had taught his contemporaries, or so he believed, to understand its limitations as well as its value. It needed to be restrained and purified by the higher sentiment of an allegiance to mankind. Nevertheless, he believed that Britain did stand for the principle of nationality and that it was right to do so. This did not stem from any innate and peculiar merits of British character but could be largely ascribed to insularity and the fact that England had attained constitutional liberty earlier than most other peoples. That commitment to political liberty had resulted in respect for the rights of every human being of whatever race. As an imperial power, Britain's record was not spotless, but what lapses there had been were from the standards the British themselves set. Britain, he further claimed, did not want to see the smaller peoples absorbed into the larger. The world would profit if there were within it a greater number of small peoples. Britain represented what he called a pacific as opposed to a military type of civilization. Such sentiments Bryce bundled together as indicating what Britain 'stood for'. He did not claim perfection or suppose that chauvinism was completely absent, but nevertheless Britain had a proud record. Such a presentation, no doubt heightened by the circumstances of war, was a classical expression of a high Liberal perspective. In the year before he died, Bryce published his last book, *Modern Democracies* (1921), a volume which did not treat specifically of Britain but looked at the way in which the experience of the older democracies might have lessons for the new states of Europe. He found, however, that he had to 'repress the pessimism of experience'. He had lost the certainty of assured progress. History showed some startling relapses and his own times now seemed to be one of these. Hatred, one of the worst of human passions, was raging all over Europe. Could Britain remain an island of relative tranquillity?

Orchestrating unity

In the year that Bryce died (1922), Mussolini headed a coalition of fascists and nationalists in Italy. Was one era ending and another beginning? What were the implications for the notion of Britain which historians tried to encapsulate? There was no one for whom developments in Italy had more disturbing ramifications than G. M. Trevelyan, who had devoted himself to writing a trilogy on Garibaldi. He had spent part of the war in Italy and read a paper before the British Academy in June 1919 on 'Englishmen and Italy'. He had been struck by how well informed continental army officers were, by comparison with British officers, on the history of Europe. It was time to stop being an old-fashioned island fortress. 'Since the war', he concluded, 'we are, whether we like it or not, a part of the Continent.' Most people still did not like it. In the 1920 edition of his book, Graham Wallas saw hideous danger that fighting might blaze up again throughout the whole Eurasian continent. Even so, he still aspired to the belief that international relations might cease to consist of a constant plotting of evil by each nation. The British, French, Germans, Russians, Chinese, and Americans should take a conscious part in the great adventure of discovering ways of living open to all. Trevelyan himself was compelled to recognize that different cultures did indeed have different understandings. A general election in Britain, he supposed, was a moral earthquake whereas in Italy it was the sum of a number of obscure intrigues. He turned back to the study of British constitutional evolution to find reassurance that the British way was the best and would last. It seemed that 'there was only one decent race on the earth—the Anglo-Saxon'. That conviction was not a new revelation, nor was it in fact special to him. Looking at Europe at the end of the war, he thought it would be a good planet to get off 'if it wasn't for the Anglo-Saxons'—by which he meant Britain and the United States.

The more he thought about the Reform Act of 1832 and about nineteenth-century Britain as a whole (about which he published a best-selling book in 1922) the more his Liberal partisanship blended into a perspective in which values and behaviour in Britain transcended party and became truly national. Four years later came a *History of England*—a volume which had sold 200,000 copies by 1949. He was already set on a path which was to make him, in his era, one of the most widely read of historians. His assumptions slipped subconsciously into the minds of his many thousands of British readers. His history had become, in the words of the *English Historical Review*, 'a national possession'. It is not surprising that an American reviewer thought his work characterized by a 'militant assertiveness' concerning the superiority of English institutions over those of other nations. A national framework for his writing came naturally to Trevelyan. His biographer points out that on six occasions he produced books with 'Britain' or 'England' in the title. It was indeed encouraging for many readers, in the year of the General Strike, to be reassured that English society and the parliamentary democracy that sustained it were 'the natural outcome, through long centuries, of the common sense and good nature of the English people, who have usually preferred committees to dictatorships, elections to street fighting and "talking-shops" to revolutionary tribunals'. In further books, articles, and lectures over nearly thirty years the same themes reappeared. Britain, he thought, stood for balance and ordered liberty. Its central political groupings were not opposed in fundamentals and their differences did not endanger the framework of the state. There was, however, an awkward disjuncture between the 'British way', as Trevelyan portrayed it, and the Britain that was developing before his eyes. He did not pretend fully to understand his evolving country, and what he did understand he did not like.

Historians did not entirely have the field to themselves. No public figure ruminated on his country at greater length and to greater effect than Stanley Baldwin. It was his gift for doing so in a reassuringly acceptable manner in the interwar period which helps to explain his political dominance. A collection of his speeches, *On England*, appeared with exemplary timing in April 1926 (the General Strike took place in the following month) and rapidly went into a number of impressions. He was, as he put it, a Worcestershire man through and through and there was nothing else like it. He came from its rich red soil and he would return to it. And, just as he saw himself as coming geographically from 'Middle England', so he sought the middle ground and saw himself as devoted to 'the binding together of all classes of our people in an effort to make life in this country better in every sense of the word'. That was 'the English way'. Baldwin was not shy about the word 'England' and told the Royal Society of St George that it was with a feeling of satisfaction and profound thankfulness that in addressing its members he could use the word without some fellow at the back of the room shouting out 'Britain'. Even so, in many of his addresses, whether in Glasgow or at a St David's Day dinner before a Welsh audience, he contrived to weave together the common strands of Britishness as he saw them. 'If you go back far enough,' he would say, his family had links throughout the British Isles. And, just as Baldwins straddled the boundaries of Britain (and, softened, had given their name in the Welsh (Trefaldwyn) for Montgomeryshire), so he reminded an audience in 1924 that another branch had gone east and one had become King of Jerusalem. In making this observation he could add that this Baldwin had thereby preceded, by 'about a thousand years', Sir Herbert Samuel. Sir Herbert, Liberal and philosopher, from a Jewish banking family, had been (rather more prosaically) High Commissioner in Palestine since 1920. Britain had added the 'mandate' in the Holy Land to its overseas responsibilities after the end of the war. That a British Jew was now in charge in Palestine, that St George (certainly no Englishman) was honoured in one of the most beautiful chapels in Venice, argued against the view that the English and the Scots (the latter being patronized by another alien in the person of St Andrew) were not in some sense intimately bound up with the world of the Mediterranean. Yet such remarks were possibly no more than references either to a very distant past or to what might turn out to be a temporary sojourn in Jerusalem. It remained the case that the very tone of British/English politics and public life was distinctive, certainly when compared with 'the Continent'.

Staying special

There was no lack of speculation as to why Britain was 'special', and there were only a few who doubted this central proposition. In 1906, in *The Governance of England* Sidney Low argued that, relatively speaking at least, what had made for a peaceable kingdom was the fact, as he saw it, that Englishmen had been able to keep their politics 'clear of all the deeper issues that touch on ethics, on theology, on religious doctrine, on the relations of the individual to his own soul'. He doubted whether this 'convenient simplicity' would be maintained—one had only to look across the Channel to see how easy it was to bring fundamental issues of this kind back into the political arena. Even so, he was relatively sanguine that even if great changes did lie ahead they would be met 'by those processes of adaptation and adjustment, with which the survey of our annals has made us familiar'. They would come about 'under the protection of the ancient usages'. There might be revolution but without revolutionary violence or revolutionary injustice. This emphasis upon change within continuity, seen as emblematically British, had a particular fascination for those who came from outside to interpret British History. A British subject since 1913, the historian Lewis Namier returned from visits to Central Europe in the early 1920s to throw himself into the study of the House of Commons. Fresh from examining the way in which parliamentary government on the European continent had collapsed or was collapsing, he came to the conclusion that 'counterfeits of organic creations do not work'. Nations and individuals could borrow devices of a more or less mechanical character but they could not usefully borrow and properly use institutions which depended for their life and functioning on the social organisms which had produced them. What distinguished British public life was the way in which the tradition of debate was thoroughly embedded in it, a prolonged debate which did not descend into bawled sloganizing with the aid of loudspeakers.

Other interwar British writers, reflecting on the largely unhappy fate of the new constitutions of Europe, were alarmed lest their failure should rebound upon Britain. For Agnes Headlam-Morley in 1929, just because institutions originally borrowed from England did not work satisfactorily among other nations it did not of necessity follow that they were not the institutions best fitted to the character and needs of the English race. The 'English system' was not a clever device of the constitutional lawyer but rather a natural product of the 'English character', a character which fruitfully combined impatience of authority with the capacity to produce and follow a chosen leader. She believed that the Germans and the Slavonic races could not produce this desirable combination. British would-be reformers should not look with disfavour upon a form of government that had served their country well. Baldwin dilated upon 'the English race' from a similar perspective. The English constituted 'a diversified individuality'. When they went overseas they exhibited 'love of justice, love of truth and the broad humanity that are so characteristic of English people'. Just as men still identified Roman qualities and virtues long after the end of the Roman Empire, so, in the future, if the British Empire should similarly pass into history, the gifts and characteristics of the English would continue to be prized.

These comforting and inspiring conclusions did not make for an easy accommodation between the British Way and Purpose and the world of continental Europe. Around the turn of the century, the question of Germany occupied a great deal of attention in the press. Conflicting interpretations were placed on its development and the extent to which, in certain respects at least, it presented a model from

which Britain could learn. Some supposed that its 'national efficiency' existed alongside political immaturity and underdevelop-
ment. There were many who continued to posit that, of all European
peoples, there was a spiritual and racial affinity between the British
and the Germans. In the middle of the nineteenth century the young
Lord Salisbury had argued that it was to Germany alone that Britain
could look for 'an alliance of a people'. On the other hand, negative
sentiments towards Germany were growing. In the context of the
First World War, in both countries, there was little good to be said.
The invasion of Belgium put an end to the Germanophile tradition in
Britain. It did not easily or swiftly revive. There was a sense, therefore,
in which the notion that there was in mainland Europe a 'natural'
partner for Britain disappeared.

There was nothing to replace this forsaken kinship. Britain and
France fought together as allies, of course, but neither politically nor
culturally in the 1920s was there much sign of any substantial convergence between the 'British way' and the 'French way'. The continuing need to emphasize detachment from the Continent found expression in the opposition in 1919 to the idea of a Channel tunnel. Sir
Maurice Hankey, Secretary to the Cabinet, was firmly of the view that
Providence—for a great purpose in the history of Europe and of the
world—had made Britain an island. Its insularity had enabled it to
save the liberty of Europe many a time. In the opinion of Lord
Hardinge, firm supporter of the pre-1914 *entente* with France, and
shortly to be British Ambassador in Paris, nothing could alter the
fundamental fact that the British were not liked in France and never
would be. France, he recalled, had long been England's historic and
natural enemy. Differences of language, mentality, and character had
always made real friendship between the two countries very
difficult—and he inferred that this would continue to be the case.

Such considerations both reflected and reinforced the sense that
the British were special. Rider Haggard, celebrated author of *King
Solomon's Mines* and global traveller, was impressed by the way in
which his fellow countrymen in foreign parts did not allow themselves to be swayed into novel behaviour. He pictured them booking
teas, playing golf, or any other accustomed game—for games were
quintessentially English—if they should find themselves on the brink
of the Styx. Their capacity to do this perhaps explained why they
remained a ruling race. A ruling race of necessity had to preserve the

habits and traditions of the fatherland. Other Europeans, however, when they tried to understand this insular yet global people, could not understand the reasons for their apparent success. Count Hermann Keyserling, for example, from a Baltic German noble family, travelled the world before 1914 searching for the basic cultural characteristics of the societies he encountered. In his diary he recounted that whenever he met one of the representatives of the British people he was shocked by the contrast between the dearth of their talents and the limitation of their horizons, on the one hand, and the measure of acknowledgement which they nevertheless extracted from him, as from everybody else. It was very galling. Even the more eminent Englishmen could not be taken seriously as intellectuals. So, what seemed to be the case was that while they were blind and incapable in many respects they did seem to control a sector of reality perfectly. That explained their power of convincing others and their superiority over the other peoples of Europe. They alone were really perfect in their way amongst all Europeans. If they had read such a diary entry it is not certain that contemporary Englishmen would have been altogether delighted by this estimate. And, between the wars, when global events began to test whether 'fitness for purpose' really did characterize the British, there was a suspicion that they might be found out.

Some supposed that the essence of Englishness was mysteriously to be found in the English language itself, which enabled the country to escape the ideological pyramids so elaborately erected elsewhere in Europe. There had long been a continental European tradition that English as a language was a handicap in polite discourse. In the late nineteenth century Lord Houghton had suggested that Englishmen said what they had to say, while Frenchmen could say anything they chose. A generous interpretation of this phenomenon was that the English language was such a composite that its native speakers appeared in public to be bumbling, but in reality they were searching for the best construction to employ. In the case of other languages there was no such choice. Such complexity or origin, however, was not held to hinder clarity of expression. English stood beautifully poised between German elaborateness and French simplicity. The very nature of its deep structures swept away ridiculous concepts and embodied a practical and empirical turn. Even if the platform exuberance of a Lloyd George or the mystical meanderings of Ramsay

MacDonald showed what damage 'Celts' might do to a vocabulary which exuded common sense, English, at least in English hands, was an enormous benefit, as the rest of the world was inexorably coming to understand. This was not merely a British conceit. Refugee scholars from Germany and Austria in the 1930s often found themselves having to adapt themselves quite fundamentally in using their new language. The art historian Erwin Panofsky, for example, came to see that his native terminology was often either unnecessarily recondite or downright imprecise. Speaking in English, even an art historian had more or less to know what he meant and mean what he said. Karl Mannheim, the sociologist, came to see the merits of a less systematic and more pragmatic approach to his subject brought about by con-tact with 'the Anglo-Saxon mind'. Karl Popper, the philosopher, reached maturity without finding polysyllables rebarbative. In Eng-lish, however, he had to learn to be repelled by them. Arthur Koestler successfully wrote in English but initially, on coming to England, he was both attracted and intrigued by a civilization whose social norms were the reversal of his. It preferred 'character' to 'brains', stoicism to temperament, nonchalance to diligence, and the tongue-tied stam-mer to the art of eloquence. There was an irony in the fact that the country he admired bought his political and ideological novels on a proportionately lower basis than any other, including Iceland.

It was this odd country, as immigrants perceived it, which had to come to terms with what was happening on the mainland of Europe in the 1930s, though it would prefer not to have had to do so. The thought that, once again, Britain would have to take sides in an envel-oping European crisis was disagreeable. Apart from the small minor-ities on the Left or the Right who could readily enthuse about the Soviet system or were entranced by fascism, the broad sweep of opin-ion was hard put to it to find a congenial identification with any single European country—even with France. The outbreak of the Civil War in Spain in 1936 led some to take sides from a distance, or even volunteer, but even the most committed had to admit the unsurprising fact that it had some distinctively Spanish features which did not readily translate. More than a decade later, the hopes of 1919 for a new European order of democratic tranquillity had largely disappeared. As the prospect of renewed continental conflict came ever nearer, the temptation to believe that the British way could be preserved by resisting close entanglement remained strong. The prospect of another major war was horrifying. It triggered an intense but in the event transient bout of pacifism.

It was in this context that 'appeasement' as an aim of British foreign policy became increasingly contentious and divisive. The notion of promoting 'peaceful change' and seeking to be an 'honest broker' seemed, at one level, common-sense and consonant with the notion of Britain as an ambivalently involved/detached player in European politics. Yet, in the last analysis, it would be the military power that Britain could deploy which might determine the extent to which it could have an effective voice in determining the course of events. If there was to be 'rearmament', however, when should it begin and what form should it take? That in turn depended on the scale and location of any conflict which might arise. The ability to send a substantial army to fight 'in Europe'—something which had been ruled out until this late juncture—was a formidable task. Might it not be better to concentrate on insular defence above all? And what about the Empire? Debate on these issues came to the centre of British politics and the set pieces of the period; the Ethiopian crisis of 1935, the Rhineland crisis of 1936, the Austrian and Czechoslovak crises of 1938/9, to name only the best-known. Whether Britain should have intervened more robustly (and how?) has been endlessly pored over ever since. The questions, in terms of high politics, diplomacy, and strategy, remain the same. When was Britain ready for war? Could a more robust and Churchillian approach to policy have deterred Hitler? Just at what point did the conciliatory aspirations which underlay early appeasement turn into humiliating capitulation before superior power? Why did England sleep?

To these and analogous questions, historians have continued to give different answers. The easy condemnations of Neville Chamberlain in his years as Prime Minister after 1937, only to be expected in the early decades after 1945, gave way to seemingly more balanced assessment and recognition of the complexity of the problems, viewed globally, which the British government faced at that time. In turn, however, there are those who think that the pendulum of understanding has swung too far. Fundamental mistakes in foreign policy were made. If so, however, they perhaps stem not from errors of planning and perception in this or that area, but rather from some of the unresolved contradictions in British self-understanding to which attention has been drawn in this chapter, indeed in this volume: the ambiguity of 'Britain in Europe', the prickly intimacy of a supposed Anglo-American special relationship, the self-centredness of an insular state, the ambivalence of its creaking imperialism. Prime Minister Chamberlain had notoriously referred to Czechoslovakia as a 'far-away country' about which the British people knew nothing. It would be encouraging, but erroneous, to suppose that he was wrong.

The war, when it came in September 1939, started in Poland—even further away. It could not in itself cure these rumbling political and cultural tensions, but the very gravity of the position in which Britain found itself in its early years suppressed their significance. This was not the time for philosophical reflection on 'Britain and the Continent': the issue was survival. Even in the Foreign Office, it made little sense, initially, to draft lengthy memoranda on the subject of war aims. And, by the time the tide had turned, it became steadily more apparent that the torch of freedom had in reality passed across the Atlantic. There was, of course, much scope for individual British emphases and policies, but the framework for the postwar world was being drawn up elsewhere.

Finest hour and future foreboding

This strange and complicated country, clutching at history in time of need, emerged in 1945, from a war which it might well have lost, with a renewed belief in the merits of the British Way. It had seen off European regimes which had boasted of their superior social and industrial organization. If the war had been between 'democracy' as it had evolved in Britain in the first half of the century and 'dictatorship' as it had become dominant in Europe, under various guises, the practical as well as the moral superiority of the former had been demonstrated. In a broadcast to the nation in January 1940 Winston Churchill had declared that as a peaceful country, governed by public opinion, democracy, and Parliament, Britain had not been as thoroughly prepared at the outbreak of the war as the dictator state whose whole thought had been bent upon preparing for it. Even so, the dictator state had not triumphed. The 'British way' was not only intact, it was indestructible. Of course it was not perfect, but its strength lay in its capacity at worst to muddle through and make do in adversity and at best to be imaginative and innovative.

These were reassuring conclusions, but they rested on the assumption that Britain had indeed 'won the war'. It was indeed the case that Britain was the only country to have fought through from start to finish without occupation. Its contribution was undeniable and honourable. The fact was, however, that the world war as it unfolded from its European origins could not have been and was not 'won' by Britain. Thus the first fifty years of British history in the twentieth century ended on a note of triumph which was to prove debilitating. It is not to deny the merits of British institutions and ideas encapsulated by the phrase 'the British way' to point out the extent to which, as with any society, the conditions under which they flourished depended upon a complex interplay of domestic and international factors. As many were uneasily aware, the continuity of past with present could not be guaranteed. It was not self-evidently the case, however, that Britain's special role was coming to an end. Men and women whose morale had been sustained through dark years of war by a belief in the distinctive greatness of their country could not be expected swiftly and completely to reassess the myths and images which had buttressed that edifice. That would take time, perhaps a long time.

In the late 1930s, a spent English politician turned his attention to history writing, though not for the first time. He was in large measure driven by financial needs but also by a passionate sense of his country's history, the part his family had played in it and also because, apparently against the odds, he had not yet abandoned the conviction that he might serve again. He first published a four-volume *Marlborough: His Life and Times* the last volume of which appeared in the month of the Munich crisis, September 1938. With the aid of young Oxford scholars, he immediately began work on what was to become *A History of the English-Speaking Peoples*. He had composed some half a million words by September 1939 when he had to put it aside 'for the duration'. He was back in a government which had gone to war. Eight months later the author, Winston Churchill was Prime Minister. The conjuncture of these events and activities was remarkable. No other war leader so completely fused past and present, in belief and action. Yet the paradox was that this dynamic exemplar of the British way had been born as far back as 1874. In the general stock-in-trade of his ideas on race, class, and gender he was a man of his time and class. He was half-American. He had a commitment to democracy that was patrician. He had the common touch but was not a common man. He still believed that there was nothing dishonourable about the British Empire. The party system was no doubt necessary to the functioning of British democracy, but he had switched between parties with little compunction and considerable facility, or so it seemed. It was as though, as has been observed, his aim in life was to avoid being classified by any simple conventional category. So, this substantially unreconstructed champion of the English race, its heritage and its history, sat somewhat uncomfortably at the moment of victory in 1945. With remarkable skill, as Aneurin Bevan, his Welsh Labour critic, subsequently admitted, he had put the case of Britain to the world and the destiny of Britain to the British. And then, though he had led his people to the broad sunlit uplands, he was not to lead them into the future. The people cut him off, though in 1951 he was to return. Then, in one last effort, the man who had a claim to being the greatest war minister in the world wanted to go down in history also as the greatest peacemaker.

In all this, as Geoffrey Best, one of his latest biographers, wisely observes, there is an irony. Within short decades, Britain would become a land in which such a man as Churchill would never again find room to flourish. His values would come to seem alien. In the first fifty years of the twentieth century, despite disputes and conflicts, the people of Great Britain, as Best puts it, still had a good idea of who they were and what place they occupied in the world. They knew that the only serious threat to their survival was what it had been in the past: foreign invasion and defeat. The British Way and Purpose could still be identified with commitment and enthusiasm. In another half century that could no longer be said.

Plate 6 Cover of the first issue of *Picture Post*, 1 October 1938. *Picture Post* (1938–57), published by Edward Hulton and edited in its heyday by Stefan Lorant and Tom Hopkinson, was one of the most popular magazines of the late 1930s and 1940s, a unique combination of populism, high-quality photojournalism, and political conscience. Many of the greatest and most evocative photographic images of the era first appeared in its pages.

Being British: creeds and cultures

Siân Nicholas

What was it to 'be British' in the first half of the twentieth century? An era that saw two world wars, the loss of global pre-eminence, and the rise of mass democracy and mass communications was also one of national introspection, when both the meaning of 'Britishness' and the 'search for England' (and Wales and Scotland and Ireland) became a cultural preoccupation.

'Britishness', apparently straightforward to describe in political terms, was a cultural minefield. The creeds and cultures that embodied British life were more complicated than ever. To be British was to be classically educated—but most British children left school at 14 barely literate and numerate. It was to be cultured—yet the British were notoriously conservative in artistic, musical, and literary tastes. It was to love sport—but British sport was among the most exclusionary in the world. British culture was Christian but also highly secular. It was imperial but insular, with flag-waving confined mostly to advertising and juvenile fiction. The British people were tolerant yet obsessed by class distinction, hostile to immigrants, and discreetly (and not so discreetly) anti-semitic. They spoke what some still referred to as the language of Shakespeare (when they did not still speak the ancient languages of Wales, Scotland, and Ireland)—but with slang picked up from American films. Their sentimentality was as axiomatic as their stiff upper lip. British cultural life was the pub but also the home, the

I should like to acknowledge support from the Arts and Humanities Research Board.

opera but also the fleapit; a nation of gardeners who lived mostly in towns.

Early twentieth-century Britain was a nation divided by its cultures. Class played its part: the conventional identification between 'high' and 'low' culture and the upper and lower classes was hard to break, and little, one might think, connected metropolitan café society with the industrial unemployed. But class, status, regional identity, gender, religious affiliation, and education—the latter itself profoundly influenced by all of the former—played their part in a national life shaped by both separate and overlapping cultures. Between early and mid-century the bounds of national culture shifted, fostered by economic, social, and technological change—above all the growth of mass communications and mass forms of entertainment, the cinema, radio, and popular press. What emerged was a popular mass 'culture of the middle' which borrowed from both high and low culture. In this new mass middlebrow culture intellectuals wrote for the popular press, sportsmen and music hall stars became household names, and the king broadcast into the homes of millions. This was not an imperial Britain on the nineteenth-century model. It was less robustly masculine in tone, even to a degree feminized. It was both modern and deeply conservative. Some claimed—and many feared—that it was in key respects American. But it offered, perhaps for the first time, a genuinely national 'British' cultural identity, which during the Second World War fleetingly seemed to find its voice.

The arts: high, low, and mass middlebrow culture

In 1900 'culture' was a divisive rather than a unifying factor in British society. The very question of what it was to be cultured presupposed a certain kind of education (classical, public school and university), which itself presupposed a certain class background and set of elite social and cultural values to which no more than 5 % of the nation—if that—could lay claim. Yet elite society did not necessarily correspond with elite culture: the upper classes as a whole were popularly considered to be culturally hidebound, preferring field sports and cricket to concert-going or artistic discussion. British high culture was regarded as European, but as lagging behind continental Europe. In the first decades of the twentieth century this split between high society and high culture became more pronounced as the modernist movement challenged the cultural establishment. This brought a new openness and a new cosmopolitanism to the notion of high culture, but also a new intellectual arrogance. Increasingly, high culture was characterized by its inaccessibility.

Nothing more exemplifies the cultural divide in Britain than Virginia Woolf's famous comment (allegedly inspired by Roger Fry's 1910 Post-Impressionist exhibition at the Royal Academy) that 'In or around December 1910, human nature changed'. Art was a key battle-ground of traditionalism and modernism. The furore surrounding Fry's exhibition appeared to confirm the conservatism of British artistic tastes. Picasso was considered a degenerate. Epstein's sculptures were vandalized. Though the horrors of the First World War seemed to legitimate the futurist trench art of Paul Nash or C. R. W. Nevinson, the interwar art public continued to resist the work of avant-garde artists such as Ben Nicholson or Wyndham Lewis.

Classical music also exemplified the increasingly rarefied nature of high culture. After the first world war a young school of composers led by Ralph Vaughan Williams, and including Holst, Delius, Ireland, and Finzi, sought to create a new 'English' music that turned away from the European classical tradition followed by the late Romantics Parry or Elgar and instead looked to English folk song for inspiration. But continental Europe again set the pace. Stravinsky, Shostakovich and Schoenberg were composers admired and to some extent emulated by the 'English moderns' (Bliss, Lambert, Walton, Britten). British audiences, however, persisted in the Victorian preference for the 'three B's' (Brahms, Bach, and Beethoven) plus (after long championing by Sir Thomas Beecham) Mozart.

If, in drama, Britain retained its conservative reputation, largely through the restrictive ministrations of the Lord Chamberlain's office that regarded Ibsen and Strindberg as dangerously continental, it was in literature that British high culture saw the most telling developments. A distinct generational shift emerged between the grand old men of late Victorian and Edwardian literature such as Wells, Shaw, Bennett, Galsworthy, and Kipling (even though they all continued to publish into the 1920s and even 1930s), and the new guard represented by D. H. Lawrence, Virginia Woolf, Rosamund Lehmann, and above all James Joyce. Even more dramatic developments occurred in British poetry. While the 'Georgian' poets (Edward Thomas, Rupert Brooke, Housman, Hardy et al.) followed the lyric tradition cemented in Sir Arthur Quiller-Couch's *Oxford Book of English Verse* (1900), the modernist poets of the 1920s (led by expatriate Americans such as T. S. Eliot and Ezra Pound) consciously moved away from Georgian simplicity and naturalism to a poetry characterized by dense allusion and complex form. Eliot's *The Waste Land* (1922) was considered an artistic watershed, redefining the postwar literary landscape. The earlier modernists were themselves challenged in the 1930s by the self-consciously left-wing coterie of 'Audenite' poets (Auden, Spender, Day Lewis, MacNeice), followed in turn by Dylan Thomas, David Gascoyne, and Julian Symons—but their worlds overlapped, a series of intersecting and almost exclusively male circles who publicized their own and each other's work through a succession of literary magazines (from *Criterion* and *New Verse* to the BBC's house journal, *The Listener*) and anthologies (such as the Audenites' *New Signatures*, 1932) that seemed to rewrite the canon year on year. They were, though, notoriously omitted from Quiller-Couch's updated *Oxford Book of English Verse* in 1939.

At the heart of high culture in the immediate prewar and interwar years was the 'Bloomsbury Group'. This clique of close friends and acquaintances professed a modernist distaste for the establishment and 'public-school' values, and exalted personal relationships and artistic sensibility against the conventions of class, family, and national allegiance. They embraced the world of art, literature, and poetry, and virtually invented literary criticism. They considered themselves the intellectual aristocracy and despised conventional high society, but were inveterate snobs as well as inconsistent critics (Virginia Woolf hated *Ulysses*). Contemporaries such as Harold Acton, Cyril Connolly, and Evelyn Waugh considered them dowdy, their successors in the field of literary criticism such as F. R. Leavis turned on them as an exclusive and intellectually arrogant coterie, and George Orwell's attack on intellectuals who 'would rather rob the poor box than stand for the national anthem' was aimed in part at them. The general public was largely unmoved: Joyce's *Ulysses* and Lawrence's *Lady Chatterley's Lover* found themselves banned alongside Radclyffe Hall's lesbian potboiler *The Well of Loneliness* in the 1920s, and Joyce found himself more appreciated in Paris and

Lawrence in Mexico than either in London. Kipling and Galsworthy, not Woolf or Lawrence, won Nobel prizes for literature in this period. But it was Bloomsbury that became a synonym for metropolitan high culture in the interwar years.

Contrast this with the very different lives, the 'low culture', of the mass of ordinary British people. Low culture was music hall and the fleapit cinema. It was sensational cheap literature and the *News of the World*, popular music and the dance hall, the pub and the working man's club, football pools and betting on the horses, seaside holidays in Blackpool or Porthcawl. In 1900 the working classes (80% or so of the population) could be identified by the way they spoke, the clothes they wore, the food they ate, even their height. Their typical educational levels and life aspirations left little time for 'culture' as experienced by the Bloomsburyites. Working-class culture was work-centred for men and home-centred for women, and local or regional rather than national in outlook. Its influences were less European (the only experience of which most working men had was the Western Front in the Great War) than American.

The archetypal low cultural form was the music hall. From its Victorian origins, music hall entertainment was considered to embody British popular culture: earthy, patriotic, sentimental, humorous. However, by the first decades of the twentieth century variety theatre was having to meet the challenge of an entirely new form of entertainment: cinema. Cinema too was a low cultural form. Early cinema films were shown either in music halls as novelty interludes between live acts or as fairground attractions in tents or other temporary locations. But, boosted by a surge of popularity for newsreels and Charlie Chaplin shorts during the First World War, by the middle of that war cinema attendances had reached twenty million a week, with live entertainment increasingly relegated to the novelty interlude. Cinema's popularity, however, lay less in the specific films shown than in the whole entertainment package: several hours of amusement, the opportunity to meet friends, a warm dark place for courting—it is not surprising that the most assiduous cinema-goers were the young, nor that onlookers regarded the cinema as a moral threat.

Given the relative poverty of British elementary education, British popular culture was surprisingly literate. Victorian Britain had witnessed the creation of a mass market for the printed word. The popularity of family- and juvenile-oriented magazines such as *Tit-Bits* and the *Boy's Own Paper*, the steady expansion of Alfred Harmsworth, Lord Northcliffe's, magazine and press empire, and the boom in new publishing houses specializing in cheap mass fiction transformed the mass reading market. By the end of the First World War, fifty years after the 1870 Elementary Education Act in England, a mass readership for light fiction was an integral part of British cultural life, as demonstrated by the huge interwar demand for lending libraries (whether public libraries, Boots, and W. H. Smith's long-established lending libraries or the new freelance 'tuppenny' libraries increasingly to be found in 1930s newsagents and tobacconists) and cheap fiction.

However, contemporary critics (most powerfully the Leavisite 'Scrutineers') deplored the lack of discrimination of a mass readership that called virtually any work of fiction, from serial magazines to pulp fiction, a 'novel'. While before the First World War 'serious' writers such as Kipling or Conan Doyle might appear in lists of the most popular novelists alongside the likes of Marie Corelli and Florence Barclay, it was noted with horror that the most popular fictional character in Britain was now Edgar Rice Burroughs' Tarzan. Men's fiction was dominated by American pulp violence. Women's fiction had moved away from the exoticism of Elinor Glyn—but only to the domestic romances published by Mills and Boon. The fact that so many people now read daily newspapers was blamed for the decline of news values, and the Sunday *News of the World* (the highest-circulation newspaper in the western world) was excoriated for plumbing the depths of popular reading tastes.

Of course, 'working-class culture' and 'low culture' were not always synonymous. Chapel culture in Welsh or industrial northern communities fostered a strong communal interest in classical music. Working men's institutes in politically radical areas ran cinema clubs showing films such as Eisenstein's *Battleship Potemkin*. Self-education, including cultural education, was an important part of many working-class communities. If changing technologies, new work patterns, and new housing developments (notably council estates) were weakening old community-based cultural ties, the steady improvement in working and living conditions for the employed (shorter hours, higher average wages, statutory holiday entitlements from 1938) gave those in work more leisure time and more disposable income with which to enjoy it.

Most telling was the division between those in and out of work.

Some regions, such as the increasingly prosperous midlands and south-east, saw boom times and flourishing cultural and leisure opportunities. Others closed in on themselves: there were no super-cinemas in the south Wales valleys. In general, however, the unemployed were not so much excluded from popular culture as constrained in their enjoyment of it. They went to the cinema—but sat in the cheapest seats of the shabbiest fleapits. They might go to the pub—but drank much less of the cheapest beer. They might go to the football, but not as often. And as George Orwell noted in depression-hit Wigan, 'everyone has access to the radio'. The year 1930, at the height of the slump, saw the largest ever annual increase in radio licences.

But in the first half of twentieth century the term 'popular culture' increasingly became associated, not with the culture of the working classes, but with a more inclusive mass culture, pejoratively termed 'middlebrow'. Upward mobility both into and within the so-called 'middle class' in this period was so widespread as to make any generalizations about cultural tastes extremely problematic. But certainly the new mass middlebrow culture was characterized by its absorption of both high and low cultural forms, popularizing elements of high culture and gentrifying aspects of low culture. It was regionally neutral. It reflected the diversity of tastes of the growing middle class, but reflected too the homogenization of mid-twentieth-century suburban Britain. Its key vehicles were the new mass media, the cinema, the national popular press, and radio, and it was exemplified in a core of cultural forms such as popular film, the *Daily Express* and *Picture Post*, popular detective fiction, and the BBC.

These middlebrow artistic and musical tastes were largely tradi-tional, representational, and conservative, the antithesis of modernist preoccupations. Theatre was generally considered a middlebrow art form; although in their different ways the aged Shaw and the youthful Noel Coward stretched the boundaries of conventional British theatre, the most radical development on the British stage in the interwar period was probably the stripped down and emotionally direct Shakespeare pioneered by Harley Granville-Barker and John Gielgud. Middlebrow literature ranged from Ivy Compton-Burnett to P. G. Wodehouse, Dorothy L. Sayers to Agatha Christie. Book clubs shored up the middle market, with Mills and Boon at one end of the spectrum and the Left (and the Right) Book Club at the other. Prime Minister Stanley Baldwin firmly cemented his middlebrow credentials with his professed admiration of Mary Webb's rustic novel *Precious Bane*. Indeed, middle-class appetites for perilously lowbrow literature were far greater than the readers themselves may have liked to admit. Literature that appears to have transcended the barriers of class and taste included Margaret Mitchell's *Gone with the Wind*, Daphne du Maurier's *Rebecca* (a publishing phenomenon), and the historical romances of Georgette Heyer.

The middlebrow co-opting of cinema was more dramatic. Suburbanization, increases in spending money and leisure time, and the technological leaps that saw films develop in barely twenty years from shaky silent black-and-white one-reelers to opulent five-reel productions in sound and colour contributed to cinema's transformation in the 1920s from a 'low' entertainment to a mass popular cultural form. The 1930s saw the transformation of the cinema building itself from, typically, a dingy and uncomfortable converted hall to a purpose-built auditorium with cafés, car parks, plush seats, and exotic décor. Yet, while cinema-going as a mass popular habit largely transcended class, 'how' one went to the cinema remained extremely class-specific: whether one went to a 'super-cinema' or a fleapit (or one of the well-understood gradations in between); whether one went as a weekly ritual, a special occasion, or to see a specific film; whether one went as a family, group of friends, courting couple, or alone; how much one paid for the seat, and whether it was at the front, the back, or in the balcony. All these factors (and others) served to differentiate the cinema audience.

Although generally accused of pandering to lowbrow tastes, the print media also played an important part in the emergence of middlebrow culture. The British popular press was one of the most energetic in the world. Already by 1920 total daily national and regional newspaper circulation was in the region of thirteen million copies. By 1947 this figure had more than doubled. Although the provincial press retained a healthy part of the market in the interwar years, the daily London press inexorably took control of the newspaper market in England and Wales (though not in Scotland or Ireland, which had their own national press), helped by the rail networks that now joined almost every corner of Britain. In the 1930s the four popular national broadsheets, the *Daily Mail*, *Daily Herald*,

Daily Express, and *News Chronicle,* accounted for over 70% of total newspaper circulation across Britain.

Despite superficial parallels, social class and newspaper readership did not easily correlate (the *Daily Herald*'s overwhelmingly working-class readership was the main exception). Across all titles content, presentation, and style were tailored to appeal to a widening spectrum of readers, simultaneously the traditional middle-class market and the soaring working-class readership. The most successful newspaper in this period was the *Daily Express,* which sustained the broadest appeal of any newspaper (aside from the prodigious *News of the World*) through an upbeat style, a balance of serious and light content, and extensive sports coverage. The *Daily Mirror*'s tabloid relaunch in 1935 made it the first paper deliberately to appeal to the young of whatever class, highlighting gossip and sensation alongside broadly progressive political coverage. Other popular features of interwar newspapers included whimsical columnists ('Beachcomber' et al.), crosswords (a craze imported from the USA in 1930), and a large dose of 'society' news. In magazine publishing, *Punch* retained its hold on the middle class, and the *New Statesman, Spectator,* and *The Listener* had some success in bridging the intellectual/middlebrow divide. There was a healthy market in general, special-interest, and especially women's magazines. But new kinds of photo-magazines, notably *Picture Post,* cleaned up in the middle market. Pitched to 'the intelligent man in the street' and with a more than passing resemblance to the American *Life* (though with a distinctly leftish editorial bent), *Picture Post* traded on its inclusivity, featuring glamour, sex, and celebrity side by side with 'ordinary life'. Within five months of its launch in 1938 it had weekly sales of 1,350,000, easily outstripping *John Bull,* the best-selling weekly magazine of the 1920s. Although usually associated with photo-spreads of exuberant and photogenic young women, *Picture Post* maintained a strong interest in politics and social issues, notably in its high-profile 'reconstruction' issue, 'A Plan for Britain', in January 1941.

Above all, there was the wireless. The creation of the British Broadcasting Company in 1922 (from 1927 the British Broadcasting Corporation) was arguably the most significant cultural event in Britain in this period. For the first time, through the power of broadcasting, a single mass audience could be reached and a 'common culture' was within grasp. Again, the common culture propounded by the BBC was an essentially middlebrow one, with both highbrow pretensions and lowbrow indulgences.

The immediate origins of the BBC were prosaic, a marketing ploy by a consortium of wireless manufacturers, supported by press interests who feared an alternative advertising medium in Britain. But the BBC's first Director-General, John Reith, soon recognized its cultural potential. Reith, a Scottish Presbyterian Unionist with an obsessive belief in public service, believed that broadcasting could 'make the nation one man', forging a link between listeners across the British Isles and providing a 'symbolic heartland of national life'. His BBC was a cultural arbiter: both interwar BBC networks, the National and the Regional, offered a middlebrow core of popular musical classics, informational talks, drama, and a distinctive style of comedy that eschewed music-hall vulgarity for wordplay and parody, balanced by intellectually challenging talks and 'difficult' music on the one hand and dance music (consigned initially only to late-night slots) on the other. Reith's ambition to provide 'the best of everything', whether of high or low character, and never to pander to public tastes, was often mocked but became the essential ideal (if not always the reality) of BBC output. Most characteristic was his attention to the spoken word. Although in part introduced for practical purposes as the one accent that all listeners could be guaranteed to understand, the clipped, upper-middle-class 'Oxford accent' became emblematic of Reith's broadcasting empire. The early BBC was also a cultural window: it provided sport, entertainment, drama, music of all kinds, religious broadcasts, and, most significantly, a single 'national' news, to listeners across the British Isles. The BBC's regional policy was an important (if often compromised) recognition of the strength of regional as opposed to national cultural allegiances. But the announcer's famous catchphrase, 'This—Is London', conveyed a far more powerful message: the capital city as truly the centre of the nation.

The BBC's influence can be overstated. Audibility was often patchy, with valley areas like south Wales barely able to receive signals at first. Wireless sets were initially an expensive luxury, as was the licence fee (although the immensely slow take-up rate in, for instance, Northern Ireland was generally attributed to non-payment rather than lack of interest). With the opening of the Daventry long-wave transmitter in 1925 the whole country was at last effectively covered, and hire purchase agreements and relay subscriptions reduced the cost of 'listening-in'. But even in the 1930s Reith's heavy influence drove many listeners to the popular continental commercial stations such as Radio Luxembourg, notably on Sundays, when he had dictated that the BBC broadcast nothing of a frivolous nature.

What characterized the mass middlebrow culture of the interwar years above all was the speed with which new cultural trends were introduced and discarded. New fashions, new slang, crazes for novelty toys like yo-yos, the fleeting celebrity of film stars or popularity of radio shows—all now long forgotten—could reach a national audience with dizzying speed and disappear just as fast. The phenomenon of the Lambeth Walk is a case in point: within a matter of weeks in 1938 a simple communal dance, inspired by a song performed in an up till then only moderately popular London stage show (*Me and My Girl*), itself a curious exercise in cockney kitsch, could be found being danced by every social group and every age group in almost every dance venue across the nation.

Yet to a significant degree the boundaries between high, low, and middlebrow cultures remained unbridged. Perhaps the most telling feature of the quasi-anthropological Mass Observation movement of the late 1930s was the way in which the Mass Observers saw themselves, in researching such topics as pub culture or Blackpool holidays, as observing quite another world. The fashion, exemplified both by Mass Observation's studies and George Orwell's *The Road to Wigan Pier*, for highly educated, progressively minded middle-class observers to 'discover' the lives of the working class, points to a 'national' culture still in many respects profoundly divided.

Sporting cultures

Above all, sport exemplifies the danger of glib cultural generalizations in this period. The British sporting tradition was conventionally seen as symbolizing the heart of British values, demonstrated at its starkest by two celebrated casualties of the First World War, Captain W. P. Nevill, killed in the advance at the Somme after kicking a football into no man's land, and Edgar Mobbs of Northampton and England, who punted a rugby ball at Passchendaele with similar results. British sporting culture was, however, a web of competing interests and loyalties, whether social, economic, or geographical.

Class and education played an essential part in British sporting culture. Of the three great British spectator sports, cricket, rugby football, and association football, the first two, conventionally associated with the Victorian public schools, were the sports of choice among the schools of the middle classes and the universities. Association football was the archetypal working-class sport. This class association was cemented in the amateur/professional divide that categorized some sports and sportsmen as 'gentlemen' and the rest as merely 'players'. By the 1920s football was fully professional at the highest level, and laboured under a social stigma as a consequence (a stigma reinforced by football's 'unpatriotic' reluctance to suspend fixtures during the First World War). Rugby had formalized its amateur/professional divide in 1895 into two codes, amateur rugby union and (mostly) professional rugby league, and the union code policed the divide with pitiless vigilance. Cricket, ostensibly the most middle-class of games, had in fact perhaps the broadest popular following of any sport in England and Wales. Its unique solution to the professional/amateur problem was to accommodate both in the county game in an uneasy compromise in which amateurs and professionals played alongside each other but were rigorously segregated when off the pitch, and to ignore as far as possible the professional one-day cricket leagues that operated in several parts of the country. That a professional might captain the England cricket team was unthinkable.

Yet local tradition cut across class. In England, football was originally strongest in the industrial north and midlands. Rugby league had an obsessive northern working-class following, its physical rigour an integral part of the northern masculine self-image. But so too did cricket: Yorkshire and Lancashire dominated the county championship throughout the interwar years, as well as supporting their own professional leagues. In Wales, sporting allegiance famously bypassed class and by the 1920s was split regionally between professional football in the north and amateur rugby union in the south (with Glamorgan maintaining a strong if anomalous cricketing tradition). Rugby union and cricket were popular in the middle-class environs of the English home counties, and football increasingly so in London and the south-east. But the south-west was, like south Wales, another working-class rugby union enclave. In Scotland, football had a strong working-class following in the cities, but cricket was barely played outside some schools, and rugby union, though enjoying a broad-based popularity in the borders, remained dominated by the Edinburgh and Glasgow public schools (the annual England/Scotland rugby fixture was as much a middle-class social gathering as a sporting occasion). In Ireland, sport was marked above all by history and religion: hurling and Gaelic football represented Catholicism and nationalism against the encroachment of the 'English' sports, cricket and association football. In fact, association football remained popular in both northern and southern Ireland, but after 1922, of the 'national' sports of the British Isles only rugby union remained organized and played on an all-Ireland basis. Team sport allegiances were so powerful because they incorporated and represented wider traditions, loyalties, and antagonisms, whether national (Wales/ England in rugby union, or England/Scotland in football), regional ('rough north' versus 'effete south'), local (historic rivalries between adjacent towns), or, most bitterly, sectarian (notably in the sometimes violent Protestant/Catholic football rivalries in Manchester, Liverpool, Glasgow, Edinburgh, and Belfast).

Of course, British sporting culture was far richer than simply football, rugby, and cricket. Boxing was immensely popular across the British Isles, with local small halls attracting highly knowledgeable and partisan crowds—and offering a way into sport for London Jewish and, later, black British boxers. Dog racing at White City and speedway at Stamford Bridge were hugely popular. Betting, though technically illegal outside racetracks, supported interest in not just horse racing but dog-racing, pigeon-racing, and competitive coarse fishing. A family interest in football was generated by the football pools, launched by Littlewoods in 1923, which by the mid-1930s were being filled in by up to half the households in Britain. The rush of ground developments in the 1920s (including Wimbledon's centre court, most major football grounds, and Wembley stadium) testifies to the record crowds witnessed in all spectator sports. Meanwhile, increased participation in sport was one of the great social phenomena of the period. Pubs still provided the focus of local football, rugby, angling, and bowls clubs, with tennis and golf clubs playing an equivalent social role for the middle class. The interwar enthusiasm for hiking was a cross-class and cross-gender phenomenon. Above all, the rapid expansion of urban municipal facilities in the 1920s and 1930s transformed sporting opportunities, with public golf courses, tennis courts, and lidos widening public participation as well as politicizing the provision of leisure facilities.

What above all transformed the late Victorian mass spectator sports into national preoccupations was the mass media. The newsreels, popular press, and—from 1927, when it first began live sports outside broadcasts—BBC fostered a new national sporting culture. Middle-class sports such as tennis, or principally middle-class sports such as cricket and rugby union, received a massive boost through media coverage. Journalists such as Neville Cardus (who famously contributed both cricket analysis and music criticism to the *Manchester Guardian*) gave cricket an intellectual, even literary status. In tennis, newsreel and wireless coverage (along with the leggy elegance of Suzanne Lenglen and the home-grown success of Fred Perry) made Wimbledon fortnight a national sporting occasion, alongside the Derby, the annual rugby internationals, and more arcane sporting rituals like the Oxford and Cambridge Boat Race. Meanwhile, working-class sports became gentrified. The cinema made the heavyweight boxer Bombardier Billy Wells a national celebrity despite his lack of success in the international ring. The King was among the estimated 200,000 who attended the first Wembley FA Cup Final in 1923. Stoke City's Stanley Matthews became a household name, and Arsenal, the glamour team of the 1930s and the first London team to challenge the north's hegemony, brought the metropolitan middle classes to the football terraces—as well as becoming the first football team to star in a feature film, *The Arsenal Stadium Mystery* (1939). The amateur/professional distinction remained, though, and was even consolidated. League cricket received far less press coverage than the county game. The BBC's decision to include (amateur) rugby union results in its national sports news but (professional) rugby league results only on its northern wavelengths contributed to the marginalization of the league code in the national mind.

'Being religious'

The Victorians and Edwardians notoriously conflated Christianity—in particular Anglicanism—with the British nation (and Empire). Dean Inge, writing in *The English Genius* (1938), was not alone in affirming the parallel between Christian virtues and the ideal of the English gentleman. Yet Britain was in practice a denominationally fragmented nation, in which religion played an increasingly passive role. At the same time, there was still a sense in which 'Christian values' were subscribed to—for instance, in relation to divorce, as Edward VIII was to find out when he married Mrs Simpson.

The pattern of religious affiliation in the first half of the twentieth century—as in the nineteenth—casts doubt on the supremacy of the Church of England in the religious lives of the British people. True, Anglican attendance peaked in the 1920s, and maintained particular strength in rural areas and southern England. But as a proportion of the population Anglicanism was already in retreat (eclipsed in the industrial north, for instance, by the Nonconformist tradition). The Church of England's adoption of increasingly High Church trappings alienated both Nonconformists and Anglican evangelicals. Scotland and Wales saw substantially higher levels of religious affiliation than England in this period. But the disestablishment of the Church of England in Wales in 1920 did little to remove its image as an alien institution, and Wales remained predominantly Nonconformist, its chapel culture (revivified in the Great Revival of 1904–5, though inevitably weakened by depression and outmigration in the 1930s) remaining a powerful community force, particularly in Welsh-speaking areas. The Church of Scotland was Presbyterian, not Anglican, and claimed to 'speak for the nation'. In reality the substantial Irish-descended Catholic presence meant that Scotland too was religiously divided—sometimes acutely so. Ireland's Protestant/Catholic divide marked all parts of Irish and Northern Irish society. Only the Roman Catholic Church experienced real growth in this period, particularly in industrialized and urban areas such as Lancashire and the West Midlands, and among some sections of the upper class. In intellectual circles it was fashionable to be agnostic. Meanwhile, specifically non-Anglican religious identity played an important part in sustaining the cohesion of immigrant communities, whether Irish Catholics in the major ports and cities, Muslim communities in London and the ports, the Sikhs of Woking, the Jews of London's East End, even the Welsh-speaking chapel-goers of London or Oxford. The interwar Anglican Church found itself caught between the progressive weakening of its institutional hegemony and the dead weight of parliamentary interference: witness the furore over the rejection by the House of Commons of the 1927 Revised Prayer Book, defeated by an unholy alliance of Tory evangelicals, Liberal and Labour Nonconformists, and the Communist Parsee S. Saklatvala.

Certainly the evidence points to a progressive decline in church attendance and observance. Twentieth-century popular culture was, it was often lamented, a secular one—or worse, if one considered the vogue for spiritualism in the 1920s and the pervasive popularity of newspaper horoscopes (which maintained an extraordinary hold especially over women readers). Yet, even if ways of 'being religious' had altered, Britain was as yet hardly a 'secular' culture. Children still went to Sunday schools, if only to give parents some rare privacy or to qualify for the traditional free party. In the new and relatively isolated council estates, churches found themselves with an important social if not strictly religious role. The enduring power of the ceremonial, especially when associated with communal singing, was demonstrated in the rapid popularity of the Christmas Eve Festival of Nine Lessons and Carols, instituted at King's College Chapel, Cambridge, in 1918 (and broadcast annually from 1928 on the BBC), of Hubert Parry's setting of *Jerusalem*, even the 'traditional' singing of 'Abide With Me' at Wembley Cup Finals from 1927. The Christian tradition remained a key mainstream cultural force, from the art of Eric Gill or Stanley Spencer to the poetry of T. S. Eliot. Indeed in the 1930s and 1940s, when conversion became intellectually fashionable again, writers like Eliot, Evelyn Waugh, C. S. Lewis, and Dorothy L. Sayers cast themselves as proselytizers of the Christian faith in poetry, novels, radio talks, and even the BBC's *Children's Hour*. Meanwhile, the BBC's daily religious broadcasts provided comfort for those unable to get to church—though in promoting a new kind of personal, broadly ecumenical, home-based devotion, they arguably also contributed to the decline in traditional church-going practice. 'You don't have go to church to lead a Christian life' was a commonplace.

But it was a sign of the times that the most prominent churchmen in
the interwar years owed their celebrity to factors other than their
piety: Bishop William Temple for his membership of the Labour
Party, Father Ronald Knox for his whimsical prose and broadcasts, or
the defrocked Rector of Stiffkey for his improper relations with
young girls and his untimely demise in a fairground tableau of Daniel
in the lion's den.

Juvenile and youth culture

Also contributing to the marginalization of the Church were the new
cultural opportunities for youth. Interwar Britain saw the development of a thriving juvenile culture, aimed predominantly at boys (but
enjoyed, it appears, equally by girls), that reflected a curious mixture
of imperial and American influences. Cinema was central to most
children's lives, with Saturday matinees providing a weekly moment
of licensed mayhem and 'cowboys and Indians' the playground game
of choice the following week. Cigarette cards blurred the distinction
between heroes and celebrities, with imperial adventurers superseded
by sporting and film stars. Juvenile publishing thrived; and if a celebrated 1927 Foyle's survey of the most popular children's authors
(which gave pride of place to such eminent Victorians as Henty,
Conan Doyle, Verne, Dickens, and Captain Maryatt) clearly represented the preferences of middle-class parents rather than their children, George Orwell was not alone in professing astonishment at the
popularity among working-class boys of the *Magnet*'s Billy Bunter or
the *Gem*'s Tom Merry in 'public-school' stories where 'the clock has
stopped at 1910'. Though most children's books remained fixed in an
upper- or middle-class setting, improving texts on the Victorian
model they were not, ranging from the xenophobic derring-do
of Sapper's Bulldog Drummond and respectable adventuring of
Enid Blyton's Famous Five to the juvenile iconoclasm of Richmal
Crompton's Just William, with his fearsome sometime adversary
Violet Elizabeth Bott. Radio provided less exciting fare (schools
programmes, 'Romany', *Children's Hour*, etc.), but it did also have
sport and, for a brief moment at the end of this period, *Dick Barton—
Special Agent.*

Likewise, teenage and young adult culture thrived in this period. Cinema and the dance hall (or, for those so inclined, lidos or hiking clubs) provided a far wider range of social opportunities for young people than their parents had ever enjoyed (and liberated 'courting' from Victorian mores). Here the American lead was even more evident. The popularity of gangster films, American slang, and 'Yank Mags' among teenage boys and of Hollywood romance, fashion, and American crooners among girls testifies to the power of transatlantic popular culture—and raised periodic moral panics among the older generation.

Women and culture

The greatest changes in British cultural life in this period, however, were in the lives of women. In an era when women were increasingly visible in the workplace, in films, as advertising copy, women were still excluded from most male cultural spaces, such as pubs or working men's (or, for that matter, gentlemen's) clubs. Women were likewise still excluded from most of male sporting culture, whether as spectators or as participants (though among upper- and middle-class circles handicapping and less cumbersome skirts respectively made mixed golf and tennis doubles interesting at last for sporting as well as social reasons). However, in the interwar years women's leisure opportunities were transformed. The dance hall offered new venues of socializing and entertainment, particularly for young working class women. The cinema revolutionized women's leisure: whether single or married, working-class or middle-class, they became some of the most regular and enthusiastic of cinemagoers, and cinema managements and film-makers alike went out of their way to appeal to them. The establishment of relatively large and comfortable cinema theatres in towns gave women a new public space, and shopping followed by a matinee became part of the home-based woman's cultural life. And there was radio: the husband may have controlled the dial in the evenings, but in the daytime women found radio a new form of domestic private entertainment, with Radios Luxembourg and Normandie in particular attracting the listening housewife with magazine programmes, variety, and light music sponsored by the principal names in British household goods. Meanwhile, the market for women's fiction, in particular romantic fiction, was one of the most thriving of the period.

The significance of gender to interwar British culture is not, though, limited to women's cultural experiences. An influential analysis has pointed to the progressive feminization of interwar British culture itself: the replacement in the 1920s and 1930s of the imperial-heroic masculine ethos of Victorian Britain with a new identification of the national with the domestic, the private, the 'feminine'. In contrast to the predominantly male exponents of literary high culture, middlebrow culture cultivated a 'language of reticence', a self-effacement that characterized popular writers as diverse as Agatha Christie and Jan Struther. In fact the feminization of British culture was something both identified and deplored by many contemporary critics (though not usually in literary terms): women were the cultural fifth columnists, addicted to American cinema, fashions, popular music, and romantic daydreams.

Yet if British culture was being feminized in this period, British women themselves were being culturally redefined in a fashion that could only be described as more 'masculine'. If European women were conventionally seen as vamps, and American women as floozies, British women in the interwar years were more commonly idealized as 'pals'. The pal was no retiring Victorian Miss. She had characteristics of the flapper, the big sister, and the public schoolboy: bright, spirited, a 'sport', faithful and true, good in a tight spot. Bulldog Drummond's Phyllis was a pal, as was Susie Dean of J. B. Priestley's *The Good Companions* (as indeed was Jessie Matthews, who played her in the film version). And she transcended class. The archetypal female pal of the interwar years was Gracie Fields (specifically, the Gracie of *Sing as you Go!*, another Priestley creation); her wartime successor was perhaps 'Forces sweetheart' Vera Lynn.

National culture or national cultures?

In so many respects interwar Britain clearly enjoyed a vibrant and confident national cultural life. Yet this was to some extent belied by some very defensive manifestations of cultural nationalism in

England, and more particularly in Scotland, Wales, and Ireland (north and south). Many historians, for instance, have noted an interwar preoccupation with the English rural tradition. H. V. Morton's *In Search of England* (1927), an elegy in travelogue form to the English countryside, set a literary trend in the late 1920s and early 1930s that chimed with both the opening out of the British landscape to travel and tourism and the increasing insularity of British political culture. Works from C. B. Ford's *The Landscape of England* or J. B. Priestley's *English Journey* to A. G. Macdonell's *England, Their England* 'searched' for England among its villages, towns, and cities, its way of life and cultural heritage, its national character. In landscape art Paul Nash, John Piper, and Graham Sutherland developed new neo-romantic modernist styles focused on the English countryside. Cecil Sharp's 'rediscovery' of English folk music fed the music of composers such as Vaughan Williams. Stanley Baldwin successfully exploited the political appeal of English character and heritage. This was, though, a modern, suburban appropriation of the countryside. It was the English suburban middle classes who read Arthur Bryant and bought Betjeman's Shell Motoring Guides to Britain, who 'rediscovered' the countryside in cars, motor coaches, and railway specials.

If the interwar 'search for England' was a largely complacent exercise in nostalgic modernity, the 'search for Scotland' in the same period was widely viewed as a product of national disintegration. National self-confidence in interwar Scotland was shaken by unemployment, the shift of economic power southwards, and emigration. The 'Scottish literary renaissance' of this period was a specific attempt therefore both to challenge the hegemony of 'English literature' and to rescue Scottish culture from the romanticized and Anglicized 'Kailyard' tradition. The Saltire Society was established in 1936 to promote Scotland's cultural heritage. In his *Golden Treasury of Scottish Verse* (1940)—itself a riposte to the *Oxford Book of English Verse*—Hugh MacDiarmid explicitly linked Scottish Gaelic with Scottish nationalism. But the language issue was divisive: attempts by MacDiarmid and others to carve out a new literary tradition in 'synthetic' or Lallans Scots were challenged by Edwin Muir, who argued that Scots writers should face reality and write exclusively in English. A simpler cultural refuge was in sectarianism, aimed in particular at the alleged tide of Irish Catholic immigrants flooding into Scotland to seek work or poor relief.

Language and religion played an even keener cultural role in Wales, similarly affected by industrial decline and depopulation. By 1911 less than half the population of Wales could speak Welsh, a figure that declined steadily throughout the first half of the twentieth century. Although the disestablishment of the Church of England in Wales in 1920 removed one of the key grievances from Welsh nationalism, Sunday observance became a new battleground for cultural traditionalists (particularly when directed at Sunday cinema opening). Sport no longer provided national solace: the memory of Wales's defining rugby victory over the New Zealand All Blacks in 1905 hardly compensated for the declining fortunes of Welsh rugby in the 1930s that mirrored Wales's economic decline. A notional 'Welsh national anthem' had been adopted by the 1890s—but would have to wait over three-quarters of a century to gain formal recognition outside Wales itself. But, as Alfred Zimmern had prophetically noted as early as 1921, there were already three Wales: 'Welsh' Wales, 'upper-class or English Wales', and 'industrial, or as I sometimes think of it, American Wales'.

In Ireland, of course, language, religion, and cultural identity were almost indivisible. While the Protestant majority in northern Ireland took their cultural and sporting lead largely from the British mainland (while maintaining an ambivalent relationship with, for instance, Irish folk music), the Gaelic Athletic Association (GAA) and Gaelic League revived 'Irish' sports such as Gaelic football and hurling to the deliberate exclusion of association football or cricket. They also maintained significant ties with the Irish nationalist movement, with the Catholic clergy, and with Irish literary circles (the revival of the ancient Tailteann Games in 1924 was a cultural as well as a sporting event, with support from, among others, Yeats and John McCormick). In fact, writers such as Synge and Yeats, both with Protestant backgrounds, sought to foster a Celticized rather than sectarian Irish national identity (both had been instrumental in the foundation of an Irish National Theatre half a century before its British counterpart). Joyce, a lapsed Catholic, was as European as he was Irish. But from sport to literature, from the quasi-religious tone of Irish political life to the aggressive patriotism of Radio Athlone, partition institutionalized cultural separation from the United Kingdom.

In fact, in Scotland, Wales, Ireland, and England alike, regional identities often outweighed national ones: witness the BBC's relation with its own regional broadcasting services in the 1930s. South Wales (and indeed West Country) listeners, for instance, objected to the single 'Wales and West' Region and called for separate services. But when Wales was given separate status in 1937, much of North Wales preferred to listen to North Region (from Manchester). The decision to treat Scotland as a single 'national region' was criticized even by the Scottish National Party as ignoring Scotland's own regional diversity. Northern Ireland Region was particularly difficult to administer, as the BBC found itself trying to accommodate both the region's Irishness and its Britishness. It compromised by carefully avoiding overt expressions of either unionist or nationalist culture on either their Northern Ireland or national services (religious broadcasts from Northern Ireland, for instance, had to take a 'common Christian platform'). But by doing so it probably contributed further to the mainland's ignorance of the Northern Ireland situation.

But whether English, Scottish, Welsh, or Irish, the same fears underpinned cultural critiques of the period. The mass book market was widely regarded (most stridently in Q. D. Leavis's *Fiction and the Reading Public*, 1932) as a 'drug habit', providing low emotional gratification rather than disinterested intellectual pleasure. The cinema was the 'dream palace', source of cheap fantasy for impressionable youth. The popular music industry was even worse. At the root of all was one pervading cultural influence: the USA.

Americanization

The fear of American influence was one of the most striking features of British cultural discourse in the interwar years. America's preeminence in world trade seemed matched by its cultural hegemony. In Priestley's *English Journey* (1934) 'the new postwar England' was symbolized above all by Woolworths. Woolworths was cheap and it was American; indeed, its Americanness and cheapness could be taken as synonymous. America represented vulgarization, massification, commercialization: seductive, but dangerous. Critics readily identified the main cultural battlegrounds: cinema, variety, and popular music. Only in radio did the cultural barricades appear to withstand the transatlantic onslaught.

The American influence on British cinema was all but absolute. By the mid-1920s the overwhelming majority of films shown in British cinemas were American. Cinema-goers regarded American films as exciting, naturalistic, and glamorous, in stark contrast to the stilted dialogue, strangled accents, and theatrical conventions of most British output. The Americanization of British popular and dance music was almost as extreme and even more critically deplored. Introduced into Britain just before the First World War, the spread of 'hot' jazz, ragtime, and the foxtrot during the wartime and immediate postwar years was a red rag to cultural critics, who noted the alien ('negroid' and 'Jewish') origins of such music. (Yet the Prince of Wales himself was filmed, shockingly, doing the Charleston.) When in the late 1930s swing and bebop hit the dance bands and dance halls, the focus of criticism shifted to the bands' singers, with 'crooning', Bing Crosby style, attacked for its intimate manner. As for variety, in fact British music hall and American vaudeville had close links, the principal difference being perhaps that American comics conventionally developed a quick-fire patter style while their British equivalents more often drew humour from drawn-out jokes and anecdotes. Certainly, younger variety artists, especially those appearing on commercial radio, borrowed American comic techniques. This did not prevent sustained and again often anti-semitic attacks on the underlying depravity of American humour.

'Being British': in defence of national culture

The British response was defensive and not always successful. The cinema industry responded with protectionism, government-legislated quotas on the proportion of British films screened that, through the institutionalization of the 'quota quickie', further discredited British films in audience opinion. American film companies circumvented the quota by establishing London bases from which they produced a diverse and highly successful range of films with British settings, from *The Proud Valley* to *A Yank at Oxford*. The music industry responded by championing difference. Music publishers were happy with whatever sold best, but popular music broadcasters like Christopher Stone refused to play 'hot' American jazz except in special programmes and concentrated on the more staid English 'white jazz' exemplified by Jack Hylton or Henry Hall that he believed his audience preferred. Music hall aficionados defended native variety traditions against 'alien' influences. Most successfully, the BBC cast itself as the antithesis of American-style populist broadcasting, to this end championing British cultural traditions from music to comedy even as some of its more progressive producers surreptitiously adopted slicker, more Americanized production styles. However, the old problem of where 'Britishness' ended and 'Englishness' began overshadowed BBC output as it did most public discourse on the subject: on the National Programme Gillie Potter, a cerebral music hall act with a passionate aversion to foreign variety influences, introduced his comic monologues from mythical 'Hogsnorton' with 'This is Gillie Potter speaking to you in English from England'.

But the 'national' role of the BBC—and other mass media—went further than this. The contribution of the newspaper press ranged from the *Express* and *Mail*'s ill-fated advocacy of Empire Free Trade to the symbolic representation of the nation in editorial cartoons (where, in a telling shift, John Bull was superseded by a host of 'little men' or 'John Citizens', the timid besuited everymen drawn by David Low or Sydney Strube). Between them, radio and newsreel effectively consolidated what some historians have called a 'calendar of national events' that shaped the national year. From the spring song of the nightingale from the Surrey woods, and the summer Promenade Concerts, to the Christmas nativity play from the Church of St Hilary in Cornwall, the BBC created its own annual broadcasting traditions that celebrated the humane diversity of British national life. Radio and newsreel together maintained a national sporting calendar, from the rugby union Five Nations championship between the four 'home' countries and France at the start of the year, via the Boat Race, Grand National, Lincoln and Derby, to the FA Cup Final, test cricket, and Wimbledon, and finally the Varsity Match in December. Together too, radio and newsreel played a central role in creating the public face—and voice—of the twentieth-century British monarchy, through newsreel coverage of royal tours, ship-launchings and openings, outside broadcast and newsreel coverage of the great royal pageants and ceremonials, and of course the King's Christmas Day broadcast to the Empire.

In sport, however, American influence was insignificant. British sporting traditions were arguably too deep-rooted, insular, and complex to be easily superseded. If Britain looked anywhere for sporting contacts it was to the Empire, to which the principal British sports were all exported with some success (the only serious incursion into British sporting traditions in this period, speedway, came from Australia). Most 'international' British sport was in fact conducted by the constituent home nations: by the end of the nineteenth century fixtures had been established in football and rugby both between the home nations and with the Dominions Australia, New Zealand, and South Africa, providing lines of competition and national identity that may have diffused more divisive political grievances. The British Empire Games were inaugurated in 1930—the same year that the Football Association spurned the inaugural football World Cup. Ironically, unless one counts cricket (where the national side played under the name 'England' at home and the 'Marylebone Cricket Club' (MCC) when touring the Empire), the only major international sporting competition in which 'Britain' participated was the Olympic Games. The England cricket team's capacity to create national gloom and despondency was axiomatic (viz. the running joke throughout Hitchcock's *The Lady Vanishes* (1938), where Charters and Caldicott's dire prognistications on England's fate are revealed as not political commentary but cricket talk), and its political and cultural significance sometimes surprisingly potent (notably during the 1932 'Bodyline series' when Australia appeared to impugn the MCC's sportsmanship). Meanwhile, the British took a proprietary interest in the Olympic Games (created by Baron de Coubertin, as everyone knew, as a tribute to the British amateur ethos). The crowd of 90,000 at the 1908 London Olympics remains the record for a British athletics event, and the fame of the Cambridge University-based Achilles Club athletes at the 1924 Paris Olympics cemented a belief in the cult of the gentleman amateur that not even the successes of the better trained Germans and Americans in the 1930s could tarnish. (British women, however, were not permitted to participate until 1932.)

Thus, the Americanization of British culture was rather less widespread and rather more superficial than cultural critics feared. The most interesting feature of cultural Americanization was perhaps less the popularity of American cultural forms among the young than their 'Anglicization' for the mainstream. (Hungarian-born) Alexander Korda successfully sold British history in lush Hollywood-style epic form to British (and American) audiences in films such as *The Private Life of Henry VIII*. British popular music established its own 'Tin Pan Alley' along the Charing Cross Road. The BBC's most American-style variety show, *Band Wagon*, reshaped an American popular music showcase as a vehicle for aural slapstick that owed more to music hall and pantomime than American variety. While British film and radio critics, songwriters, and gag merchants worried about Americanized tastes, the British public often surprised them with their parochialism. The most popular film of 1937 was *Victoria the Great*, the most popular song and dance of 1938 the 'Lambeth Walk', the most popular male film star in Britain, George Formby. The influence sometimes worked in reverse. Charlie Chaplin adapted British music-hall slapstick into an American cinematic formula. Alfred Hitchcock moved from dark British to darker American thrillers. Ronald Colman and Leslie Howard created the Hollywood hero as archetypal sensitive Englishman. The Lambeth Walk was danced in New York.

What 'American Britain' did offer, however, was a new, more popu-list and more inclusive version of Britain itself. Whether in the palais de danse or the Café de Paris, American-influenced dance music appealed to people in all classes. America provided the bulk of the films that people saw in the cinemas that catered to every class. America was not, as Europe had been, the cultural arbiter of an elite, but the source of fashion and glamour for the mass. And Hollywood's filmic idealization of Britain, British history, and the heyday of the British Empire (not to mention the writings of such Americanized Englishmen as P. G. Wodehouse) synthesized an image (or series of images) of Britishness that British audiences simultaneously scoffed at and connived in, but that the conflicting ties of English, Welsh, Scottish and Irish culture had arguably never themselves managed to provide.

The Second World War: national culture and national identity 1939–1945

During the Second World War interwar formulations of national culture and identity found a new resonance. Whereas cultural critics had once sought solace in the belief that British cultural traditions were the antithesis of American values, the whole nation now found strength in the conviction that they were in fact the antithesis of German ones. British characteristics such as tolerance, friendliness, improvisation and the volunteer spirit were compared explicitly and implicitly with Nazi oppression, cruelty, and calculation. A *Picture Post* cover of July 1940 juxtaposing a photograph of a bright-eyed, tousled lad wielding a cricket bat with one of a uniformed and unsmiling Hitler Youth cohort spoke for a national culture that was now a resource of war.

Britain was of course hardly a homogeneous culture. Evacuation threw disparate communities together, exposing the continuing sharpness of class, regional, religious, and ethnic cultural differences. The elision of 'England' and 'Britain' in so much public discourse was as offensive to subnational minorities during the war as before (was it really enough simply to say, as J. B. Priestley did in his BBC *Postscript* after Dunkirk, 'and when I say English I really mean British'?). But the wider danger encouraged national unity. The prewar fascist sympathies of Saunders Lewis were an embarrassment that the Welsh-language cultural world did its best to forget. Most Scottish nationalists threw themselves behind the war effort. Although the Irish Free State was neutral, 50,000 Irish citizens joined up in the British armed forces. During the war greater care was taken with the vocabulary of nation and national identity. Regional, class, and gender differences were acknowledged and accommodated as never before. And the understated, inward-looking interwar formulations of Britishness found a new purpose. Strube's 'little man', now tin-hatted, anxiously emerging from his Anderson shelter to check on his prize marrow, embodied the muddling through, peaceable nation of suburban gardeners of Orwell's writings.

The idea of Britain as a united national culture was a constant motif of wartime propaganda. Humphrey Jennings's fascinating 1943 propaganda film *Listen to Britain* featured an iconic sequence of Dame Myra Hess, accompanied by the RAF Orchestra, playing Mozart's Piano Concerto in C in the foyer of London's National Gallery, to a lunchtime concert audience ('tickets 1/-') of ordinary Londoners, uniformed women, wounded servicemen—and the Queen, anonymous (if instantly recognizable) in the front row. The theme of inclusiveness was central to British wartime film-making and broadcasting. Never before had so many 'ordinary people', with such a carefully compiled cross-section of British accents, been brought to the microphone. Never before had film-makers worked so assiduously to script into their stories representative characters from the different nations and regions of Britain (from *The Foreman Went To France* to *Millions Like Us*). Never before had the various British cultural strands come together to address a common audience. The wartime work of CEMA (the Committee for Education in Music and the Arts) and ENSA (the Entertainments National Service Association) were two sides of the same coin: high and low culture organized for the people.

But cultural inclusiveness was not simply a propaganda fiction. Leading national composers followed William Walton into films, most famously perhaps Ralph Vaughan Williams, who made his cinematic debut at the age of 70 with his score for *Forty-Ninth Parallel*. Walton's music for *Henry V* was soon a concert piece in its own right, and Richard Addinsell's 'Warsaw Concerto' (written for the film *Dangerous Moonlight*) a hugely popular addition to the classical repertoire. War artists did their bit, recording for the wartime public and for posterity sleepers in the London Underground (Henry Moore), bombed architecture (John Piper), or women factory workers (Laura Knight). The liberal intelligentsia appeared in force in the pages of *Picture Post* or on BBC talks programmes (or more recklessly on *The Brains Trust*). The theatre world moved into film, Noel Coward most successfully of all with *This Happy Breed* and *In Which We Serve*. If war poetry seemed surprisingly absent, this was perhaps because so many of the poets were writing and producing at the BBC—Louis MacNeice, for instance—although John Pudney (another BBC man) achieved a certain regard when his 'For Johnny' featured in the film *The Way to the Stars*.

Although it was widely reported that the war had raised cultural standards nationwide, the practical effects of such crossovers on national culture are hard to measure. The BBC's wartime Proms were the most successful ever, but the attention given, for instance, to the London premiere of Shostakovich's 'Leningrad Symphony' in 1942 may have had more to do with its propaganda value than its musical appeal (the score had been smuggled from Moscow by diplomatic bag to mark the first anniversary of the USSR's entry into the war). Similarly, increases in concert-going can be attributed in part to programme organizers' increased willingness to feature the popular classics. Although reading was more popular than ever—a recommendation of *Anna Karenina* on the BBC saw the title sell out in days— the most popular type of reading on the home front was light and escapist fiction, and among the troops detective novels, thrillers, and 'soppy love stories'. (To the critics' despair, the most popular book of all during the war was the American pulp writer James Hadley Chase's quasi-pornographic *No Orchids for Miss Blandish*.)

Certainly, wartime high culture did not replace 'lower' forms of enjoyment. Cinema attendances rose steadily despite the blackout, Average weekly cinema attendance increased, from an estimated nineteen million in 1939 to a peak of thirty million in 1945, with 70% of the nation now counting themselves cinema-goers. The greatest box-office success of the entire war was *Gone with the Wind* (an American epic featuring two British stars), which opened in London in April 1940 and was still playing on D-Day. But British films also enjoyed a new popularity with audiences, both the realist dramas co-produced through the Ministry of Information's Film Division and the Gainsborough studio's lavish costume melodramas (the outstanding popular favourites of the mid-1940s). Meanwhile, sports fixtures, even race meetings, were maintained. Inter-service matches were popular and even path-breaking, with rugby union and league players temporarily permitted to play together. The establishment of 'Unity Pools' maintained yet another popular element of peacetime. Dance halls enjoyed unprecedented popularity, and armed services dance bands competed against each other in a rivalry that matched that of the service football teams (the RAF's Squadronnaires, for instance, notoriously managed to conscript almost the whole of Jack Hylton's band).

The wartime BBC became an ubiquitous feature of national life, presenting not just a communal cultural experience but one that came in the public mind to embody wartime 'Britishness' itself. The

BBC saw itself as both the preserver of national culture and the principal medium of cultural provision during the war. But for the first time it accepted an active responsibility to attract and keep audiences (partly to maintain their morale and partly to discourage them from listening to enemy stations) that resulted in a far more populist approach to broadcasting. Audiences noted the BBC's distinctly more popular tone and style, the new (comparative) informality of the BBC announcers—now named—and the enlivening of BBC news with war correspondents' eyewitness stunts. With the Regional Programme suspended, regional diversity was preserved by assiduous programme planning, and programmes in Welsh and Gaelic were given their place in the national schedules. When the BBC augmented its wartime Home Service with a second station, the Forces Programme, in early 1940, it made the most dramatic shift in its broadcasting philosophy since Reith's day, devoting an entire network to deliberately populist 'light' fare aimed at servicemen, factory workers, and housewives.

Most striking of all was the increased self-confidence of populist broadcasting. The place of dance music became entrenched, and the band leader Geraldo made national headlines when in an edition of *The Brains Trust* he challenged conductor Malcolm Sargent to swap batons to find out whether classical orchestras or dance bands had higher standards of musicianship. Wiser heads within the Corporation persuaded the BBC Board of Governors that Vera Lynn's sentimental singing style would not undermine servicemen's fighting spirit (in fact it 'seemed to cheer them up'). The most celebrated wartime radio programme of all was a variety show—*ITMA*—praised by intellectuals for its surrealism and wordplay, but loved by the mass listening public for its delirious silliness.

Interestingly, religious observance did not increase markedly during wartime. Early attempts to characterize the war as a Christian crusade were downplayed so as not to offend imperial multi-faith sensibilities. But the Anglican archbishops had a high wartime profile (especially 'the People's Archbishop' William Temple, whose Christian socialism chimed well with the 'reconstruction' mood of the times), and National Days of Prayer were given great publicity. Herbert Mason's celebrated photograph of St Paul's Cathedral in the Blitz ('The war's greatest picture') demonstrated the continued symbolic importance of religion in national life.

Again, one of the great cultural fears during the war was of Americanization. The arrival of GIs in Britain was numerically the greatest invasion of any nationality into Britain in its history. It was a culture shock to all concerned, whether the British amazement at American brashness or American shock that the British might disapprove of segregation. Children learned American slang and begged passing GIs for American gum. British women, it was alleged, would do much for a pair of American nylons. The casual manner and ready money of the incomers fascinated and appalled their British hosts. But again, 'low' American influences were less extreme than some alleged. The American Forces Network broadcast on a limited frequency that barely penetrated beyond US bases. Broadcasts on the BBC by American comics such as Jack Benny and Bob Hope were popular, but not as popular as those of Will Hay or Tommy Handley. The most dramatic cultural backlash against the Americans was probably the BBC's decision to vet popular songs for 'inappropriate lyrics' (particularly with respect to 'feminine faithlessness') and popular singing artists for 'effeminate' delivery (i.e. crooning), for which it was heartily criticized in the music and popular press. But the American contribution to the national culture of wartime Britain was undeniable: in films like *Mrs Miniver* Hollywood resold to British audiences every cliché of Britishness that the British had formerly exported to the USA, and the song 'White Cliffs of Dover' (written by Americans Walter Kent and Nat Burton) became part of the soundtrack of the People's War.

Thus, partly as policy, partly through necessity, the war saw the consolidation of a shared national culture on a scale never before experienced in Britain. One might cite *ITMA* and *The Brains Trust*, *Picture Post* and the *Daily Mirror*, *The Way Ahead* and *The Man in Grey*: there had arguably never been so many common cultural reference points. But perhaps the most stunning example was on D-Day, 6 June 1944, when at 9 p.m. a staggering 80% of the population listened in to the BBC to hear the King address the nation. There had never been such a collective national experience before, nor is there likely to be again.

A new world coming

The so-called 'austerity years' saw the greatest mass participation in popular culture yet seen in Britain. Cinema-going reached a peak, and the British film industry attracted unprecedented critical and popular acclaim. Sporting interest hit a new high, with football attendances in England peaking at 41.2 million in 1948–9, cricket in the ascendant (the 1948 'victory tests' between England and Australia), and the 1948 London Olympics putting Wembley at the sporting heart of the world. Newspaper circulation reached its highest ever, the *Daily Mirror* just pipping the *Daily Express* to the giddy milestone of four million daily sales. The BBC basked in its wartime reputation.

Yet the cultural backlash began almost immediately. Critics attacked the mindless populism of wartime culture. From the right, Evelyn Waugh's *Brideshead Revisited* gave voice to those who deplored the ascendance of the ignorant lower classes. On the left, the wartime example of collusion between state and artist became the blueprint of a new cultural policy: high culture for the people through state organization of the arts. CEMA became the Arts Council of Great Britain. The BBC Third Programme added a self-consciously elitist top tier to British broadcasting. The foundation stone was laid for the National Theatre of Great Britain. The 1951 Festival of Britain was conceived as a celebration of innovation in design and technology. That it became, rather, a celebration of tradition and national identity (and as such attracted eighteen million visitors) testifies to the power of both populism and the past in British national culture.

Britain in 1950 was still a nation of competing and contested creeds and cultures. Even its wartime sense of national identity and national pride was built on the paradox of an imperial power fighting a 'people's war'. But interwar and wartime formulations of national culture were already under challenge. In 1948 the arrival of the SS *Empire Windrush* brought the first great influx of Caribbean immigrants to Britain. England condescended to appear for the first time in the 1950 football World Cup—and lost, shockingly, to the USA. Gillie Potter, comic raconteur of 'old England', retired from live performance after playing the London Palladium to an audience impatient for the headliner, Danny Kaye. In 1953 the coronation of Elizabeth II marked not only a return to national pageantry but the advent of nationwide television. A new world was coming.

Plate 7 After the sacrifices of the war years and the austerity of the immediate postwar era, spectator sports enjoyed their heyday. Here, the fans of Fulham Football Club stand to attention in 1952. By that date Britain had, according to many commentators, experienced a political and social revolution. But the crowd pictured here—overwhelmingly male—seems an unlikely agent of that revolution.

5

Unity and disunity: the price of victory

David Dutton

A genuine victory

At first sight it would appear perverse, absurd even, to suggest that Britain in 1945 was anything other than an unequivocally victorious power. A moment's contemplation of the situation which would have arisen from a successful Nazi invasion and occupation of the British Isles should be enough to set the respective characteristics of victory and defeat into context. The only Great Power, apart from Germany, to fight through the two world wars of the twentieth century from beginning to end, Britain had emerged on the winning side from both. Her triumph, in military terms, was absolute in 1945 in a way that it had not been in 1918. Indeed, there were many who regarded the victory of the later year as finishing the job left incomplete at the end of the earlier contest, resolving the German Question once and for all. The destruction of Britain's enemies was total. The German military machine had been eliminated, the charred remains of its leader in the ruined bunker in Berlin a symbol of the final eclipse of the thousand-year Reich of which he had boasted. On the other side of the globe Japan lay prostrate, the victim of the only occasion on which nuclear weapons have ever been used in anger. There was no scope in 1945 for those worthy notions of a peace without victor or vanquished enunciated a generation earlier by the American President, Woodrow Wilson. Both Germany and Japan had had to accede to the doctrine of unconditional surrender (though Japan was allowed to retain its Emperor).

In arriving at this state of affairs Britain had played a not inconsiderable part. Her declaration of war against Germany had come just two days after the Nazi invasion of Poland in September 1939. For a year after June 1940 Britain, almost alone, had kept alight the torch of freedom in the face of crushing German advances in continental Europe. When the tide of military affairs began to turn, Britain had participated actively in the major land campaigns which led to victory—in the deserts of North Africa, in the conquest of Italy, in the advance through northern Europe, and in the jungles of the Far East. In addition, she had contributed substantially to the war in the air and on the seas. And it was to a British general, Bernard Montgomery, that a delegation from Admiral Dönitz, Hitler's designated successor, surrendered the German forces in North Germany, Holland, and Denmark on 4 May. As the conflict came to a close in 1945, Britain stood undisputed as one the three Great Powers straddling the world stage, a position confirmed by her presence at the top table of international diplomacy in the conferences at Yalta (February) and Potsdam (July–August), intended as preliminaries to a forthcoming peace conference. Great Power credentials were reinforced by the country's position as a permanent member of the Security Council of the newly constituted United Nations Organization, with the right of veto over any proposed course of action of which she disapproved. The British army in the summer of 1945 had a commanding presence in many parts of the globe, not least the Middle East, where there was scarcely a country between Libya and Iran in which British troops were not in occupation. Meanwhile, the historic symbol of British greatness and national power, the Royal Navy, was larger in 1945 than at any time in the nation's past. Notwithstanding the exertions of six years of global conflict Britain remained among the richest nations on earth, far outstripping the shattered economies of continental Europe. In terms of military, technical, and industrial resources only the United States and the Soviet Union surpassed her. Perhaps most important of all, the end of the war saw the British Empire and Commonwealth restored to its full territorial extent. Even territories such as Hong Kong, which the Americans had hoped the British would now give up, reverted to their former status after the interlude of Japanese occupation. If all this did not constitute 'victory', total victory indeed, then it was difficult to know what did.

But at what price?

In later decades, however, as the 'decline of Britain' became, after about 1960, a historical if not a national obsession, the picture began to appear more ambiguous. Commentators became more conscious of the price paid for victory in two world wars and, in the context of the rapid dissolution of the British Empire and the equally rapid economic and industrial advance of the defeated powers of 1945, Germany and Japan, ready even to suggest that, in some senses at least, 1945 represented a British defeat. Victory in 1918 had quickly given way to a feeling of disillusionment in the 1920s, the inevitable consequence of the enormous human sacrifice which it had entailed and of the recognition that the world which had emerged from the war was not noticeably an improvement on that which had preceded its outbreak. By contrast, at the end of the Second World War, as the full horror of Nazi atrocities became apparent, there can have been few people living in Britain who doubted that the war which they had fought and won had been both necessary and just. Most would have gone further and agreed that a 'good war' was followed by a 'good peace', as the Labour government of Clement Attlee proceeded to create that land fit for heroes to live in which the politicians of the early 1920s had singularly failed to construct.

Many later observers, however, particularly those belonging to the New Right of Conservative politics, have been less convinced. Among the most eloquent advocates of this line of thought, Correlli Barnett suggests that, in opting for the temptations of a 'New Jerusalem' after 1945, Britain wasted a unique opportunity to tackle the root causes of her long-term industrial decline. Desirable though many of the features of Labour's Welfare State undoubtedly were, they should not have been the country's priority in 1945. By giving precedence to the creation of 'New Jerusalem' over the pressing needs of industrial regeneration, the postwar government created a dependency culture or, in Barnett's vivid phrase, 'a segregated, subliterate, unskilled, unhealthy and institutionalised proletariat hanging on the nipple of state maternalism'. Taken a stage further, the same line of argument has led some writers to question whether Britain was right to enter the war in the first place. Its most obvious consequence, after all, was to free the states of Central and Eastern Europe from Nazi tyranny, only to transfer them to half a century under the scarcely less brutal yoke of Soviet communism. According to Maurice Cowling, by staying on the sidelines—though the notion of peaceful coexistence with Hitler's Germany remains a questionable proposition—Britain could have averted the 'disestablishment of the Empire and the establishment of Socialism'.

At the very least the nature and cost of Britain's victory in 1945 deserve closer analysis. Objectively, it is difficult to sustain the idea that the victory was truly British. The war which began in 1939 was a European one. Had victory been secured by the Anglo-French alliance which declared war on Germany that September, the resulting peace would have been largely a British one. But France fell in June 1940 and, fortunately for Britain, the struggle widened. In the process, however, it became ever less a British war. The Grand Alliance that brought the conflict to a successful conclusion was one in which Britain became increasingly the junior partner; the overall thrust behind the alliance less and less the securing of specifically British war aims and objectives. More importantly, Britain's capacity to continue the struggle was now almost entirely dependent upon the inflow of American financial assistance. She had become, in Peter Hennessy's graphic phrase, 'an economic subsidiary of the United States'.

The British military effort peaked in about 1943, and after that date American and Soviet military power rapidly eclipsed Britain's own. The conference at Teheran that year was, as its historian has written, the turning point. At this first wartime gathering of the leaders of the Grand Alliance, it became clear that, notwithstanding Churchillian rhetoric about Britain's Special Relationship with the United States, the American President was now ready to give priority to his partnership with the Soviet Union. Roosevelt's vision, writes Alan Bullock, was of a 'world settlement to be achieved through the new international organization and guaranteed by continuing cooperation, a condominium between the two Great Powers of the future, the USA and the USSR'.

In sheer military terms the war was won by the inexhaustible human resources of the Soviet Union on the Eastern front and the amassing of America's military armoury, including ultimately the atomic bomb, in the Far East. Within this context the British contribution to victory begins to appear somewhat marginal. Thus Britain occupied a position in the international arena in 1945 which was distinctly different from that which she had held as recently as 1939. Before the war she had been one of a number of Great Powers within a multipolar world, her position given exaggerated prominence after 1918 by the retreat of the United States into a state of isolation and the preoccupation of the Soviet Union with her domestic affairs. After 1945 Britain clung to the triumvirate of Great Powers on the basis of her recent record, particularly between 1940 and 1941. But in the long term the position was unsustainable within what was essentially a bipolar world, dominated by the only two superpowers to emerge from the Second World War.

But if Britain's contribution to victory in 1945 had been somewhat less than contemporaries liked to imagine, it had nonetheless been made at an enormous cost. The most tangible loss of the First World War had been in terms of human life. The British armed forces lost more than 700,000 men between 1914 and 1918, excluding those of the Empire and Commonwealth. Over the same period more than a million and a half men were wounded, many so badly that they could never play an active role in society again. By comparison, Britain escaped relatively lightly from the Second World War. The armed forces sustained about 270,000 fatalities and about the same number of wounded. To such totals should be added figures for civilian casualties which were considerably higher than in the earlier conflict. Overall, though the human cost to Britain of the First World War had been infinitely greater than had been expected, that of the Second was altogether lighter than 1930s predictions had suggested.

In economic terms, however, the impact of the Second World War was very much greater than the First. The cost of the Great War was bad enough. About 10% of Britain's overseas assets had had to be sold to pay for it. Overall, something like 15% of the country's wealth was wiped out. Britain's central position within the international economy was ended for ever. The pattern of her export trade was severely damaged and, in a reversal of the nineteenth-century relationship between the two countries, she ended the conflict with a substantial debt to the United States, which now replaced her as the world's leading economic power. Yet the Second World War liquidated as much as 28% of Britain's national wealth. The country's capital account showed an adverse movement between 1939 and 1945 in the region of £4700 million. By the end of hostilities Britain shouldered the largest external debt in her history. The total deficit came to about £10,000 million, more than half of which had been financed by Lend-Lease. In August 1945 Keynes, warning of a 'financial Dunkirk', noted that the country was living beyond its means to the tune of £2000 million per annum. If the two wars are taken together, the accumulated economic catastrophe becomes all too apparent. Alec Cairncross calculated that, over a period of nearly forty years between 1913 and 1951, there was no net increase in the nation's total real wealth.

Still a world power

There is a logic, especially as imposed by later generations, that Britain's dire economic circumstances in 1945 should have compelled a radical rethink of her international role. As Keynes put it in August 1945, 'our external policies are very far from being adjusted to impending realities'. Arguably, Britain had been overstretched as an international power throughout the twentieth century. 'The Weary Titan staggers under the too vast orb of its fate,' declared the Colonial Secretary, Joseph Chamberlain, as early as 1902. By the end of the First World War Britain was certainly pursuing a role in world affairs which was beyond her capacity. The victim of the United States' refusal to assume the mantle of the world's leading power, which economic realities and the circumstances of the time naturally bestowed upon her, Britain found herself the mainstay of the international settlement, the potential factotum of the League of Nations. Much of British foreign policy in the 1920s and early 1930s was about trying to define the extent and limits of British commitments, especially to the continent of Europe (imperial obligations were still taken for granted), though, ironically, by the end of the interwar era she had taken on military guarantees in parts of Europe where, even in her heyday, she had never exercised any particular influence. By the late 1930s she also faced the nightmare scenario of a possible three-front war against Germany, Italy, and Japan, a combination of powers which would have severely taxed her warlike capacity even at the height of the Pax Britannica. As has been seen, the experience of the

Second World War merely confirmed—objectively at least—that the era of British greatness which began with the triumphs of the Duke of Marlborough in the early eighteenth century had finally closed.

Such, though, was not how things seemed to most Britons in 1945. The very fact of winning the war made it difficult for contemporaries to accept that the conflict had eliminated the country's capacity to play a leading role in world affairs. 'The new Labour government', writes Kenneth Morgan, 'was convinced that Britain remained a great power, whose strategic and financial importance on the world stage would be important for decades to come.' The euphoria of victory served to conceal the country's underlying economic weaknesses, notwithstanding the government's recognition of the urgent need for an American loan when Lend-Lease was abruptly terminated immediately after the final defeat of Japan. Britain's predicament was interpreted as a short-term difficulty, whose rectification would be the prelude to the resumption of former glories rather than the beginning of an era of more modest pretensions. As the Foreign Secretary put it in 1947: 'we must free ourselves from financial dependence on the U.S. as soon as possible. We shall never be able to pull our weight in foreign affairs until we do.' In this type of thinking, argue critics such as Correlli Barnett, lies the evidence of Britain's 'defeat' in 1945—or at least proof that military victory was not an unqualified advantage. 'Britain had not been conquered or invaded,' recalled Jean Monnet, one of the founding fathers of the movement for European union. 'She felt no need to exorcize history.' With no obvious incentive to rethink her traditional role in world affairs, Britain embarked for a further generation upon a hideously costly but ultimately futile quest to sustain her pretensions to great power status, in the process diverting much-needed funds from the urgent tasks of industrial regeneration, while making inevitable her remorseless slide down the world's economic league table.

Ultimately, Britain's role in the postwar world would be that of a subordinate partner to the United States in the evolving Cold War against the Soviet Union. The continuity of the so-called Special Relationship from the war years to the 1950s seems in retrospect obvious enough. But in the immediate postwar era Britain faced the prospect of an American withdrawal from Europe, and Bevin, whose ultimate legacy was the interdependence of the Atlantic alliance, had for a time to think in terms of independent British action. Quicker than the

United States to appreciate that the spread of Soviet communism might pose a threat every bit as grave as that which had so recently been overcome in Nazi Germany, Britain found herself taking the lead in resisting Russian encroachments in areas such as the Middle East. Total expenditure on the armed forces in 1946–7 came to £1091 million, equivalent to 15% of the country's Gross National Product. This compared with only 7% in 1938, when Britain was rearming for a possible war with Germany at a rate which the Treasury believed threatened the country's financial stability.

It was in the spirit of possibly having to go it alone that a secret Cabinet committee decided in January 1947 that Britain, deprived of American technical cooperation by the passage through Congress of the 1946 McMahon Act, should proceed with its own programme to develop a nuclear bomb. Bevin's reported words sum up better than any others the mood in which the government decided that it must acquire this supreme symbol of great power status in the modern age: 'We've got to have this thing over here, whatever it costs. We've got to have a bloody Union Jack flying on top of it.' The Truman Doctrine and Marshall Aid saw the United States returning to centre stage, but American leadership in the Cold War provided little real relief for the over-stretched British economy, even though a further injection of American financial sustenance made the burden more easy to bear. Even before the creation of NATO in 1949 and the outbreak of the Korean War a year later, Britain was probably spending a higher proportion of her GDP on defence than any other Western country. There were, of course, contemporary voices of dissent. According to Sir Henry Tizard, writing in 1949, 'We are not a Great Power and never will be again.' 'We are a great nation,' he insisted—though quite what he understood by the distinction is not entirely clear—'but if we continue to behave like a Great Power we shall soon cease to be a great nation.' This, though, was very much a minority point of view in the late 1940s. By the end of the Labour government in 1951, difficult choices were having to be faced between spending in the international arena and the demands of the New Jerusalem at home.

A European or an imperial destiny?

Britain's wartime experience, and her determination to see herself as one of the world's three Great Powers in the postwar era, played an important role in determining what it meant to be British in this period. In effect it precluded a European identity at a time when the first moves towards European integration were taking place and when, critics have argued, the opportunity existed for Britain to seize the leadership of that movement. Spared both invasion and occupation, the British people (with the exception of the inhabitants of the Channel Islands) had not had to cope with the moral dilemmas of resistance and collaboration. On the Continent such experiences induced a readiness to question prevailing assumptions about national identity which was almost entirely absent in Britain. Countries such as France, Italy, and Germany were consequently more inclined than Britain to adopt radical solutions to the economic, social, and political problems which they encountered at the end of hostilities. These included supranational solutions. The difference was compounded by the stronger intrinsic position of the British economy in 1945 and its more rapid short-term recovery when compared with the states of continental Europe. Officials from the Treasury, Board of Trade, and Foreign and Dominions Offices, meeting at the beginning of 1949 to consider the stirrings of continental integration, concluded that 'there is no attraction for us in long-term economic co-operation with Europe'. Britain's national income was, after all, still twice that of the German Federal Republic in 1950 and nearly two and a half times that of France. In the circumstances it was hardly surprising that Britain kept her distance from the Schuman Plan of May 1950. From it emerged a year later the European Coal and Steel Community, consisting of the six countries which in March 1957 became the original signatories of the Treaty of Rome. The importance of the British government's decision in terms of determining the nature of British identity over the next half century can hardly be exaggerated. Whether this, above all else, constituted the 'price of victory' in the sense of a tragic lost opportunity is a question too bound up with ongoing perceptions of the European movement and British relations with it for the mere historian to pass judgement.

If not 'European', what in fact was the 'Britain' which faced so uncertain and ambiguous a future on the international stage after 1945? The first half of the twentieth century was the last period in which Britain's identity was inextricably intertwined with that of her worldwide empire, though some might argue that the imperial Gordian knot would not finally be severed until Britain joined the European Economic Community in 1973. At the beginning of the century there could be no doubt that Britain owed its world role to the existence of the Empire. Indeed, there were those such as Joseph Chamberlain who sought the means to endow the imperial edifice with a new and permanent apparatus of unity. Such dreams of imperial federation had quickly faded as the Dominions made it abundantly clear that they wanted to achieve individual, nationalistic identities rather than a common imperial one, however arrived at. Much had changed since the First World War, even though the Empire had reached its greatest territorial extent following the inclusion as League of Nations mandates of the colonial possessions of Britain's former enemies. It was unlikely that the situation of 1914, when the component parts of the Empire, including the nominally independent ones, had found themselves at war with the Kaiser's Germany by simple virtue of the fact that Britain herself was involved in that conflict, would ever be repeated. The Statute of Westminster of 1931 had confirmed the sovereign status of the Dominions. They were now fully independent, in no sense subordinate to the mother country, though accepting allegiance to the British monarch as their own. Yet the Empire still counted for much. Britain's solemn acts of remembrance rightly focused on the war dead of the entire Empire and not just those of the British Isles. In 1938 it was as a token of the 'lasting gratitude of his fellow countrymen throughout the Empire' that King George VI invited Neville Chamberlain to join him on the balcony of Buckingham Palace on the latter's return from the Munich Conference. A year later all the Dominions, with the exception of Eire, which in any case did not regard itself as such, declared war on Germany of their own volition, in Britain's support. Their contribution to the war effort was considerable, not least in that interval between the fall of France and the Nazi invasion of Soviet Russia, when Britain would otherwise have been fighting alone. At the Yalta Conference Stalin used the parallel of the British Empire to justify his claim to seats at the General Assembly of the United Nations for the Ukraine,

Byelorussia, and Lithuania, as if the subordinate relationship of the Soviet republics to Moscow was comparable to that of Canada and Australia to London.

With hindsight, 1945 clearly marks the beginning of the end of Britain's imperial era and, as Alan Sked has written, 'the easiest, most straightforward and least controversial measurement of Britain's decline is the disappearance of the British Empire'. It has become a truism to point out that the sinking of the *Prince of Wales* and *Repulse* in December 1941 and the surrender of Singapore the following February were not mere passing setbacks but long-term hammer blows to British prestige which could never be reversed. Though Japan was driven out of its conquests in 1945, the psychological underpinnings of empire, based on the presumption of Western superiority, had been destroyed. In 1947 the Indian subcontinent achieved its independence. 'As long as we rule India we are the greatest power in the world,' Lord Curzon had declared in 1901. 'If we lose it we shall drop straightaway to a third-rate power.' Within twenty years the British Empire had all but disappeared, the extinction of the Colonial Office in 1967 symbolically marking its demise.

Yet this was not how matters seemed as the Second World War came to a close, and there are good grounds to be sceptical of so deterministic an account, not least because it was for the most part those territories which had escaped Japanese occupation which first achieved independence; those which had fallen to the enemy remained longest under postwar British control. A more important long-term consequence of the interlude of Japanese supremacy in the Far East was probably the decision of Australia and New Zealand to seek their future defensive salvation from the United States rather than from Britain, a change which culminated in Britain's exclusion from the ANZUS pact of 1951. The granting of independence in the Indian subcontinent was inevitable, given the Labour party's long-term commitment to this outcome which went back to the days of Keir Hardie and Ramsay MacDonald. Yet it is striking that in other respects the postwar Labour government remained deeply committed to Britain's imperial role. Clement Attlee had himself declared in June 1943: 'if we are to carry our full weight in the postwar world with the US and USSR it can only be as a united British Commonwealth'. Thinking inside the party focused on the notion of imperial partnership and development. Decolonization was seen to lie several generations in the future. The leading figures in Attlee's Cabinet were convinced Empire men, especially in relation to Africa. Developing the untapped mineral resources of this continent could, hoped Foreign Secretary Ernest Bevin, solve Britain's dollar shortage and even make the United States 'dependent on us'.

Even Indian independence was not seen as the end of the road for the ties which bound the subcontinent to the mother country. Labour's task was to oversee a transition of power which left the Commonwealth connection in place. An independent India (partition was not part of the plan) would take on a status not dissimilar to that of South Africa or New Zealand. Even when India insisted upon a republican constitution in 1950, legal devices were found to enable her to remain a full member of the Commonwealth. Indeed, as that body now developed multiracial characteristics which had been largely absent when it had comprised only the old white Dominions, it acquired new virtues in the eyes of the British political Left which had not been apparent hitherto. Significantly, when the Labour government placed the British Nationality Act on the statute book in 1948, it defined 'Britishness' in terms of the self-governing Dominions. Under its provisions, citizens of the independent Commonwealth were accorded the right of entry into the United Kingdom. History may have been ready to impose a finite and short-term duration on the imperial dimension of Britain's history, but as the century reached its half-way point that dimension still seemed genuine enough.

A united kingdom

More generally, the first half of the twentieth century saw Britain achieve a degree of unity unprecedented in its history. In this process the impact of two world wars played a decisive role. As at earlier times, the state of war and the existence of an 'Other' in terms of a mortal foreign foe helped to define and heighten what it meant to be British. For a year after June 1940 it was almost as if the rest of the world was Britain's 'Other'—and the sense of British national identity had probably never been stronger. By the beginning of the twentieth century the processes of national unification were already well advanced. The growth of mobility and the revolution in the systems of transport, the standardization of time throughout Britain in 1880, the increasing numerical preponderance of the English population within that of the United Kingdom as a whole, the decline in the use of native languages in Scotland and Wales, successive extensions of the franchise together with a widening of political participation, and the fact that the whole political system operated on a recognizably British, rather than a specifically Scottish, Welsh, or even English, basis had all served to hasten this development. The result was that the onset of European war in 1914 was met by a response of British national unity, expressed in a collective will to win which was as total as could reasonably be expected. Rates of voluntary enlistment before the imposition of conscription in 1916 suggest that Scotland and Wales were as capable of expressing a sense of British patriotism as was England. Ireland, though, remained a special case, and it was striking that it was the only part of the kingdom upon which conscription was not imposed.

Whatever has been said by its later critics, the postwar partition of Ireland allowed the new United Kingdom to achieve a far greater degree of national consciousness than had its predecessor. British Unionists found it surprisingly easy to reconcile themselves to the establishment of a separate parliament in Dublin. As John Turner has put it, 'the retreat from the Irish Union was seen, even at the time, as a process of decolonisation rather than as a dismemberment of the integrity of the United Kingdom'. The state of Northern Ireland remained recognizably different, the activities of its devolved government largely ignored by most observers on the British mainland, but at least the majority of its inhabitants had no doubts as to their (admittedly idiosyncratic) British identity. The disappearance of those constitutional issues which had been to the fore in the politics of Edwardian Britain—the House of Lords, female suffrage, and the Irish question itself—opened the way for a consensus about the fundamentals of British political life in the interwar period which stood in marked contrast to the experience of most continental countries. There was nothing comparable in Britain to the deep divisions which scarred the histories of France, Spain, and Germany in the 1930s. In an era characterized at the international level by the growth of political extremism, it is striking just how moderate British politics remained and how successful were the established parties in weathering the storm. No member of the British Union of Fascists was ever elected to the House of Commons; the Communist Party of Great Britain succeeded in securing just one seat in the general election of 1935.

None of this is meant to suggest that separate Scottish and Welsh identities disappeared altogether. This was particularly true of Scotland where separate legal, ecclesiastical, and educational systems persisted, indeed flourished. Separatist political parties did emerge after 1918, though their success at the ballot box was extremely limited. But for the majority of the inhabitants of Wales and Scotland there was nothing incompatible in being both British and Welsh or Scottish. The two identities could exist side by side although, particularly in times of crisis, the concept of a united British nation was strong enough to overshadow any alternative focus of allegiance. In four of the seven general elections between 1918 and 1935 the Conservative and Unionist Party secured more Scottish parliamentary seats than any other party. For the Protestants of Northern Ireland the existence of an Irish (and Catholic) 'Other' to the south was sufficient in itself to perpetuate their Britishness.

The Scottish–British relationship perhaps worked best during the Second World War, when Thomas Johnston was Scottish Secretary of State. A regime emerged in which specifically Scottish interests were allowed their head to a possibly greater extent than for more than 200 years. Yet at the same time Scots (as did Welsh) contributed to the British war effort and were proud to do so. The Scottish National Party did win its first by-election at Motherwell in April 1945, but the seat was lost again at the subsequent general election and no other SNP candidate came remotely near to success. In Wales Plaid Cymru's electoral fortunes were equally unremarkable. In the immediate postwar period two million Scots did sign a new covenant calling for a Scottish parliament, and high-profile acts such as the theft of the Stone of Scone from Westminster Abbey suggested embryonic separatist tendencies, but home rule did not figure prominently in the general elections of 1950 and 1951 and the Conservatives were still able to win a majority of Scottish seats as late as 1955. Scottish and Welsh voters in the immediate postwar era seemed largely content with the capacity of the British state to deliver greater social and economic prosperity within the context of a united kingdom. Few at the century's half-way point would have predicted that the possible dissolution of the United Kingdom would become a live political issue before the century was over. Overall, it seems reasonable to conclude that 'the relationships between the component parts of the United Kingdom were more stable during this period [1931–56] than they had been in the past or were to be in the future'.

Pulling together for the common good

The experience of the Home Front in the Second World War should also be seen as an important factor in uniting the nation and confirming a British identity. This is a more controversial statement than would once have been the case. Much recent writing has challenged the traditional picture of a united country, all its citizens pulling together in a common endeavour in the face of a common foe. As Paul Addison ruefully remarks, 'Once full of neighbourly Cockneys defying the Blitz, the home front has been repopulated with factious politicians, incompetent managers, malingering workers, unfaithful husbands and wives, racists, looters, black marketeers and other prototypes of Essex Man.' To offer one specific example, as many as 4,585 cases of looting were recorded in London in 1941, a large proportion from homes destroyed by the German Luftwaffe. It is all part of a process by which the whole concept of a 'good war' has been called into question. The difficulty derives from generalizing about the experiences of literally millions of individual citizens. But, as with much revisionist writing, there is some danger of throwing the baby out with the bathwater if the orthodox proposition is rejected in its entirety. Human nature did not change overnight, nor was the country's social structure completely overturned. But the general trend between 1939 and 1945, and more especially after 1940, was towards a more united, homogeneous, and egalitarian society. Even after sixty years it seems unnecessary to challenge George Orwell's observation that 'War is the greatest of all agents of change ... Above all it brings home to the individual that he is *not* altogether an individual.'

The Second World War, far more than the First, was a total war in terms of involving the civilian population in the same sort of experiences as those encountered by their colleagues at the front. 'Patriotism was no longer limited to the front line; it became a generalized quality of all citizens who endured the deprivations and dangers of total war.' The rhetoric of the war, including that propagated by the government, was focused on ideas of shared sacrifice—and also shared objectives—which must have done something to promote egalitarian attitudes. Such feelings were at their sharpest in 1940 itself when Dunkirk, the Battle of Britain, and the Blitz brought the population together with a sense of common purpose and dogged defiance in the face of adversity which was probably unprecedented. 'We were a united nation,' recalled the historian A. J. P. Taylor. 'Despite our fears we remained unshakeably convinced that we should win in the end.' This sort of mood could not be sustained indefinitely, at least not at the pitch of 1940, and succeeding years inevitably saw some waning of enthusiasm and of the full sense of community.

Towards a new Jerusalem

Yet the feeling that the war must lead to a better world, specifically for the ordinary man, remained strong. National unity, stemming from 'the determination of the British democracy to look beyond victory to the uses of victory' and to ensure that a people's war was followed by a people's peace, was, declared Sir William Beveridge in 1943, the great moral achievement of the conflict. As early as August 1940 the War Cabinet set up a War Aims Committee, one of whose objectives was 'to consider means of perpetuating the national unity achieved in this country during the war through a social and economic structure designed to secure equality of opportunity and service among all classes of the community'. This chimed well with a growing popular sentiment, increasingly shared by the political elite, that there could be no going back to the social conditions of the 1930s, especially the mass unemployment which had scarred that decade. It was indicative that Blake's 'Jerusalem' was adopted as the anthem of Britain's Women's Institutes with their 288,300 members. It expressed, as *Picture Post* commented, 'the Members' resolve to work for a better Britain'. When Beveridge published his report at the end of 1942, the blueprint for the construction of a postwar welfare state, it became a best-seller, a status not normally enjoyed by a government report. But Beveridge's 'vision of a comprehensive social insurance system, binding private philanthropy and state provision into a uniform system, came close to embodying a national consensus about the purposes of the war'.

Churchill's elevation to the premiership in 1940 was undoubtedly important in cementing the sense of national unity. There was, of course, something profoundly ironic about a man born into aristocratic privilege and tracing his ancestry back to the first Duke of Marlborough coming to epitomize the 'forward march of the common people', and we are frequently reminded that there always remained working-class communities where Churchill's name was more readily associated with the Tonypandy riots of 1910 and the General Strike of 1926 than with his duel to the death with Adolf Hitler. Yet the fact remains that in July 1940 a public opinion poll showed Churchill enjoying an approval rating of 88%, a figure which did not fall below 78% before Germany's final defeat. Any lingering class antagonism may well have been softened by Churchill's inspired appointment of Ernest Bevin, leader of the Transport and General Workers' Union, to the Ministry of Labour. The Churchill–Bevin axis developed into the most significant within the wartime government. Be that as it may, Churchill enjoyed a position in national esteem which none of his successors in Downing Street has ever come near to emulating. Isaiah Berlin put the relationship between leader and led in these terms: 'After he had spoken to them in the summer of 1940 as no one has ever before or since, [the British people] conceived a new idea of themselves which their own prowess and the admiration of the world has since established as a heroic image in the history of mankind.'

Assessing the wartime mood is, almost by definition, extremely difficult and the results inevitably impressionistic. But there is statistical evidence to show British society becoming more internally cohesive. 'The long-run tendency to a redistribution of income in the twentieth century has been very greatly accelerated by the two wars.' The gap between salaries and wages, which provides a broad guide to the separation of classes in society, narrowed significantly during the Second World War. It has been estimated that something like 30% of the purchasing power of the top sixth of the population was transferred into the hands of the rest of society, increasing the purchasing power of the latter by about 25%, though the benefits secured by the very poorest sections of the community from this redistribution of capital appear to have been minimal. A Rowntree survey in York suggested that the percentage of working-class households living in poverty fell from 31.1% in 1936 to just 2.7% in 1950.

None of this is meant to imply that Britain was somehow transformed into a classless society by the two world wars. The ethos of the Great War—the sacrifice of the individual to a higher good in the form of king and country—was not designed to hasten the breakdown of class barriers. As many revisionist writers have shown, the upheavals of the Second World War—conscription, bombing, evacuation—were as likely to lead to the intensification of class prejudices and differentiations as to their eradication. Orwell had described England (he could probably just as well have written of 'Britain') as the most class-ridden society under the sun in 1941, though he had also noted the capacity of its inhabitants to come together in moments of supreme crisis. It is doubtful if much had changed by the end of the conflict. Britain was still very much a hierarchical society. But it was also one in which social groups seem largely to have accepted their lot and the demarcation which it implied. The actual social composition of the population in which something like three-quarters of all adult males were engaged in manual work in 1945 provided an element of uniform stability. Richard Hoggart, his perceptive observations sharpened by his own humble origins, described the structure of society at the mid-point in the century. 'Most working-class people', he insisted, 'are not climbing; they do not quarrel with their general level; they only want the little more that allows a few frills. They learn the importance of this early.' If some had sensed the possibility of violent revolution in Britain at the end of the First World War, it was hard to see where such a development would come from a generation later.

To what extent did the heightened sense of wartime unity survive the ending of hostilities? Churchill clearly believed that it would, telling members of the wartime coalition that he was taking 'My good friend, Clem Attlee' with him to Potsdam to show that 'we were a United Nation'. Partisan politics (never entirely absent during the war years) returned with a vengeance, even before victory over Japan had been secured, with the Labour party registering a landslide general election victory in July 1945. But we should be wary of the notion of a united nation signing up for some sort of socialist revolution. The electorate's votes were more evenly distributed between Labour and Conservative candidates than the division of seats in the new House of Commons suggested, and when abstentions are taken into account, it becomes evident that Attlee's party managed to secure the support of little more than one in three of those entitled to vote. 'Idealism on a mass scale was prominent by its absence,' concludes one sceptic.

A postwar consensus

Yet there are good grounds for arguing that many of the aspects of national unity, which had reached a peak during the course of the war, were sustained into the years of peace. In the first place the intrinsically consensual nature of the political debate continued. Indeed, it became more marked. The concept of a postwar consensus has been much criticized, particularly by those who have a more rigid idea of what this concept implies than do those who subscribe to it. After the war Britain's main political parties operated within a broad framework, a set of generally accepted parameters in which certain key assumptions were shared across most of the political spectrum and in which policy options were consequentially limited. Consensus never meant total agreement and inter-party disputes remained intense—though they were often more about the ritualized rhetoric of party political debate than about fundamental differences. Real disputes tended to focus less on absolutes than on questions of 'more or less'. The key assumptions shared by the parties included the pro-vision by government of a wide-ranging welfare state; the mainten-ance through government action of a high and stable level of employment; and the acceptance of a mixed economy. As a result of their wartime experience, leading figures in both parties had come to believe that government had it within its power to avoid any repeti-tion of the mass unemployment of the 1930s and to offer protection to its citizens in their times of need. Arguably, the major achievement of the Labour government after 1945 was to complete and consolidate the work of the wartime coalition. In the process, many of its reforms took on shapes which would not have been exactly matched had the Conservatives been in power at this time—the National Health Ser-vice is perhaps the best example—but it seems at least probable that

Britain would still have moved in broadly the same direction under a government headed by Winston Churchill. The main thrust of Beveridge's proposals had, after all, been endorsed in the election manifestos of all the leading parties in 1945. Even the majority of Labour's nationalization measures were carried through with minimal controversy, broadly accepted as logical extensions of the controls evolved during the war years. Strikingly, when the country next went to the polls in 1950, the Conservatives emphasised their commitment to the major achievements of the Attlee years. The welfare state and full employment would be safe in their hands. Conservatives talked much about removing unnecessary controls but, returned to power, left Labour's edifice of nationalization largely untouched.

Paradoxically, this coming together of the political parties—never total but clearly evident by the century's mid-point—was matched by a marked polarization among the electorate, who divided unambiguously and unhesitatingly between the two main parties, often on class lines. Labour and the Conservatives between them monopolized almost 97% of the total vote at the 1951 general election. Yet it would be wrong to take this political affiliation, committed though it was, as evidence of a deeply divided society. As the Attlee government progressed, newspapers and periodicals abounded with complaints from middle-class readers about the changes the government had introduced and the continuing austerity which they were obliged to endure. But endure it they did. Perhaps Orwell got it right when he noted that, whatever differences existed among the British people, 'somehow these differences fade away the moment that any two Britons are confronted by a European'. Many contemporary observers remarked upon a sense of unity in postwar society. The country remained orderly and peaceful. In stark contrast to what had happened after the First World War, there was a marked absence of industrial unrest. Between 1918 and 1923 as many as 178 million working days were lost; between 1945 and 1950 the corresponding figure was just 9 million. 'The privations of rationing, queuing, and the like were borne quietly and with good humour,' writes Kenneth Morgan. They had to be. In some senses conditions became worse rather than better in the immediate postwar years. Bread was rationed for the first time in July 1946; potatoes in November 1947. A generation later commentators would begin to ask whether Britain was becoming ungovernable. This question could not have been posed in the 1940s.

Peter Hennessy makes the point most effectively: 'The way in which an open society *voluntarily* transformed itself into first a resistance then a reconstruction machine is the most striking feature of the history of Britain from 1940 to 1950.'

A mid-century audit

What then was the state of the nation as the century reached its half-way point? It is easy, in the light of the country's subsequent rapid decline and the attention which New Right critics have focused upon the economic underperformance of the war and immediate postwar years, to reach an overly pessimistic conclusion. Always it must be remembered that we are looking at a process of *relative*, rather than absolute, decline. Taken in isolation it may be argued that, once the war was over, the British economy entered upon a long-term boom which lasted until the early 1970s. That boom produced unprecedented levels of consumption and prosperity, and it is only the faster growth rates of Britain's competitors in the 1950s and 1960s which created the perception of decline. Indeed, in opposition to Barnett's picture of muddled incompetence, antiquated equipment and practice, and technological and educational backwardness, it is possible to present a much more positive image of the state of the British economy at the end of the Attlee government. By 1950 the country had a current account surplus of £297 million. Benefiting from the slower recovery of the German and Japanese economies Britain's share of the world market in manufacturing goods stood at a very respectable 25.5% in 1950. The country was still responsible for 38% of the world's total ship-building between 1949 and 1951. These achievements were secured against a background of full employment unprecedented in peacetime. At the opposite pole from Barnett's gloomy diagnosis, Jim Tomlinson concludes that 'the economy inherited by the Conservatives in 1951 was in a fundamentally healthy state, even if there were many areas where Labour's modernizing intent had not fully succeeded'. Kenneth Morgan too argues that, before being thrown off track by the outbreak of the Korean War, the British economy showed all the signs of steady, sustainable growth without latent inflationary pressures.

Where lies the truth? It would seem indisputable that the exertions of involvement in two world wars had transformed the British economy and that, notwithstanding such positive factors as advances in theoretical science and engineering and some gains in productivity, the majority of these changes had worked to the long-term disadvantage of Britain's relative position among the world's leading industrial powers. At the same time, many of the seeds of relative decline pre-dated even the outbreak of the First World War and are connected to Britain's modest pattern of growth and her poor record of investment in her own industrial plant and infrastructure. So rapid was the process of relative decline *after* the century's mid-point—Britain's share of manufactured exports fell to 16.5% in 1960, 10.8% in 1970 and just 9.7% in 1980—that it seems unrealistic to suggest that all was well as Attlee's administration came to a close. Yet the simple thesis that industrial decay was the inevitable consequence of Britain's spending on welfare provision looks less than convincing when it is realized that her social security expenditure in 1950 as a percentage of the country's GNP was little more than the average of that of the countries of western Europe and considerably less than the German Federal Republic. When social security spending is added to that involved in the maintenance of an understandable, yet ultimately unrealistic and unsustainable, world and imperial role the argument becomes more compelling.

But the fortunes of a nation should not be judged in purely material terms. There is a strong case for seeing Britain's history in the first half of the twentieth century as a record of success and continuity, resulting in a greater sense of unity and belonging among her population than existed in most other European countries. Britons in the middle years of the century believed they knew who they were. The United Kingdom was genuinely, if imperfectly, united, though unity did not imply total uniformity. The component parts of the kingdom were largely at ease with one another. The problems posed by large-scale immigration from the New Commonwealth lay in the future, though the unexpected arrival of the *Empire Windrush* at Tilbury in 1948 with some 500 immigrants from the West Indies was a portent, and two years later the Labour Cabinet admitted that the pressure of a large non-white population could pose problems for the country's future domestic harmony.

The country's major institutions—the monarchy, Parliament, the political process, the civil service, the trade unions, the press, and the legal system—had all evolved while remaining fundamentally unchanged. The cynicism which became so apparent in later decades was on a much smaller scale. There was in Whitehall and Westminster an optimism and enthusiasm about what government could do which were, on the whole, shared by the British people. As an astute and well-placed American observer put it, 'I am persuaded that the most important thing that happened in Britain was that this nation chose to win or lose this [Second World] war under the established rules of parliamentary procedure . . . Representative government, equality before the law, survived.' Symbolically, the Representation of the People Act of 1948, by abolishing plural voting, finally enshrined the principle of 'one man one vote' demanded by the Chartists a century before.

Victory in 1945 convinced most Britons that their way was, indeed, best, 'that somehow or other, things in their country were arranged much better than elsewhere in the world—even if, in limited directions only, there might be some room for improvement'. Britain was a liberal, tolerant society with an innate capacity for compromise. It was also a conservative and moderate society with little taste for extremes whencesoever they came. The population took pride in the Festival of Britain, celebrating the country's achievements a hundred years after the Great Exhibition of 1851. There were some rumblings in the press about the expenditure involved, but on the whole the contrast with the experience of the Millennium Dome half a century later is instructive.

There was, of course, a narrow dividing line between justifiable pride in Britain's achievements and a tendency towards complacency and too great a readiness to take future success for granted. We can recognize the latter without the need to accept uncritically the thesis that Britain had entered upon an inexorable spiral of rapid decline. Certainly it seems unreasonable to suggest that Britain should have responded to her victory in 1945 in a manner comparable to that in which Germany and Japan reacted to defeat. Five or six years later Britain had, it seemed, recovered well from the trauma of war. At home the Welfare State and the National Health Service had been established as lasting monuments to the Attlee government; abroad the Empire remained, for the time being at least, a reality, while Britain's still extensive role in world affairs could not be disputed.

The British people were reasonably prosperous. Only the United States, Canada, Australia, Switzerland, and Sweden enjoyed a higher per capita GDP, and the gap between Britain and the last two countries was not great. At the same time Britons enjoyed better health than ever before.

A half-century in perspective

Hindsight imposes some final reflections. In a relatively short time much of the unity and sense of identity evident in 1950 would begin to unravel. The country's imperial dimension now seems light years away. Logically, with the passing of generations, even the white Dominions were likely to feel themselves less British than they once did. Britain's loss of great power status would increase this trend on the grounds of simple self-interest. The New Commonwealth was never likely to take on a British identity in the first place, except in the most superficial sense. After decades of being at the centre of a worldwide Empire, Britain would soon be on her own again, forced to reassess her position in relation to the continent of Europe, upon which the accident of geography had always imposed a fundamental ambiguity. That continent lay devastated at the end of the Second World War, but would soon recover, its economies rapidly overtaking Britain's own. In a context of relative decline it was inevitable that Britons would become less self-confident about their own way of doing things and about their basic ideas and institutions. The revival of nationalism, even separatism, in Wales and Scotland and renewed debate about the relationship between Britain and Ireland were altogether less predictable in the immediate aftermath of the war. But so great have been the changes of recent years that they inevitably place the mid-years of the century in a new light. Against the background of the establishment of a parliament in Scotland and an assembly in Wales, and the re-creation of an all-Ireland dimension in British–Irish relations, it may well be concluded that the first half of the twentieth century marked the high point of Britain's history as a unitary state.

Plate 8 Aspirations and achievements: Low's perception of the enduring struggle.

6

Declining advantage: the British economy

W. R. Garside

The success and stability of the British economy during most of the 1990s masks the extent to which there has been growing concern since at least the last quarter of the nineteenth century over the country's economic performance compared to that of Europe and America. Indeed, relative as opposed to absolute economic 'decline' has been the dominant framework of interpretation of economic change for the greater part of the twentieth century. If we limit ourselves to an aggregate measure of economic output, Gross Domestic Product (GDP) per head, fluctuations in which affect the economy's overall rate of growth, it is clear that the country's performance for the greater part of the century in real terms has been good in relation to its own past but less favourable when compared to other major industrialized nations, as Table 6.1 shows.

Any effort to assess the extent or reality of such relative economic

Table 6.1 GDP per capita ($ in 1985 relative prices)

	1870	1890	1913	1950	1973	1989
UK	2,610	3,383	4,024	5,651	10,063	13,468
USA	2,247	3,101	4,854	8,611	14,103	18,317
France	1,571	1,955	2,734	4,149	10,323	13,837
Germany	1,300	1,660	2,606	3,339	10,110	13,989
Japan	618	842	1,114	1,563	9,237	15,101

Source: A. Maddison, *Dynamic Forces in Capitalist Development* (Oxford, 1991).

underperformance is bedevilled by the fact that 'decline' is a very contested term, influenced as it is by perceptions of Britain's place in the world, by the construction of different types of evidence to interpret the experience, and by the continuing debate over which policies might be or should have been adopted to reverse or at least manage the process. What is generally conceded is that for the twentieth century as a whole, living standards for the majority of the British population and levels of industrial productivity and aggregate growth improved despite clear evidence of decline (sometimes absolute) in particular areas of economic, and especially industrial, activity.

Whether the political construct of a 'national economy' or the notion of 'national competitiveness' as distinct from the competitive prowess of industries or firms is of any intrinsic importance in this context is a source of keen debate among academic purists. But such considerations cannot erase the influence that Britain's preoccupation with relative economic disadvantage has had on policy choices and political posturing over this century and before. The angst of informed observers has arisen from a juxtaposition of absolute decline in Britain's self-sufficiency and status as a world power with the compelling psychological and cultural capacity of the British people to believe that their condition, from the turn of the century at least, was decidedly worse than it should have been, whatever contrary evidence or appropriate comparative yardstick might have been deployed to argue otherwise.

The Edwardian era: 'high summer' or latent decline?

Some forty years or so ago, economic historians of decline focused their attention largely upon the supposed failures of British entrepreneurs who allegedly lacked the dynamism and drive of their Industrial Revolution counterparts, failing in particular to attain during the period 1870–1914 the increases in output, exports, and productivity that were being achieved in America and Germany. Much of the debate about economic performance in late Victorian and Edwardian Britain concentrated on the country's over-commitment to a narrow range of staple export industries such as coal, cotton, and iron and steel catering for relatively low income markets, and the subsequent retardation in the development of potential growth sectors such as vehicles, chemicals and electrical engineering. By contrast, rising competition from America and especially Germany was seemingly grounded in more productive investment- and science-led industrial activity.

Despite the intellectual heat that such exchanges have generated, the 'economic decline' debate for 1870–1914 period remains inconclusive and unsatisfactory, partly because of the fragile and contentious statistical data upon which such generalizations depend and because of the counterfactual assumptions upon which the notion of blame or failure rests. It has proved difficult to substantiate total failure in the late Victorian and Edwardian economy with Britain by 1913 still the most productive economy in Europe. Insofar as an alleged technological backwardness in Britain is concerned, detailed industry case studies, notably in cotton and steel, demonstrate that pre-1914 entrepreneurs probably acted as rationally as the contemporary scale of resources, costs, and technological knowhow permitted. There is no robust evidence to substantiate the earlier claims of historians that Britain suffered a severe check to her rates of growth of output or productivity from the turn of the century. Even if the growth in productivity after 1899 was lower than in any earlier period, the country still retained a leading place among industrialized nations, and was only gradually beginning to reveal within specific industries and particular regions evidence of relative economic stagnation. Britain's export lead in this period was being closed, but only slowly. Although the balance of trade down to 1913 was almost always in deficit, growing surplus income from 'invisibles' such as services and interest and dividends strengthened the balance of payments overall—this despite substantial exports of capital abroad. Growth rates were understandably faster in countries undergoing those industrial and economic transformations that Britain had already experienced, but few such developers caught up with Britain in absolute terms. If mine owners in 1913 were sending coal abroad in quantities that were never to be surpassed thereafter they were making profits, even if productivity within their industry was declining. The first signs of foreign superiority in steel and engineering were beginning to emerge in 1914, but entrepreneurs in general appeared to have been alive to new investment opportunities when it appeared profitable to pursue them. Moreover, in the decades before 1914 an enormous number of changes occurred in the balance between different types of economic activity and at an uneven pace throughout the economy.

This rather lofty assessment did not appear thus to contemporaries. A growing awareness of relative economic decline in the early decades of the twentieth century prompted calls for political action and obvious remedies, not least, as in America and Germany, the adoption of a protective tariff. Although such a move would have challenged one of the cardinal tenets of the liberal economic order in Britain—free trade—protectionists saw the organization of industry behind tariff barriers, accompanied by a degree of discretionary imperial preference, as a necessary bulwark against rising foreign competition for which free trade appeared to be seriously inadequate. Tariff reform, it was argued, would reduce our dependence on paying for increased food and raw material imports from invisible income and the revenue from particularly successful exports such as coal, whilst a system of colonial preferences would stimulate in those areas a demand for British manufactured exports. Agriculture would be afforded a degree of protection, imperial solidarity would cement Britain's military and political strength in the world, the country would possess a bargaining weapon in trade negotiations, all while industry reaped technological and resource advantages from being protected against outside competition.

Free traders, however, proved triumphant. Tariff barriers, they argued, would promote inefficiency, delay industrial reconstruction, and invite retaliation, thereby reducing profitable outlets overseas. Moreover, shifting the tax burden on to commodities purchased by poorer income groups in favour of protection for producer interest groups raised the spectre of 'dear bread' and an unwelcome intrusion by the state into the conduct of economic affairs. It was not a fall in real wages and retaliatory trade wars that Britain should be encouraging, it was contended, but a further strengthening of free international exchange from which Britain could only benefit in terms of cheap imports and a derived demand for British exports. Protection might force American and European countries, who had previously imported goods from primary producing countries from the surpluses earned by exporting to Britain, to compete more abroad in order to sustain their level of primary producer imports. Free trade, in other words, afforded its own degree of defence against foreign competition.

In any event, it was by no means certain that tariffs were an answer to competitive pressure, given the need to encourage even greater technological advance and a more thorough transfer of resources towards newer, capital-intensive sectors. The forces acting upon the Edwardian economy were rather more subtle and complex than might have appeared to proponents of protection. The typology of industrial activity was undergoing a rapid and significant transformation that was to have lasting effect. The first long wave of the Industrial Revolution had been associated with the cotton textile industry of the north-west, involving the growth of urban manufacturing centres. The Victorian boom and the so-called 'Great Depression' of the late nineteenth century were led by a more diverse combination of heavy industries located around the coalfields of northern England, central Scotland, and south Wales. In the third wave, leadership passed to the light engineering and metal trades of the West Midlands.

The industrial regions were undoubtedly important, but none the less they made a rather poor showing in terms of nineteenth-century and early twentieth-century relative incomes. Labour-intensive methods of production had encouraged the search for competitive low-cost operations, which further served to depress income levels in the traditional industrial regions. By contrast, the higher than average level of regional income in the south-east set it apart. Its comparative advantage resulted not from transfers or spillover effects from traditional industries such as cotton, heavy engineering, shipbuilding, or coal but from a service-orientated regional growth sustained by the income and wealth from trade, finance, overseas investment, and the consumer spending of the landed elite. The City of London, as an international financial centre down to 1914, furnished the growth of a complex of financial institutions and international connections that created sources of substantial wealth. This in turn generated demands for goods and services, freeing the south-east from the limitations of low incomes. It was there that high levels of service provision generated an element of self-sustained growth. Much of the increase in employment in Britain from 1851 to 1911 was channelled into this region. Whereas the textile and mining economies depended essentially upon demand external to their regions, the metropolitan economy enjoyed internal generation of employment growth sustained by structural diversity, a dense concentration of population, a preponderance of middle-class occupations, and conspicuous consumption. This proved to be of long-term advantage. When faced with the economic turbulence of the post-1920 period the southeast, unlike the more vulnerable specialized, export-orientated sectors of the north, south Wales, and central Scotland, could generate all types of new firms because of the size of its potential market, both regional and European, and its favourable levels of local purchasing power.

It was the increasing complexity of both the national and international economy, therefore, that appears in hindsight to be the more dominant influence upon British economic progress down to the eve of the First World War, rather than any overarching entrepreneurial failure. Britain was experiencing a changeover from pre-eminence to being one of several growing, dynamic economies each determined to marshal their economic and human resources to greatest effect. It has even been argued that, far from failing, Britain down to 1914 displayed considerable foresight in transferring entrepreneurial energy away from industrial activities, for which the country was not always best suited, towards commerce and finance, where her real comparative advantage lay.

Although historians might be prepared to accept details of sectoral advantage or disadvantage and the periodicity of 'success' and 'failure' in the decades before 1914, the most potent sources of the country's declining advantage have been seen by some as more deeply embedded and of much longer-term origin. Perhaps the most ready explanation of why Britain performed less well than her industrial competitors as the twentieth century wore on was because she was shackled by her past success and by the legacy of political, social, and cultural structures that were established in the nineteenth century but carried over unreformed into the next. In the absence of revolution, one argument runs, the industrial bourgeoisie gained political influence without undermining the *ancien régime* of the nineteenth century. Thus, a commercial class combined with the remnants of the landed aristocracy to ensure the political subordination of industrial capital. As the public schools were opened up to the sons of northern industrialists, the middle class was distracted from the pursuit of production and profit and encouraged to hanker after an essentially southern rural idyll. Recent refinements of this view stress the extent to which the metropolitan power elite in southern England, landed and mercantile in its origins, operated through the House of Commons, the civil service, the Treasury, the Bank of England, and the City to ensure the primacy of financial capitalism rather than industrial modernization. There is little evidence, however, that the British ruling class was any more anti-industrial than in countries singularly more successful in developing their economies. The sons of the wealthy were not overwhelmingly educated in public schools; nor did public school graduates spurn science or industry. The idea that the British elite embraced a negative anti-industrial bias is by no means proven. Assertions to the contrary are frequently based on impressionistic evidence and do little to address the perpetuation throughout the nineteenth and early twentieth century of successful, innovative entrepreneurship.

Other historians have stressed the persistence in Britain from the nineteenth century of independent, family-owned firms devoid of sufficient resources to develop appropriate research, marketing, or diversification strategies. Thus during the first half of the twentieth century, it is alleged, Britain failed to develop the larger, vertically integrated, and intensely managed corporate business structures that enabled Germany and the United States in particular to make greater progress, particularly in the new high-technology sectors of chemicals, pharmaceuticals, and electricals. In truth, a number of traditional industries in Britain embraced technical and organizational change during the first four decades of the century. Moreover, smaller-scale, family-dominated manufacturing concerns were not as inefficient or such a drag on economic performance as this approach suggests. British firms had to respond to particular internal and external sources of demand and often displayed a degree of flexibility that greater capital-intensive methods of production or bureaucratic corporate structures might have inhibited.

Nevertheless, even in the 'high summer' of Edwardian prosperity, there was no guarantee that the gains still being derived from the export success of staples such as coal or the bifurcation of economic activity between a predominantly northern industrial base and a south-eastern metropolitan financial and service sector economy would continue to serve the needs of the country in the face of a considerable shock to the system. The outbreak of war in 1914 delivered such a blow, restricting Britain's ability to adapt to the shift in leadership among the major industrialized nations.

The wartime economy, 1914–1918: strains and opportunities

When war broke out in 1914 the British government assumed that fighting Germany was compatible with 'business as usual'. The war was expected to be of short duration, but by the end of 1915 it was obvious that the mobilization of economic and financial resources would have to be undertaken on an entirely different scale, beyond the capacity of the free market economy alone. The 'Great Shell Scandal' of 1915, arising from the scarcity of ordnance at the front, graphically illustrated the limitations of existing forms of economic control and direction. The creation of the Ministry of Munitions in June 1915 reflected a new sense of urgency and realism. Survival was not merely a military matter; the state had to contemplate extending its authority to a degree previously unimagined if the needs of both the army and the domestic population were to be met in any prioritized way.

During the early years of the war, mass production techniques and economies of large-scale production were notable for their absence. Many essential industries were still underdeveloped and major industrial sectors were subject to trade union job controls. As the needs of the wartime economy became apparent, the authorities concentrated on directly influencing the supply of skilled men to industry and on raising productivity through greater specialization and mechanization of production in a way that enabled other sources of labour (particularly women and the semi-skilled) to be used without significant damage to productive efficiency. The Ministry of Munitions established state-owned factories and shipyards were equipped with electric power and new production processes. Similar general advances were made in assembly-line techniques in factories from 1916. In general, the war economy encouraged industrial change and practices on a number of fronts through, for example, rationalization, the breaking down of trade jealousies and secrecies, especially in the engineering sector, and more active scientific research in industry, as well as new forms of management.

These specific developments were but part of an extensive array of state economic control. The first total war gave rise to logistical and organizational demands of unprecedented magnitude, particularly the need to blend a free market approach to production and the allocation of resources with the need for intervention when the market was clearly failing the nation. Previous reliance on limited state intervention, the efficacy of private enterprise, and the laws of supply and demand had to give way to the economic and financial priorities of a mass army engaged in a major European land war. What had begun as a trickle of strategic intervention in the affairs of industry during 1915–16, concerning labour, prices, and investment, became a deluge from 1917 as government became determined not to supplant private capitalism but to steer it more systematically towards a coordinated and disciplined response to pressing economic need.

The extension of state interference and influence was considerable. By 1918 two-thirds of the economy and nine-tenths of imports were subject to direction by bodies authorized by the government. The country had some 200 government-owned plants. Military expenditure had risen from about 4% of GDP in 1913 to 38% in 1916–17. Wartime production schedules placed a new premium on the maintenance of industrial peace. Business and labour interests became more involved in the conduct of the war economy as each strengthened their own position numerically and institutionally. The Ministry of Munitions recruited business leaders as senior administrators. In 1916 the Whitley Committee on Relations between Employers and Employed argued for the establishment of Joint Industrial Councils in industries as diverse as motor vehicles, chemicals, and pottery and by 1918 twenty-six councils were in existence. Likewise the Ministry of Reconstruction, established in August 1917 to embrace social reconstruction after the war and to improve business organization and industrial efficiency, placed great stress upon enhanced cooperation between workers and employers.

The Ministry of Reconstruction spent considerable time and effort during the closing years of the war addressing issues of industrial efficiency, scientific and technical education, and improved industrial relations. By 1917 there was growing support for the view that the role of the state should be expanded in peacetime in order to encourage the development of more efficient productive practices, closer empire unity, and the protection of the economy from export 'dumping'. The fear that jobs and industry could be threatened by renewed German export aggressiveness spurred key industrialists such as Dudley Docker, a prominent Birmingham businessman wedded to industrial modernization and tariff protection, to urge the safeguarding of industries like engineering which already had been subject to severe German competition before the war. To Docker, the war provided Britain a critical opportunity for social and economic reconstruction to preserve its world prominence and leadership. Likewise, 'social imperialists' called for a revitalized imperial strategy whereby Britain could retire behind a heavily protected Empire dominated by British industry.

The faltering peacetime economy

Despite these developments, each of the principal economic agents failed to build upon the opportunities afforded by the war to foster a more progressive form of industrial reconstruction and modernization. In the immediate aftermath of war little consideration was given to the utility of economic control and direction as a continuing feature of the peacetime economy, even though some parts of British industry had gained from an acceleration of technical progress both in products and processes. If lessons had been learned during the war about the preferred means of organizing capital and labour to more productive use and about the putative role of the state as an agent of industrial and economic rejuvenation, they were quickly forgotten. Wartime profits were frequently fed into shareholders' dividends rather than into productive investment. There was a clamour for industry to be free of government interference. Technological advance was not entirely halted (many firms in growth sectors such as chemicals and electrical engineering came to display research and development capabilities at least equal to European standards), but fundamental constraints on industrial reconstruction persisted. Industrial relations soured after the collapse of the short postwar boom as employers sought both to lower wage costs to improve competitiveness and to reassert their managerial authority in the face of an expanded and determined trade union movement. In the newer mass production sectors, employers adopted informal patterns of firm-specific skills which hastened the decline of the already beleaguered system of formal apprenticeship without any compensatory advance in vocational or technical training.

Wartime experience and its immediate aftermath exposed a deeper malaise, namely the reluctance of employers, labour, and the government to broker the terms of postwar reconstruction. The invention and innovation of the war years, the cooperation of employers and employed, and the control of key sectors of the economy could, debatably, have been the catalyst for a policy of industrial and economic modernization had the principal actors been willing to concede some of their vested privileges and established practices to facilitate structural adjustment. Had that occurred to an extent sufficient to have encouraged the development of newer expanding sectors of industry based on developing technologies, adaptive forms of collective bargaining, and agreement on how the gains from economic progress could be divided amongst competing claimants, then the adjustments which have conventionally been seen as the 'inevitable' outcome of Britain's economic maturity and fading status might have proved less painful. Unfortunately, the ability of an expanded but traditional industrial structure to absorb large numbers of demobilized workers, thereby diffusing the sensitive political and militant atmosphere of the immediate postwar period, pushed discussion of a new industrial and economic order into the background.

Contemporary political and economic circumstances narrowly prescribed the opportunities for fundamental change. There was little hope of creating a new cooperative industrial environment when neither the employers nor organized labour was willing to seek consensus unless its perceived adversary conceded a measure of real power. Moreover, hopes of securing agreement over the differential development of old and new sectors or of imposing general tariffs were never likely to be fulfilled. Whatever support had developed within manufacturing towards protection since 1903 was compromised thereafter by an intellectual and moral hegemony in favour of free trade, and by a gap between the attractive form of 'constructive imperialism' outlined earlier and the likely impact of any concomitant food duties on the working class. As a consequence, the fight for tariff protection dragged on into the interwar period amidst similar competing claims about its likely effect on Britain's industrial competitiveness and hegemonic status.

In addition, there was deep suspicion of government within business whilst industrialists in general remained fragmented and divided, unable as a consequence to speak with any authority on a strategy for national economic survival. And there was a further, more fundamental difficulty in the way of forging an effective modernizing strategy in the immediate aftermath of war. Industrial consensus and the drive for more scientific and technologically based business activity, had rested earlier upon fears of a very different economic outcome to the war. Once the resurgence of postwar German economic and industrial power had receded, the restoration of the liberal economic order had greater attraction than extended economic control and state intrusion into the affairs of private capitalism. Germany's sudden collapse in the closing months of the war removed one essential justification for a programme of state-initiated economic development.

The immediate impact of the war was to generate during 1919–20 a speculative boom and subsequent deep slump, demands for new forms of wage determination, industrial organization, and ownership, and, through a process of rapid economic decontrol, a free-market deflationary solution to competitive decline. And there were other strains. Expensive reconstruction expenditure worried the Treasury, the City, and the Bank of England. Although Britain did more than most countries in terms of imposing additional taxes, the major part of the cost of the war had been met by borrowing at high rates of interest. The comparative advantage Britain had formerly derived from the acceptance of sterling as an international medium of exchange was compromised by the government's need to borrow short to finance the war. Apart from the government's own internal borrowing, the country had liquidated investments in the USA and had run down gold reserves to a substantial degree. Britain's wartime financial plight had been eased by America's entry into the war in 1917 because it enabled a renewal of public and private loans that had previously been restricted in the face of Britain's increasing indebtedness. But by the end of the war Britain had borrowed $3.7 billion (about two-thirds of Europe's debt to America).

Although the war clearly disrupted much of Britain's normal productive activity, many industrial sectors did rather well under the stimulus of buoyant demand and rising incomes in an insulated domestic market, including motor vehicles, rubber, soap, pharmaceuticals, artificial fibres, tobaccos, chemicals, electricals, glass, iron and steel, and shipbuilding. Had Britain's staple industries continued to develop at their prewar pace the problems that subsequently developed in terms of excess capacity and high unemployment, though unlikely to have been eradicated, might have borne less heavily. But the huge increases in productive capacity undertaken during 1914–18 in sectors such as iron and steel, coal, and shipbuilding for the sake of supplying armaments and other essential military requirements bequeathed to the peacetime period excess plant and inflated prices. Employers in addition faced increased unit costs as the length of the working week was reduced in 1919 without reductions in pay.

Beyond this, many firms in the immediate postwar period were encouraged by the prevailing domestic market and financial environment to engage in ill-informed acquisition, amalgamation, and over-capitalization which, when coupled with wage concessions, proved crippling. Although manufacturing industry enjoyed a profits bonanza during the war, the returns were not always wisely used. Steel indulged in extensive acquisition and amalgamation while other staple trades, instead of reducing capital liabilities, expanded capacity within existing technologies and on goods destined for very traditional markets. Up to £550 million of credit was made available by the banks for industrial purposes during the short-lived boom. There was also frantic buying and selling of industrial concerns at vastly inflated prices. Little attention was paid to altering business organization or the concentration of ownership as a way of encouraging improved practice and efficiency.

In the circumstances, grandiose ideas for domestic reconstruction aimed at building upon the enforced change in state/industry relations during the wartime period fell foul of the financial authorities' determination to rescue London's international reputation. With industry and the trade unions unable to offer a coherent strategy of national renewal, the Treasury in particular was able to reassert its influence over the priorities of economic policy that put domestic reconstruction behind the needs of international financial prowess. This was all the more unfortunate because the economic slump which followed the collapse of the postwar boom in 1920 created a gap between actual and potential industrial production. Though industrial output grew thereafter, the gap between potential output (extrapolating pre-1914 growth trends) and actual production persisted so long that industrial production levels did not exceed their 1879–1913 trend until 1937. In addition, the real exchange rate for British industrial exports is estimated to have peaked at 46% above its 1913 level in 1917–18, imposing upon industry a major readjustment problem.

Facing the global economic environment: Britain in the 1920s

The principal source of Britain's changing competitive advantage lay less in the Edwardian period than in the years following the First World War, largely as a consequence of the damage inflicted upon world trade and the international balance of payments. Although the immediate strains of war focus attention on the 'wartime economy' strictly defined, it was the impact of the war in accelerating the emergence of a hostile global economic environment that cast the longest shadow over Britain. The United States was consolidating its international position while sterling as a leading international currency was under serious threat, all against the background of a fundamental shift in the balance of power between the leading industrialized nations. There is little doubt that the declining competitiveness of British exports, already evident before 1914, worsened thereafter. The country was caught between the twin blades of competition and complementarity. Countries which had formerly depended upon British exports became more self-sufficient under the exigencies of war whilst others, notably the USA and low-wage Japan, capitalized on the disruption to European trading patterns to invade markets, especially those in Asia and Latin America. The war had stimulated import substitution in non-European countries such as Canada, Australia, and India, reducing the markets upon which a considerable part of the prewar export output of Britain had depended. The coal industry, for example, faced both the development of indigenous mines in the Netherlands, Spain, and other former importers and increased competition in existing markets from Germany and Poland, at a time when technical advances in fuel technology and the growing use of substitutes (such as oil for coal in shipping) were further reducing demand. In short, the opportunities that the war provided to rivals compressed into a few years a relative deterioration in Britain's trading situation that would otherwise have been a more protracted process.

This was particularly worrying for a country such as Britain whose manufacturing sector as a whole before the war had depended on overseas sales for 45% of its markets, in the case of cotton textiles for 75%, and in the case of iron and steel for roughly one third. By 1920 export volumes of all kinds were about 30% less than they had been in 1913. Economic dislocation in Europe provided Britain with a brief postwar respite in terms of her share of world trade, but for the remainder of the 1920s her relative decline as an exporter was accentuated by the collapse of prices and earnings in those primary producing countries that had previously been such an important source of demand for British manufactures. With growing import volumes in the 1920s coinciding with a drastic slump in invisible income, Britain was cruelly exposed to an international economic environment that offered little hope of immediate economic betterment.

The British authorities, bereft of any strategy for economic restructuring attuned to the realities of the changed national and international economic environment, searched instead for traditional symbols of normality and stability such as balanced budgets, free trade, and the gold standard, the restoration and operation of which seemed to promise a measure of economic certainty for the future. The gold standard's system of fixed exchange rates, it was tacitly believed, provided through the free movement of gold a means whereby a country's monetary circulation, incomes, and prices would adjust automatically to produce balance of payments equilibrium. In truth, the war had so transformed the economic and financial strength of America that the terms upon which international economic relations were to be restored offered little hope for Britain. Although the USA emerged from the war as the leading creditor nation, it did not seek as a deliberate act of policy to aid financially the reconstruction of European economies to peacetime production. Moreover, the United States was determined to restore a full gold standard. Britain argued at the Genoa Conference in 1922 for sterling or the dollar to be allowed to act as a reserve asset rather than gold, permitting European currencies to be stabilized on a gold exchange standard. The idea was vetoed by the Americans. Once other countries, including the Dominions, also moved towards a full gold standard, Britain was obliged to follow suit as a necessary step to re-establishing a dominant role in the international financial community. The transformation in international indebtedness and economic power resulting from the war thereby imposed upon Britain years of enforced deflation as she struggled to adjust her internal costs and prices to enable the gold standard to be restored and with it, from her point of view, the financial strength and stability required to sustain industry and jobs.

This blind faith in the recuperative powers of the gold standard was attacked by the economist John Maynard Keynes and his few followers as both myopic and dangerous, given the fundamental deterioration that had occurred since the war in Britain's trading, industrial, and financial pre-eminence. Calls for a managed currency, expanded public investment, and the imposition of a revenue tariff were ignored in the 1920s in favour of the restoration of 'normality' based on free trade, sound money, and private enterprise. The relatively high interest rates imposed on the country following the restoration of gold in 1925 and the emergence of an intractable pool of increasingly long-term unemployed in industrial sectors and regions unlikely to benefit from any cyclical upturn in economic activity were worrying enough signs even before the outbreak of world slump in 1929/30. Although most contemporaries saw a return to fixed sterling–dollar parity as the guardian of international confidence, balance of payments stability, and ultimately the sustenance of employment, it imposed a further competitive burden upon traditional export sectors undergoing secular decline.

Turbulent times: slump and recovery in the 1930s

Given what we have discussed so far, it is not surprising to find that the 1920s witnessed little systematic modernization of the industrial structure or willingness to contemplate new priorities of economic policy. It was the relative neglect of those industrial sectors growing fastest in terms of world trade and technological advance that became especially apparent in the interwar years. The fact that Britain by 1939 was still over-reliant upon the output and trading performance of her nineteenth century industrial giants while newer sectors of the economy struggled to catch up on lost ground both at home and abroad, demonstrated how little systematic thought had gone into equipping the country with the means of gaining and sustaining a place in the new industrial order.

Those historians who take an optimistic view of Britain's economic performance between the wars regard such an indictment as seriously misleading. Newer industries, such as motor vehicles and electrical engineering, might not yet have effected a sufficient structural transformation of the economy to benefit of the country as a whole, it is maintained, but they came by the 1930s to exert an increasingly important influence upon productive potential, demonstrating an impressive range of technical achievement, scale economies, and productivity growth. Moreover, if the new industry sector suffered 'growing pains' in the 1920s and 1930s it was instrumental nonetheless in laying the basis for a more permanent structural transformation in British industry, albeit delayed until after the Second World War. Analyses of Britain's cyclical recovery from depression in 1932 have also accorded the new industries a significant role. Under the stimulus of rising real incomes for those in employment, it was a combination of the expansion of the newer home-market industries benefiting from the fruits of technological change and a building boom that brought Britain out of the slump earlier than most other nations.

Nonetheless, it was clear to many politicians and outside observers by the end of the 1920s, as it had been much earlier to those not blinded by the hope of a ready return to prewar economic normality, that competition and technological change had made industrial reconstruction imperative, either by the rationalization of the older trades or by a deliberate shift into a broader range of newer, expanding sectors, or both. The onset of the slump in 1930 dashed any lingering hopes of a spontaneous revival of the traditional export sectors that were situated mainly in northern England, Scotland, and Wales. However, those depressed areas had little to offer new and expanding industries that could not better be obtained elsewhere. Two of the most important factors influencing the location and pattern of growth of the newer industries between the wars were those of proximity to markets or distribution networks and the supply of a particular type of workforce better suited to mechanization than to a craft. Spatial development, in other words, was more a product of a new set of industries with different locational determinants than of the relocation of existing firms. New and expanding sectors were more positively drawn towards the Midlands and the South East than to Wales, Scotland, and the North. In the former areas they drew increasingly upon a pool of juvenile and female labour with a background and aptitude best fitted to semi-skilled and unskilled work at the ruling wage. The conditions permitting the establishment of branch plants of new industries across the country as a whole had not yet emerged; branch expansion tended to be for the purposes of obtaining extra capacity rather than labour, and such demands could often be met from within already prosperous areas without benefiting areas of secular industrial decline.

The decline of the 'old' industries and the rise of the 'new' were not, therefore, interdependent developments. The process was a largely disconnected one, with the result that structural adjustment, rather than converting capital and labour to fresh activities, simply left the depressed areas to decline. A more rapid growth of the developing sector could not, therefore, be relied upon to solve the problems created by secular decline in a basic industry such as coal mining. Since the developing industrial sectors were growing in ways that did not depend crucially upon adjustments in the older sectors, industrial decline in the depressed regions was reinforced. In different circumstances this might have galvanized governments into facilitating more rapid structural change. In 1930s Britain the discontinuous adjustment process had precisely the opposite effect, convincing officials that older industrial sectors had to be protected and sustained.

Officials were aware by the early 1930s of how little industrial reconstruction was actually occurring within coal and other staple trades. By then, however, the government had shifted its attention away from the pursuit of efficiency and competitiveness towards cartelization and output and price control in an effort to limit the spread of unemployment. It was more prepared to prop up the existing industrial structure and to curtail competition to prevent instability than it was to seek reforms that lowered costs. The coal mining industry provides a good example. The Labour government legislated in 1930 to quicken the pace of reorganization in coal at the same time as it made provision through regulated prices, output quotas, and producer-controlled marketing schemes for marginal collieries to gain a share of the dwindling market rather than be forced out of business. This inherent contradiction stifled structural change. In the wake of the slump, however, it seemed a far more urgent matter to support the finances of a politically and socially sensitive sector such as coal mining than it was to promote greater industrial efficiency. For the greater part of the interwar years, therefore, Britain's comparative advantage continued to lie in the labour-intensive 'older' staple industries already in decline as traded goods, whilst its 'new' industrial output proved insufficiently competitive to provide adequate compensation. This situation reinforced the authorities' predilection to sustain those vulnerable sectors likely to cause the greatest political, economic, and social damage if allowed to suffer even further hardship.

If the impulses towards enforced modernization were weak within government itself, they were hardly powerful on the outside. For their part the banks showed a concern for industrial affairs only when narrow financial interests were at stake or, in the case of the Bank of England, when it seemed necessary to stem undue political interference in the private sector. Industrialists since the mid-1920s had proved extremely lukewarm towards proposals for rationalization, and had exploited the many opportunities available to them (some of them supplied by the government itself) to stall effective progress. Few were convinced of the supposed benefits that industrial restructuring was meant to deliver. Doubts remain still as to whether the rationalization schemes proposed at the time would have improved the performance of the staple trades, especially since they were operating under conditions of depressed demand, fluctuating markets, and rising protectionism. It would be unwise to assume retrospectively that an off-the-peg solution to industrial uncompetitiveness such as rationalization lay ready to hand if only the political will could have been mobilized to make use of it.

Such circumstances enabled other vested interests to solidify their position. With industry too divided to speak for itself with any authority, it proved relatively powerless to counter the view, forcibly expressed by the City and the Treasury, that the most effective way of restoring Britain's economic fortunes was to maintain London's financial position in the international community. The highly preferential system afforded to the Dominions under the terms of the Ottawa Agreements is one example of this preoccupation with confidence in the pound. Empire countries were often considerable borrowers, and many of them would have had great difficulty in meeting their debt obligations unless access to sterling was improved. It was in Britain's interests to afford colonial debtors preferential treatment in the British market to enable them to obtain sterling and thereby forestall default or any other repudiation of financial obligations. Concessions on tariffs, therefore, were part of a strategy for maintaining international financial stability. In consequence, the country continued to be locked into an archaic trading pattern that reinforced the existing industrial structure.

This emphasis upon the subordination of domestic economic development to the demands of finance has itself a long pedigree. Much was made at the turn of the century of the supposed gulf between the banks and industry, with the former failing to nurture the long-term relationships necessary to support investment and development, and the latter obliged thereby to maximize only short-term returns to satisfy the financial markets. It is not altogether certain, however, as the American case demonstrates, that economic success is dependent upon a close relationship between finance and industry. Moreover, there is telling evidence that the financial sector would have been prepared to offer long-term finance to British industry both before and after 1914 had there been a strong demand for it and had it been demonstrated that such investment was likely to be profitable. On neither account did British industrialists prove conspicuously proactive.

From another perspective, it is likely that Britain's economic problems over much of our period were compounded by a low level of investment in human capital and a relative indifference to formal technical and managerial education. Although conventional neoclassical growth models stress the importance of enterprise and technological improvement, it is clear that nations sustain high rates of economic growth over the long term only if they invest in the health, numeracy, literacy, and personal living standards of their population (the 'human resource') and provide adequate social and cultural capital in the form of communications, an information infrastructure, and adequate social security and housing provision. Britain had long failed to obtain any comparative advantage in human capital-intensive products. Faced before 1914 by overseas competition from countries with a greater commitment to technical and vocational education, the British political class was wedded to minimum state activity in economic and social affairs. It is true that the last decade before the First World War witnessed a significant shift in social policy with the establishment in 1903 of a national education system and later the creation of insurance-based national, if restricted, social security schemes for health, old age, and unemployment. The principal departments of state responsible for developing human resources between the wars, however, fell foul of the retrenchment in public expenditure forced upon the country by its international orientation of financial policy and its determination to safeguard sound finance and balanced budgets.

Orthodoxy versus radicalism: policy priorities before 1939

The deterioration in Britain's economic and financial situation during the world slump finally forced her to abandon the gold standard and to adopt tariffs as a means of raising revenue, protecting vulnerable sectors, and bargaining for trade. But if confidence at home and abroad in the wake of the world slump was to be maintained to enable London to rebuild its internationalism without a threat to the value of sterling, it was necessary to eschew radical fiscal and economic policies in favour of the more pragmatic sustenance of prices, output, and employment, given the political constraints facing deflation. Although Britain after 1931 was freer to abandon orthodox economic policy than at any time since 1925, the thrust of policy remained one of safety first. Much of the reason for this was the fact that Britain's recovery from depression was earlier than most comparable countries and proved to be more sustained. As Fig. 6.1 shows, whereas the USA only regained its 1929 level of real GNP by 1937 (only to see it fall again), Britain had regained its level by 1934, while France did not recover until after 1945.

Although the development of capital-intensive, consumer-orientated 'new' industries is a feature of the British interwar period, the extent of structural change in manufacturing production at that time, though faster than it had been between 1900 and 1913, still lagged in comparison with the post-1945 period. Moreover, the 'new' industries do not seem to be as distinctly identifiable or as characteristically expansive and less labour-intensive as was previously thought.

Although there is evidence of increased industrial concentration and merger activity in Britain in the 1920s, neither development did much to diminish the perpetuation of federations of autonomous family enterprises capable, via holding companies, of enjoying

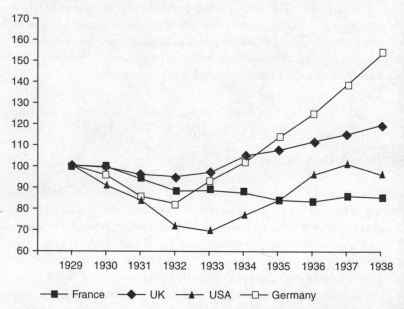

Figure 6.1 Index of real GNP, 1929–1938 (1929 = 100)
Source: D. Baines, 'Recovery from Depression' in P. Johnson ed., Twentieth Century Britain (Longman, 1994).

substantial market power without much threat from government. Hostile take-overs were not a prevalent feature of the business world. The economy, however, lacked effective mechanisms to remove inefficient firms, allowing restrictive practices and a growth of craft rather than managerial control on the shop floor to reinforce existing structures and attitudes. In a political and economic climate that gave greater priority to raising prices relative to wages via cartels, tariffs, and exchange rate depreciation and to safeguarding jobs rather than improving productivity, it was easier for bargains over work effort and manning levels inimical to longer-term economic performance to prevail. In key sectors employers and workers were often unable to strike beneficial agreements about work patterns and new technologies, thereby stalling the adoption of overseas (largely American) production and managerial practices which, if not necessarily applicable to all sectors of British industry, were nonetheless more prominent features of corporate strategy amongst Britain's major competitors.

Low interest rates ('cheap money') and the existence of tariff protection, together with a home market recovery from 1933, might in different political circumstances have encouraged ways of combining economic recovery with industrial modernization. But it was not to be. Even the break with free trade was seen in part as a way of safeguarding the currency. Reduced imports would diminish the trade gap, while increased revenue from import duties would enable the budget to be balanced, allowing foreign confidence in sterling to be maintained. Ideologically, the hegemony of economic liberalism may have been badly bruised by the crisis of 1929–32 but it was not destroyed. Finance remained supreme, and although the primacy of production was articulated and the need for reconstruction acknowledged, the influences playing upon state policy ensured that systematic modernization would be delayed if it threatened the financial, budgetary, and political status quo, that guardian of confidence at home and abroad and therefore of metropolitan, if not necessarily national, interests.

Although there were other factors affecting Britain's industrial performance before 1939, not least deficiencies in marketing and inadequate investment in technical and managerial education, it should not be too readily assumed that the structural problems facing British industry were amenable to any immediate or short-term solution. The collapse of exports and declining competitiveness facing the staple trades were endemic, while the potential expansion of the 'new' industries geared to the domestic market was constrained by the scale and depth of prevailing consumer demand. There was a general scepticism, moreover, over the capacity of the state to raise industrial efficiency and competitiveness and little by way of coherent industrial strategies from other quarters, save the spirited actions of the 'planners' who rashly assumed that there existed a core of entrepreneurs anxious to foster a more progressive industrial regime.

Radical economists and politicians such as Maynard Keynes and Oswald Mosley respectively clamoured before and after the world slump for a more proactive state, one that would be prepared to 'prime the pump' via planned programmes of national expenditure. Their presumption that a break from financial orthodoxy would actually enrich the economy by setting in train a multiple increase in national income, a reduction in wasteful expenditure on the unemployed, and a necessary redress to the north/south divide met stern opposition, not least from the Treasury. Such proposals, it argued, threatened budgetary stability and a crisis of confidence at home and abroad. Moreover, they were regarded as impracticable. Deficit-financed schemes of public works, for example, were unlikely to harness labour and capital where and when they were most needed because of their lopsided emphasis upon a narrow range of industries; they were, moreover, essentially short-term in effect, and posed a direct threat to the 'natural' forces of recovery.

When the Treasury finally sanctioned increased borrowing from 1935 it proved to be a temporary lapse from orthodoxy occasioned by the urgent demand for rearmament. In consequence, previously depressed areas gained from the strategic placement of government investment projects where capacity and labour were plentiful. This hardly amounted to a 'Keynesian' conversion; the rearmament programme down to 1939 was limited and controlled by the overriding desire to preserve national and international financial stability. With deterrence, diplomacy, and appeasement to the fore, defence expenditure was kept under close scrutiny, limited to what was thought to be required in the light of the international situation and with regard to its anticipated effects upon costs, the balance of payments, and the sterling exchange rate.

The fact remains that in the aftermath of the world slump the political economy of industrial policy put greater emphasis upon consensus than upon modernization. Britain's comparative strength down to 1939 continued to reside in the older staples, where productivity levels were low and where human capital was inadequately developed. Despite the merger boom of the 1920s and indications in the developing contacts between government and industry of a very modest shift towards the corporate economy, British industrial policy produced neither full-blown competition nor coordination. Instead it mollified vested interests and promoted collusion and cartelization in order to minimize both the shake-out of capital and labour and any latent threat to financial and budgetary stability, thereby delaying structural change and the elimination of excess and inefficient capacity.

It would be unwise to assume that such cartelization fostered a degree of featherbedding or a weakened competitive climate wholly inimical to industrial progress. Policy-makers in the 1930s were aware that restriction and collusion could prove harmful. They were equally aware, however, that faith in market forces had been shaken by the world slump, and that there were occasions when competitive excesses had to be held in check without undermining private enterprise. In an era when distrust of both the state and the market was clearly evident, it was not altogether surprising that official action designed to safeguard so many different industries in varying national and international competitive environments should have given rise to free competition, voluntary restriction, and compulsory cartelization at one and the same time. Moreover, the British chemical industry probably gained more than it lost from international cartels through the sustenance of capacity and access to strategic information. Nor did British efficiency suffer greatly from these developments, since the British/US and British/German manufacturing productivity gap was very similar in the later 1930s to what it had been at the end of the Edwardian period. One might have wished for more fundamental structural change between the wars and for the earlier emergence of competitive sectors better able to sustain Britain's longer-term future, but the patchy, pragmatic progress made over the very uncertain economic terrain of the time certainly did not engender endemic decline.

War and reconstruction again

Whether by 1939 Britain was on the brink of a breakthrough in official thinking, building perhaps on the lessons of slump and recovery to reappraise the fundamentals of macro- and micro-economic policy, will never be known. The outbreak of war soon redirected policy and resources to the sole pursuit of national survival. This is not the place to detail the economics of the war economy; what is significant from our point of view is the extent to which the disruption of another major conflict affected Britain's subsequent relative economic performance. Measures of direct and indirect economic loss as a consequence of war are notoriously suspect. It is generally accepted, however, that Britain emerged from the war in a relatively favourable position in comparison with most of her continental neighbours. Although Britain suffered a loss of external capital assets and reserves, which when added to internal capital loss amounted to a reduction of almost one-quarter of her prewar national wealth, the setbacks in direct and indirect costs (including imputed loss of income per head of those who were sacrificed), whilst greater relative to the USA, compared favourably to most European countries, excluding Russia.

That is not to deny the serious economic problems faced by Britain. Although the country had benefited enormously from the supply of military and strategic aid from the USA under the terms of the Lend-Lease system, the latter left Britain at the end of the war with massively depleted international reserves, with external liabilities at least six times greater than her gold and dollar reserves. Not surprisingly, the country was saddled in the immediate postwar years with a serious balance of payments problem. The Labour government's economic and social agenda is usually remembered for its nationalization programme and the inauguration of the welfare state. But the perceived urgency was to make good the country's prewar export position and especially to fill the gap created by a substantial fall in invisible income. Considerable effort was spent in trying to raise industrial productivity so that relatively scarce resources could be used to greatest effect. It was essential to eliminate the external deficit, to sustain a high level of industrial investment, and to keep inflation low if Britain was to gain a secure place in an increasingly uncertain and competitive trading environment. The Attlee administrations of 1945–51 benefited from the high levels of world demand that American financial aid helped to sustain. They were able thereby to turn their attention to correcting the balance of payments problem rather than having to be preoccupied with maintaining full employment. In consequence, much of the foreign aid the country received went into clearing the foreign balance rather than into industrial restructuring. With the economy running at high levels of demand, manufacturing industry and particularly the building and capital goods sectors were often under strain and compelled to delay necessary investment. Strict controls on civilian consumption were combined with strenuous efforts to temper the growth of money incomes.

The difficult task of economic management in the aftermath of war, which included a devaluation of sterling in 1949, was performed with commendable success, inasmuch as the country rode out the various short-term crises to which it was subjected whilst avoiding the severe economic setbacks that would have arisen from any serious deterioration in the overseas account. Some industrial sectors, notably metals and engineering, expanded and modernized on the basis of new scientific knowledge at the same time as domestic export-oriented staple sectors suffered disinvestment and the loss of skilled manpower and expertise. But it was the success in boosting Britain's share of world commodity exports that put her in good stead. The transformation in the balance of payments is detailed in Table 6.2.

Overall assessments, however positive, rarely tell the whole story. Historians debate whether Britain, emerging from war as the victor,

Table 6.2 Britain's balance of payments: current account (£m.), 1939–1950

	Exports	Imports	Visible trade balance	Invisible balance	Current balance
1939	500	800	−300	50	−250
1945	450	700	−250	−620	−870
1950	2,261	2,312	−51	358	307

Source: C. H. Feinstein, National Income, Expenditure and Output of the United Kingdom, 1855–1965 (Cambridge, 1972).

had sufficient will to forge a dominant place in the new international economic and political order. Whether long-established attitudes among management and men towards innovation and expansion had altered sufficiently to meet the challenges of the postwar world was a matter of concern, even for contemporaries. How far the legacy of the interwar years had effected real and lasting changes in the mutual relationship between, and responsibilities of, the individual and the state had yet to be fully demonstrated. Moreover, little had been done to address the problem of the balance of activity within the economy. It was, after all, Britain's loss of leadership in services that had distanced her over the longer term from Germany and the United States, rather than differences in comparative manufacturing productivity.

Fundamental problems remained. We have already remarked upon the extent to which Britain between the wars sought to resurrect the 'normality' of Edwardian prosperity in an economic environment that demanded far more flexibility and insight than was demonstrated at the time. A fortunate combination of circumstances enabled Britain to recover early from the world slump, but that major shock had not led to any fundamental reappraisal of the priorities of economic policy. Britain's determination to secure a leading role for sterling and her sense of commanding a pivotal role in world affairs remained—as well they might in the years before loss of Empire. But Britain's anxiety in the late 1940s and early 1950s to promote sterling as a reserve currency for the sake of buttressing her world role, combined with a determination to sustain a level of defence expenditure which the nation could ill afford in order that she could police the non-communist world, imposed substantial costs that were assuaged only by American financial aid. These circumstances merely courted future exchange rate and balance of payments crises of potentially lasting damage.

The Treasury was, however, obliged by the original Bretton Woods agreement of 1944 and later by its obligations to the Sterling Area to remain sensitive to the needs of external balance and short-term stabilization for the sake of preserving sterling as an international reserve currency. Given the Treasury's central role in policy formulation, it was understandable too that attention would regularly be drawn away from the long-term growth prospects of the 'real' economy. (Exchange rate crises in later decades were regarded more as a *consequence* of the neglect of productivity and competitiveness.)

With Britain wedded to seeking an international power role in the shadow of the USA and with the Treasury committed as it had been in the 1920s to the belief that internal economic stability depended on the ruling exchange rate, it was little wonder that sporadic efforts to redirect policy towards structural modernization remained just that.

The Labour government's much-vaunted export drive, though critically necessary, did little to divert trade away from staple industries and from a dependence on soft Dominion markets. Britain's willingness to keep Europe at arm's length might have satisfied an ingrained sense of knowing where best to forge a special relationship (across the Atlantic), but it distanced the country from the region of fastest growth, allowing other western European countries, not least Germany, to reap the benefits of intra-European trade. On the domestic economic front, the nationalization of coal, rail transport, electricity, and gas merely completed a process that had begun before the war. It did not presage a strategy for industrial modernization. The defence of sterling, the commitment to large defence expenditure, and a continuing concern to sustain what was already a fading role in international events ensured that the tension between the external and the internal needs of the country, replete in her immediate economic past, continued almost unabated.

The Treasury remained the dominant force in Whitehall, determined to retain control over economic policy and ever watchful of any long-term domestic commitments by the spending departments. Productivity drives in the early postwar years were long on rhetoric but short on results. Neither employers nor unionists were bent on technical and organizational changes that would fundamentally alter existing work practices or collective agreements. Economic advice within government favoured macro demand-side management, not supply-side reforms designed to tackle endemic industrial weakness and the neglect of human capital formation. As for the latter, wartime developments had hinted at a fundamental reform of education and one that would pay greater attention than hitherto to vocational training. However, the 1944 Education Act, for all its benefits, did little to oust the status attached to intellectual, abstract activity in grammar and public schools.

Before the 'golden age': the British economy by 1950

If, as suggested, Britain successfully met some of the immediate economic problems of postwar transition without tackling other potential sources of industrial and economic weakness, this in itself might be regarded as understandable, even salutary, considering how much more was being done to create the 'New Jerusalem' of social welfare, itself a potential source of economic betterment. However, the welfare illusion was less critical than the liberal illusion that market forces without state encouragement and correction could deliver growth and rising competitiveness. British spending on social welfare as a share of GDP was already outstripped by Germany, Austria, and Belgium by 1950, by France and Denmark by 1952, and Italy by 1954. Moreover, the share of the public sector was declining in Britain in the 1950s when Britain was already on a relative downward path of economic performance and competitiveness. More worrying was the fact that, despite the ambitious schemes of educational and welfare provision promoted in the mid- to late 1940s and implemented in the decades thereafter, the country had reached the 1950s without having made any substantial political commitment to investment in the health, security, and education of its citizens as a necessary foundation of national economic success.

The brief references made so far to the conduct of economic policy abroad might suggest that Britain could have improved her lagging industrial competitiveness by drawing lessons from the experience of other countries. The Japanese comparison was intriguing, since its national policies were generally regarded as having played an important part in creating comparative advantage. The central role of government in strategic planning, 'picking winners' in sectors or firms, orchestrating cartels, and protecting or subsidizing industry stood in stark contrast to British practice. Recent literature is beginning to challenge these perceptions of the conduct of Japanese policy, shifting attention away from earlier descriptions of a powerful and sophisticated bureaucracy judiciously able to utilize incentives and administrative guidance to steer the economy, towards a more critical view of a divided, ineffective, and at times counterproductive political and bureaucratic apparatus. Nonetheless this revisionism has not entirely removed the 'strong' view of the role of government in Japan's postwar economic success.

Even if Britain's major competitors, including Japan, gained much less from state involvement than has previously been thought, it does not follow that Britain had nothing to learn from them. The problem was that the management practices, labour organizations, forms of education, and training which the western Europeans and the Japanese in particular were using to such positive effect were a product of complex historical circumstances and prevailing social and cultural norms that were not available in pre-packaged form for adoption elsewhere. That is not to imply that countries are forever wedded to their past, as the rapid economic convergence of the postwar period demonstrates. Japan was very willing to adapt, borrow, and refashion against past practice. The critical point is that the industrial, political, and financial will was there to be exploited for the purpose of national growth and success. Britain, by contrast, consistently failed to create a coalition for growth, as costly defence expenditure and a failure to modernize the state machine led the powerful interest groups most likely to be affected by intervention— the unions, businessmen, and investors—to defend their own positions of power and influence, leaving the state to mend the economy rather than to modernize it. The essential difficulty facing Britain was not so much the existence of organized producer groups able to veto policies they opposed as the unwillingness of government to broker the terms upon which industrial modernization could proceed.

The countries which capitalized on their postwar opportunities to gain and retain comparative advantage did so by considering the adaptive capacity of their industrial structures and by examining how they could mould and alter inherited structures, markets, and technology to medium and long-term advantage. What Britain's competitors realized more clearly than she did was that the state could undertake selective intervention in growing, tertiary, and declining industries; that it could shape tax and research and development expenditures, especially in high technology sectors; and that it could invest in human capital accumulation. The cumulative effect of doing so, as competitor countries found, was that they could maintain their competitive advantage in international markets to such a degree that over time they were able to reshape the comparative advantage of the nation as a whole.

Within Britain there was for the greater part of our period a constant tension between the priorities of international economic policy and what action might be required to foster domestic economic change. Although by 1950 a case could be made for Britain having missed important opportunities for fostering greater economic progress, the most noticeable signs of relative economic decline were yet to appear. Real GDP per person in 1950 in the UK was double that of 1870. In 1994 it was five times that of 1870, but by then the UK had fallen behind other industrial nations to a much greater extent than it had done before the Second World War. Moreover, before 1950 its principal competitors were, with one exception, non-European countries, whereas thereafter more western European countries overtook the UK. It was a source of anxiety for Britain to find that over the course of the twentieth century the country had fallen down the international league table of economic performance. As we noted at the outset, British GDP per capita in 1890 was the highest in Europe, greater than that of the USA and in excess of the rest of Europe even in 1913. But as the century wore on Britain lagged behind not only the USA but more and more other countries, including by 1989 France and Germany but also Denmark, Norway, Finland, Sweden, and Switzerland.

What stands out above all else over the first fifty years of the century is the huge relative advantage of the USA in terms of her rate of growth of output and productivity and her dominance of world markets, having been able for so long to exploit greater resource endowments and to transfer labour more effectively from agriculture to higher-productivity sectors. Over the same period, Britain fared far better economically than is customarily believed, given the trauma and dislocations imposed by two world wars and the constant need to adapt macro- and micro-economic policy to an ever-changing national and international economic environment. The notion of British 'decline' in the historiography of the post-1945 period has remained potent largely because the nation has been driven by higher and higher expectations of material wealth which have rarely been able to be satisfied as swiftly or as comfortably as were the simpler and smaller wants of earlier generations. By 1950 a 'golden age' lasting some two decades was about to dawn, only to give rise thereafter to renewed angst about Britain's declining advantage. Even then, the measurable shifts in relative performance masked more overarching evidence of the material advance that had occurred in the country over the course of the century.

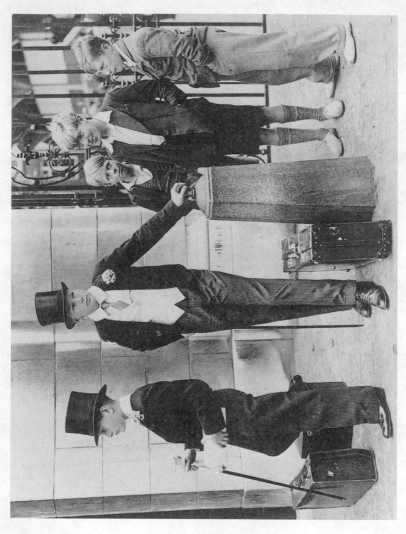

Plate 9 Harrow public schoolboys, in their formal uniform, are watched with amusement by local children. This photograph in 1937 illustrates that, although class divisions remained great throughout the period, they became far less oppressive.

Riches, poverty, and progress

Rodney Lowe

Three publications encapsulate the changing condition, and perception, of British society in the first half of the twentieth century. The first, *Riches and Poverty*, was published by Sir Leo Chiozza Money in 1905. It argued, from an analysis of taxation records, that inequality in Britain was greater then than in any comparable European country and, most probably, than at any other time in the country's history. Just under 900,000 people, who together with their dependants accounted for just 10% of the population, owned 87% of private property. The second, Seebohm Rowntree's *Poverty and Progress*, published in 1941, remains the most respected of the house-to-house poverty surveys carried out between the 1890s and the 1950s. By the strictest standard of 'primary' poverty, by which 'not a farthing was allowed in the course of the whole year for anything beyond mere physical needs', it calculated that poverty in the allegedly typical town of York had declined between 1899 and 1936 from 15.5% to 6.8% of the working-class population. However, by a more realistic poverty line (which allowed for people's social as well as physical needs) some 31% of the working class were in poverty; and, most damning of all, this included half of all working-class children under the age of 5. In contrast the third publication, Rowntree's final survey of York published in 1951 as *Poverty and the Welfare State*, was far more optimistic. It estimated that the percentage of the working class in poverty had dropped to a mere 2.8%. There was one overwhelming reason for this—the implementation of the comprehensive system of state welfare as proposed by the 1942 Beveridge Report. Had welfare services not improved since 1936, so Rowntree argued, just over a quarter of the working class would still have been in poverty.

These three publications testify to a remarkable transition in the material condition of British society. They were themselves part of an exceptional social initiative to survey wealth and poverty systematically. Their findings were also exceptional. In 1900 Britain was characterized by extreme inequality and deprivation, but by mid-century, again for the first time in British history, poverty appeared to have been eradicated. Not only did this transform most people's lives, by lifting a fear that had long overshadowed and diminished them, but it also represented—in the words of T. H. Marshall—a major political step towards the attainment of 'democratic citizenship' or social equality. Individual social rights, implicit in the government's guarantee of a national minimum of civilized life, complemented—and made fully effective—the individual civil and political rights attained more famously in the seventeenth and nineteenth centuries as a result of the Civil War and successive Reform Acts. Contemporary evidence suggests, therefore, that the first half of the twentieth century was a period of exceptional change in terms of both short-term achievement and longer-term significance.

How well has contemporary evidence and optimism stood the test of time? In relation to the measurement of poverty and wealth, both the concepts used in the surveys and the precision of their calculation have been challenged. Consequently their findings have been frequently revised. Doubts have been also raised about whether a diminution of poverty, to the extent that it actually did occur, can be taken as a sufficient measure of 'progress'. After all, as the then Labour government acknowledged, the distribution of personal wealth—the other key social measure—had changed little by 1950. Moreover, there are other measures of progress, such as greater regional, gender, and racial equality. Finally, what of the agency of apparent progress? In 1900 Britain had had one of the most decentralized systems of government in Europe, with voluntary and locally elected bodies established as the natural means by which issues such as individual welfare should be resolved in 'civic' society and away from Westminster. In contrast, against all expectation, it had acquired by 1950 what Jose Harris has identified as 'one of the most uniform, centralized, bureaucratic and "public" welfare systems in Europe, and indeed in the modern world'. Was this progress? To many at the time, such as Hayek in *The Road to Serfdom* (published in 1944), and to many since, it was not. Rather, it represented a backward step which threatened individual initiative and thus both economic efficiency and democratic vitality.

The purpose of this chapter, therefore, is to review the record of social change between 1900 and 1950 in the light of present-day concepts and reservations. It will focus first on the distribution of wealth and poverty, then on the other measures of equality, and finally on the welfare role of government. Analysis of the period has too often been foreshortened by the two world wars and tainted by interwar depression. Taking the period as a whole, however, from the intellectual ferment at the turn of the century (which drove forward the scientific investigation of 'the social question') to the administrative innovations of the 1940s (which established Britain as the world leader in welfare provision), the evidence seems to exist to demonstrate that this was a period of exceptional social change and achievement. Can so positive an interpretation be sustained?

The distribution of wealth and income

Since the 1974–9 Royal Commission on the Distribution of Income and Wealth the concepts of wealth and income, and the means for their precise measurement, have become ever more sophisticated in Britain. As a result, all earlier estimates must be regarded as tentative. This includes popular contemporary impressions, such as those of Chiozza Money or John Hilton in *Rich Man, Poor Man* (1944), and the increasing number of academic investigations in the 1930s and 1940s by statisticians such as Bowley. No consistent series of wealth or income distribution can be constructed for the period as a whole.

Personal wealth was traditionally assumed to consist of property, savings, and consumer goods. The Royal Commission argued, however, that the right to social services also constituted a significant form of wealth. Such rights, of course, were not so extensive before 1950, but there was an increasing range of services targeted on the less well-off, including free means-tested pensions in 1908 and contributory pensions in 1925. No accurate estimate of their value can be made.

Measuring the distribution of traditional forms of wealth is also, to this day, problematic. Social statistics are typically the by-product of routine administration. Britain, however, has never had a wealth tax, and reliance has had therefore to be placed on administrative procedures triggered by death, such as the listing of assets (probate records) or the assessment of tax liability (death or estate duty returns). Neither is fully satisfactory because they exclude people below a certain exemption limit, cover individual rather than family wealth, and are distorted by attempts to minimize tax liability, both legal and illegal. Most seriously of all, they also provide only one snapshot of an individual's wealth and give no guide to its size or variation over time. The Royal Commission determined that estate duty returns provided the best basis for calculation; but to generalize their data yet another potential source of inaccuracy has to be introduced. People dying in any one year are assumed to be a representative sample and categorized by sex, age, and locality. The appropriate multiplier is then applied to their estate in order to produce an estimate of aggregate wealth. Such calculations and the shortcomings of the evidence tend to exaggerate the recorded degree of inequality.

With these reservations in mind, the Royal Commission's estimates for the distribution of personal wealth in England and Wales are presented in Table 7.1. They have since been revised by Atkinson

Table 7.1 Distribution of personal wealth in England and Wales (%)

% of population over 25	1911–13	1924–30	1936–8	1954
Top 1%	69	62	56	43
Top 5%	87	84	79	71
Top 10%	92	91	88	79
Top 1%	69	62	56	43
Top 2–5%	18	22	23	28
Top 6–10%	5	7	9	8
Remainder	8	9	12	21
Total—Population (m)	18.7	22.3	25.6	
Total—Wealth (£b)	6.0	13.7	15.2	

and Harrison, who argue that the figures for 1911–13 are strictly incomparable and, in addition, lower the figures for the top 5% in the 1930s and raise them in the 1950s, thereby modifying the apparent impact of the Second World War. This does not, however, affect the main impression to be gained from the table which—in accordance with Chiozza Money's findings—is one of extreme inequality. The share of wealth owned by the top 1% may have decreased over time but it still greatly exceeded comparable figures for the USA, which were 32% in 1922 and 21% in 1949. Their 'losses' were also largely distributed (no doubt for tax reasons) amongst the top 10%, whose share of wealth before 1914 was some 10% higher than in other comparable European countries. It only declined marginally between the wars and then arguably fell more sharply in the 1940s.

The inevitable corollary of such a concentration of wealth was that there were a large number of 'propertyless' people. Hilton calculated, for instance, that in the late 1930s an equal distribution of aggregate wealth would have resulted in each family owning £15,000. In reality, one-third of the twelve million families owned nothing, and a further third less than £100 (at a time when the average male industrial wage was about £150 p.a.). Even as late as 1953 it was estimated that a third of people had no liquid assets. There was, however, one small but significant change which is reflected in Table 7.1 by the increasing share of wealth owned by the bottom 90%. After 1900 there was a doubling, from 17%, of the number of estates which required a probate return because they exceeded £100, and a sizeable number of these ranged up to £500. This gradual generation of modest estates was a consequence of a historic turning point in *income* distribution between the wars.

Personal income, as specified by the Royal Commission, derives from three sources: employment, ownership of assets (such as interest from savings), and government transfers (such as state pensions). It can also be received in either cash or kind (such as free school meals) and is, of course, reduced by taxation. There are inevitable difficulties in making precise calculations, particularly of income in kind, but most can be resolved by official figures derived from the sampling of tax returns and from regular annual surveys of expenditure and earnings. Unfortunately, these figures only go back to 1938. The rough estimates of income in cash that are available suggest that the share of pre-tax income of the top 1% of earners declined steadily from 30% in 1914 to 17% in 1938 and then to 11% in 1949. Their post-tax share fell between the latter dates from 12% to 6%. As with the distribution of wealth, the share of the top 10% fell less sharply, but nevertheless it did fall between 1938 and 1949 from 39% to 33% (pre-tax) and from 35% to 27% (post-tax). Figures for the bottom half are available only for 1949 and reveal that they received approximately one-quarter of income. Considerable inequality, therefore, remained, but a record of sustained redistribution was established between the wars.

Reasons for redistribution

What accounts for and what was the social significance of this historic turning point? A key background factor was increasing national wealth, with GDP per capita almost doubling in real terms between 1900 and 1950; but for redistribution to occur these gains had to be enjoyed disproportionately by salary and wage earners. The latter did indeed so benefit because, although they declined as a percentage of the occupied population from 78% to 66% during the period, their share of national income remained constant at around 40%. They therefore enjoyed an enlarged share of increasing national wealth. The two world wars played a major part in this transformation. The principal engines of change were inflation, which hit those on fixed incomes; structural economic change, which, although it deskilled some, generally moved people upwards into better-paid clerical or semi-skilled jobs; trade union power, which was able to exploit labour shortages and raise unskilled wages from an average of under 60% to 80% of skilled earnings by the 1940s; and government regulation which, especially during the Second World War, controlled income derived from the 'ownership of assets' as opposed to employment.

All these wartime changes benefited wage earners more than salary earners; and they were broadly maintained in peace despite mass unemployment between the wars. Salary earners, in their turn, benefited more from the peacetime structural change and in particular from the explosion in the number of white-collar jobs as all sectors of society became more bureaucratic and the service industries expanded. The upward movement into jobs with higher and more regular incomes is illustrated by David Glass's finding that by 1949 one-fifth of the sons of manual workers were employed in non-manual work. In contrast, income from more traditional sources such as agriculture, rent, and overseas investments stagnated or even declined for most of the period. Higher-income receivers were thereby disadvantaged.

There was one other major redistributory mechanism: taxes and transfers. The First World War increased the acceptability of income tax; and this helps to explain why, following the resistance to Lloyd George's prewar land taxes, it was clearly deemed politic to tax the income derived from wealth rather than wealth itself. Tax rates became so progressive that a bachelor on an income of £10,000, who in 1913 would have retained £9,242, was left by 1922 with only £5,672. This sum rose in the interwar period but it was cut to a mere £3,587 by 1950. Wartime inflation also, of course, reduced the real value of such an income, so the high rate of taxation was in effect hitting people lower down the income scale. Manual workers largely avoided paying income tax even in the 1940s, but they did not escape taxation altogether. A relatively high percentage of their income was consumed by indirect taxes (on, for example, beer and tobacco); and although the Beveridge Report referred to the 'established popularity of compulsory insurance', unemployment and health insurance contributions—by making small incomes even smaller—aroused considerable anger after their introduction in 1911. In compensation, however, considerable benefits were targeted on those with incomes below £250 p.a. in the interwar period and, in contrast to the Edwardian period, their value exceeded by some 25% the taxes paid by that group. They consequently represented a transfer of resources to manual workers, estimated at the time by Barna as between 8% and 14% of their aggregate income. The irony was, of course, that the replacement of selective benefits by universal social rights in the 1940s (which entitled everyone, for example, to free health care and contributory pensions) reduced their redistributive nature.

The impact on class

The continuing concentration of personal wealth and the sustained trend towards greater income equality reflected the transitional nature of society as a whole. The upper class, which centred around the aristocracy and landed gentry and numbered some 40,000 during the period, lost its former predominance in relation to the ownership of land, wealth, and political power. As late as the 1870s a mere 7,000 families owned half the land in the UK, but in the first quarter of the twentieth century a transfer occurred on a scale equivalent to that following the Norman Conquest or the dissolution of the monasteries. Land was bought mainly by existing tenant farmers. Sales on this scale were indicative of the decline of land as a source of wealth, a fact underlined by the estimate that of all millionaires and half-millionaires dying between the wars only 29 and 62 respectively were 'landed'. The wealth of the other 153 millionaires and 349 half-millionaires was derived largely from finance, manufacturing, and (as evidence of rising national affluence) consumer industries such as brewing and tobacco. Together with the extension of the vote, such changes eroded the bases of political power. Sales of land by larger landowners and the impoverishment of the landed gentry who were unable to diversify, for example, decreased involvement in local politics; and declining relative wealth eroded the undisputed authority of the aristocracy at a national level.

The upper class nevertheless remained throughout the period a core of wealth and political *influence*, thus helping to mask the pace of change elsewhere. Diversification from landownership into more profitable activities such as finance and company directorships, where this was possible, was a rational decision which sustained and even enlarged 'landed' fortunes. Political influence was retained both in Cabinet (where as late as 1935–55 a quarter of Conservative ministers were peers) and on the back benches (where the independent country member could still be influential). Businessmen were neither ennobled in large numbers (despite Edwardian fears) nor dominated politics (despite Lloyd George's experiments with men of 'push and go'). However, as McKibbin has shown, most significant to the continuing existence and influence of the upper class was the role of 'society'. Largely orchestrated by Anglo-American hostesses such as Lady Cunard, its glamour enabled the upper class to win a sympathetic press and mix with leaders of popular fashion, such as film stars, thereby 'enchanting' the general public. This was in direct contrast with continental Europe, where popular and political antagonism towards the aristocracy was considerable. The identification of 'society' with appeasement and even fascism briefly broke this spell during the Second World War, but again, unlike on the Continent, the upper class survived. Favourable decisions, such as that not to tax wealth, were influenced in no small measure by a sympathy for 'landed' values amongst those in 'high office', especially within the civil service.

The most dynamic social change occurred within the middle class. Conventionally defined as all non-manual workers with an annual income below £10,000, it grew from approximately one-fifth to a quarter of the population over the period. The range of incomes covered was wide, as initially were its political and social values. Greater homogeneity was achieved between the wars, however, in relation to occupation, manners, and aspirations. It was then, as has been seen, that there was the greatest occupation change, with a growth of clerical and managerial jobs. This change lay at the root of the historic shift to more equal incomes, a redistribution abetted by taxation falling least heavily on those with incomes between £250 and £1,000. It also assisted the acquisition of small estates, not least because by the mid-1930s 60% of non-manual workers had either bought or were buying their own homes.

Both world wars, however, plunged the middle class into crisis. Income was redistributed in favour of the working class, and both its political and social values were challenged by organized labour. Both wars generated, therefore, an antagonism towards manual workers which helps to explain the determination of middle-class strike breakers during the 1926 General Strike and the defeat of the Attlee government only six years after its landslide victory in 1945. The First World War particularly hit archetypal small Edwardian savers who derived their income from either rented housing or 'safe' investments in utilities at home and abroad. The returns on neither recovered fully. Moreover, until 1923 inflation reduced not just the relative but the absolute value of many salaries. This caused, albeit on a lesser scale, a resentment similar to that which generated support on the Continent for fascism. The Second World War represented the triumph of collectivism over middle-class individualism. It also led to a relative decrease in middle-class income. Genteel shabbiness fuelled anti-American feeling, especially as it was widely felt that transatlantic affluence rested on the unfair exploitation of wartime conditions. More importantly, it also fuelled anti-labour feeling as several areas of expenditure, critical to middle-class status, were hard hit. Aggregate expenditure on domestic service, for example, fell between 1938 and 1950 from

£265m to £85m (at 1948 prices) and on private motoring from £250m to £160m.

Wartime resentment of labour, however, was perhaps only an intensification of a feeling which many have argued was *the* defining characteristic of the middle class. It was accentuated by the changing nature of work between the wars when, as McKibbin has argued, a 'genuine fissure of social experience' opened between the two classes. With the regular receipt of income above the subsistence level and less threatened by unemployment, salary earners could plan ahead and save. In other words, they could literally afford greater independence and dignity. The same was also true of their experience at work. They were generally employed in small units, where relations with senior management were friendly and promotion was possible. In contrast, manual work was being increasingly deskilled and concentrated in larger units which fostered alienation from both the work itself and employers. Below the superficial calm of interwar Britain, therefore, there lay a deep mutual hostility; and this helps to explain, at least from the middle-class point of view, the solidarity of electoral support for the Conservative Party.

The working class was not only the largest grouping in Britain but also, because of the relatively small rural economy, the largest such class in the world. As has been seen, however, it was being steadily eroded by the drift into non-manual work. It was also divided by gender and by differences in the size and regularity of pay which, on incomes close to the subsistence level, could be critical to individual lifestyles and wellbeing. Irregularity of pay was caused initially by underemployment, which was endemic in many Edwardian occupations, but after 1918 principally by mass unemployment, which affected workers in the depressed regions more seriously than those in the prosperous Midlands or southern England.

Nevertheless a greater class homogeneity developed for economic and political reasons. Economically, mechanization and the decline of the staple industries reduced the relative earnings of skilled workers whilst, as has been seen, those of the unskilled rose. State transfers also effectively gave the poorest a safety net which reduced the depth of poverty. Until the 1940s there was undeniable distress, as the next section will show, but nevertheless there was a general levelling up of manual earnings which has enabled Rubinstein to claim that by the 1930s 'normal working class income' had risen above subsistence 'for possibly the first time in British history'. This made the government's commitment to a national minimum income in 1948 all the more practicable. Politically, the working class also became more united in its latent hostility towards the middle class, be it represented by employers or by 'parasitical' clerical workers. In Edwardian Britain (with falling real wages) and again between 1917 and 1921 (in the aftermath of the Russian Revolution and with the onset of mass unemployment) this hostility turned to militancy. In the Second World War a renewed economic strength brought more tangible gains in relation to income, status, and power. This has led historians to divine yet another social milestone. As McKibbin, for instance, has concluded, 'the working class in the 1940s in its prosperity and political influence had no historical precedent'.

Poverty

Poverty was more extensively studied than either wealth or income before 1950. Surveys were pioneered by the philanthropists Charles Booth and Seebohm Rowntree, who respectively investigated London in the 1890s and York in 1899, 1936, and 1950; and their lead was followed by academics, whose surveys included the five 'representative' towns of Reading, Northampton, Warrington, Stanley, and Bolton (1912–14 and 1924), and London (1928–30), Liverpool (1929), Merseyside (1929–31), Southampton (1931), Sheffield (1933), and Bristol (1938). The results of those which best permit comparison over time are presented in Table 7.2.

Professional though these studies were by contemporary standards, both their definition of poverty and their technical accuracy have been criticized retrospectively. In 1899 Rowntree famously identified two levels of poverty: primary poverty, 'when total earnings are insufficient to obtain the minimum necessities for the maintenance of merely physical efficiency', and secondary poverty, where earnings would have been sufficient 'were it not for the fact that some portion of it was absorbed by other expenditure, either useful or wasteful'. The former was a measure of 'absolute poverty' because it was based on the minimum cost of a finite list of 'necessities' with regards to food, clothing, fuel and light, household sundries (such as cleaning

Table 7.2 The extent of poverty, 1889–1950

Date	Survey	Area	Poverty		% working class population	% working class household	Real value of poverty line	Poverty line as % of average income
			% Population					
1889–1902	Booth	London	30.7		–	–	–	–
1899	Rowntree	York	27.8	*Primary* 9.9 *Secondary* 17.9	15.5	12.7	100	61
1911	Bowley and Burnett-Hurst	5 Towns	–		12.6	11.0		
1924	Bowley and Hogg	5 Towns	–		6.5	6.5	106	61
1934	Llewellyn Smith	London	12		–	6.0 *(1899 Standard)* 9.8 21.0 (HNOL)		
1936	Rowntree	York	17.7		6.8 *(1899 Standard)* 31.0 (HNOL)		148	67
1950	Rowntree	York	1.7		2.8 *(8.6)*	4.6 *(11.8)*	176	67

Note: Italicized figures are alternative measures advanced at the time or in later recalculations.

materials), and personal sundries (such as burial insurance). It has alternatively been termed a 'minimum subsistence level'. Secondary poverty, being based on the visual observation of a household's lifestyle, was much more impressionistic.

Both have been unfavourably contrasted to the postwar concept of 'relative' poverty whereby, on the current European Union definition, the poor are those 'persons whose resources (material, cultural, and social) are so limited as to exclude them from the minimum acceptable way of life in the member state in which they live'. This places the emphasis not on physical need or living conditions but on social exclusion. Consequently it has been alternatively termed a 'minimum participatory income level'. This level is dynamic, rising in line with average living standards, and is conventionally expressed as a percentage of mean disposable income. Within the present-day European Union, for example, anyone with an income below half the national mean is deemed to be in poverty.

Rowntree's concept of a minimum subsistence income dominated other interwar surveys, but it evolved further towards the notion of a minimum participatory income than many postwar critics have admitted. Rowntree initially chose a restricted definition to prevent the public response to his findings being diverted by accusations that his poverty line was too high. If anything it was too low, because it concentrated on physical, not social, need and the poor—as he himself admitted in *The Human Needs of Labour* (1936)—could not just 'live on a "fodder basis". They crave for relaxation and recreation just as the rest of us do.' Consequently he built into his later poverty budgets the cost of additional personal sundries, such as savings for holidays. This explains the rise, detailed in Table 7.2, of his poverty line both in absolute terms (so that its real value in 1950 was 76% higher than in 1899) and in relative terms. By present-day standards, Rowntree's calculations still understate the extent of poverty. His range of sundries remained, on his own admission, limited, and was designed to reflect working-class rather than average lifestyles. Moreover, his calculations remained tied to a list of needs rather than to a percentage of mean national income—although it should be noted that this is the method still preferred in the USA.

What of the technical accuracy of the interwar surveys? The methods employed ranged from the collection of impressions from local officials (as in the Booth survey), through house-to-house surveys in working-class areas of individual towns (as organized by Rowntree) to a 10% sample of working-class homes in a representative range of towns (as pioneered by Bowley). As this progression suggests, many of the technical weaknesses of the earlier surveys were recognized and remedied by later ones. Reliance on visual impressions, for instance, which lay at the heart of his 1899 estimate of secondary poverty (which trebled the overall figure for poverty), was dismissed by Rowntree himself in 1936 as 'too rough to give reliable results'. Doubts over the typicality of evidence from a single town such as York were also countered by Bowley's representative sample. Serious doubts still remain, however, over such issues as the criteria for the selection of working-class areas of towns, the accuracy with which individual household schedules were completed, and the way in which the final calculations were made. Some of the existing original schedules have, therefore, recently been reworked, and this has led to some major revisions. In 1950, for example, it is now suggested that the proportion of working-class households in poverty was almost 11.8% rather than 4.6%. However, house-to-house surveys as carried out in York did have some advantages over current national surveys. In particular, they were able to record the value of non-cash income, such as home-grown vegetables and meals provided by family or neighbours, and in that respect provide a more realistic estimate of actual living standards.

The statistics presented in Table 7.2, therefore, must be treated with care. Nothing, however, can disguise the extent of poverty in Edwardian England. Almost one-third of the *whole* population in arguably the richest country in the world was living in primary or secondary poverty. In absolute terms, the impact of the First World War was remarkable. All interwar surveys agree that—as in the five representative towns—the number of working-class households in primary poverty was reduced to about 6%. By the improved standard endorsed by *The Human Needs of Labour*, however, poverty remained widespread—varying in the 1930s as a percentage of working-class households from 21% in London through 31% in York to 43% in Southampton. It required another major wartime redistribution of income to make a significant improvement.

Such aggregate statistics disguise variations in poverty between regions and over an individual's lifetime. In 1924, for example, primary poverty in the five representative towns varied from 4% of working-class households in Northampton to 11.3% in Reading. Interestingly, as with the figures for the 1930s, a town in southern England had the worst record. Moreover, a poverty cycle was identified in which individuals became particularly vulnerable to poverty at three times in their lives: in childhood, as a parent of non-working children, and in old age. This meant that the experience—and fear— of poverty affected far many more people than the bald statistics suggest. On a more positive note, however, the depth of poverty within individual households diminished after 1918. Many more incomes clustered around the poverty line, which helps to explain why small retrospective recalculations can produce startling results. The barefoot urchin, who characterized the desperation of Edwardian poverty, was largely consigned to the past—although the arrival in the countryside of an unquantified number of ill-clothed, lice-infested, and bed-wetting evacuees in 1940 is evidence of continuing urban deprivation.

Children were the major cause—and therefore victims—of poverty. This is demonstrated by the summary of Rowntree's findings in Table 7.3, which identifies a 'large family' of four or more children as the cause of over a fifth of primary poverty in 1899, whilst the needs of smaller families were frequently not met by *regular* manual wages. These two factors still accounted for two-fifths of poverty, broadly defined, in 1936. Their relative importance, however, had declined for the poorest mainly because of a fall in average family size—which was a crucial factor in rising living standards of all households but particularly benefited the poorest, which tended also to be the largest. Between 1900 and 1930, for example, the proportion of families with five or more children was cut by two-thirds to 10%. For the poorest, unemployment had become by far the greatest cause of poverty by 1936; but for Rowntree's broader sample it tended only to exacerbate poverty arising from other sources. Increasingly important amongst those was old age, for which there was also a contributing demographic cause. The percentage of the population over 65 doubled during the period.

Social consequences

Poverty, therefore, remained widespread despite the rise of average working-class income above the subsistence level. Consequently there

Table 7.3 The causes of poverty, 1899–1950 (%)

	1899 primary poverty standard		1936 standard	
	1899	1956	1936	1950
Inadequate wages in regular work	52	9	42	1
Large family	22	8	28	–
Unemployment/irregular employment of chief wage-earner	5	50	–	6
Death of chief wage-earner	16	9	8	6
Death of chief wage-earner through illness	5	6	4	21
old Age		18	15	68
Miscellaneous	–	–	3	3

persisted both a poverty culture, which had so exercised Edwardian social investigators, and serious inequality of opportunity, which became the particular concern of later reformers. Working-class saving and spending habits were commonly condemned by middle-class investigators as irrational and immoral. Savings typically concentrated on mutual societies, with traditions of extravagant display, and commercial policies with high administrative costs and lapse rates. Spending simultaneously favoured the purchase of goods by instalments, gambling, and drink. However, given the fact that working-class earnings were typically small and irregular, each of these habits can be portrayed as rational and moral. Saving with a bank, for instance, would have been irrational, since money could only be withdrawn on notice. A sudden loss of income, therefore, could not be made good. A public display of savings, on the other hand, ensured status and thus creditworthiness in the corner shop during such crises. Persistent attempts to save—however unsuccessful— also demonstrated a determination to reject a dependency culture. Similarly, the purchase of goods 'on tick' enabled a temporary surplus of income to be enjoyed, status to be enhanced, and ready cash to be obtained from a pawnbroker when earnings again failed. Pastimes such as gambling and pub drinking can also, in moderation, be defended as rational rather than self-indulgent because they provided, amongst other things, mental stimulation and a wider network from which to learn of job vacancies. A poverty culture persisted, therefore, because of the smallness and irregularity of income; and it was only as the nature of manual earnings changed that it was gradually, and with distinct regional variations, eroded.

Major inequalities of opportunity, however, remained. They are also extremely difficult to quantify because, in the course of routine administration, such imprecise definitions and measurements were taken of key indicators that they were acknowledged even at the time to be largely valueless. This was particularly true of nutrition, which became highly politicized in the 1930s when governments sought to disguise the social impact of mass unemployment. Most famously, the 1936 Boyd Orr survey—following the League of Nations' lead— defined a minimum level of diet which would not just 'keep people alive, but . . . keep people in health'. By this standard it estimated that over one-tenth of the population (and one-fifth of all children) were chronically undernourished and one-half of the population had some deficiency. Its findings were dismissed, however, because of the perceived generosity of the standard and the meanness of the sample. Similarly, in housing, the term 'slum' was a politically elastic one which each local council tended to define in relation to the amount of housing it felt able to replace.

Some reliable evidence, however, is available from contemporary reports and key statistical series. At the start of the period, for example, the 1903–4 Committee on Physical Deterioration authoritatively dismissed fears of permanent inter-generational degeneracy as a result of increased urbanization. It did confirm, however, that some 40% of recruits for the Boer War were unfit for service and, more significantly, that in London alone 60,000 children were insufficiently nourished to benefit from schooling. At the end of the period, regular surveys also started to classify housing by four 'essential' amenities: piped water, a cooking stove, a flushing lavatory, and a fixed bath; and the fact that in 1951 over half of households—and thus over half of the working class—lacked one of these essentials testifies to the low quality of earlier provision.

Of the key statistical series, infant mortality is conventionally regarded as a sensitive indicator of parental wellbeing and environmental conditions. Its figures reveal a dramatic improvement, with deaths per 1,000 live births in England and Wales dropping from 138 at the start to 36 at the end of the period. One consequence was that life expectancy for children born in the early 1950s was twenty years greater than those born in Edwardian England (66 for boys and 72 for girls). Within such overall improvements, however, class inequalities remained and even intensified. In the late 1940s, for instance, the mortality rate for Class 5 (manual workers) remained more than double that for Class 1. Children's heights and weights have recently been adjudged an even more objective measure of wellbeing. Here the available figures do not suggest a dramatic improvement until after 1945. They do, however, re-emphasize class inequality—with children at Eton having reached their present level of height by 1900 whilst working-class children remained much smaller even in 1950. Whatever the exact pace of change, therefore, the majority of working-class children were born into poverty; and, although their chances of survival undoubtedly improved, a combination of poor housing and nutrition impaired their health and led subsequently to educational deprivation. In such circumstances there could be no equality of opportunity.

Regional, gender, and racial inequality

Inequality and individual wellbeing are affected not just by class but also, as postwar studies have increasingly emphasized, by location, gender, and race. Analysis is hampered, even more than is the case with wealth and poverty, by a paucity of contemporary evidence; but this does not mean that the issues were any less keenly felt. The regional programming of the BBC, as well as the establishment of Plaid Cymru in 1925 and of the Scottish National Party in 1934, testify to the strength of regional and incipient national feeling. Women's interests were also articulated by a wide range of organizations from the Edwardian suffragettes onwards.

Regional inequality

Perceptions of regional differences are still dominated by the interwar contrast between the prosperous Midlands and south-east of England and the depressed 'outer' regions of the north-west and north-east of England, Wales, and Scotland. The more sensitive accounts also include Northern Ireland and rural England within the latter category. This contrast, and the structural economic change which underlay it, was epitomized by the 'adoption' for charitable purposes of 'outer' communities by either areas or occupational groups in the south. Thus Worthing and Surrey respectively adopted Brynmawr and Jarrow, whilst the staff of the Ministry of Health and of the BBC adopted Crook and Gateshead.

Individual welfare was undoubtedly influenced by regional variations in the economic structure and inherited social infrastructure; and where areas of traditionally low wages and poor social provision were hit by the interwar depression, they were doubly disadvantaged. The Depression, as is well known, hit the economies of 'outer' regions particularly hard. Wales duly experienced the largest migration of any comparable region in Europe, with a net interwar loss, from a total population of some 2.5 million, of 430,000 people. Scotland suffered a loss equivalent to 70% of the natural increase in its population, while Tyneside lost 8% of its population in the 1920s alone. Those left behind in areas deprived of their most economically active members experienced some of the worst social conditions. In 1935, for example, the infant mortality rate in Wigan was treble that in Oxford; and Richard Titmuss calculated for the 1930s that, had living standards in the depressed and prosperous regions been similar, half a million 'premature' deaths could have been avoided. It was in such urbanized areas that poverty, and a poverty culture, lingered longest.

Rural Britain was also an area of traditionally low wages and poor social provision—and one which, except for a brief period around the First World War, had experienced depression since the 1870s. It was here, therefore, that some of the greatest deprivation existed. *Average* manual wages in the mid-1930s, at 35 shillings (£1.75), were 6 shillings (30p) below the *Human Needs of Labour* minimum, even though Rowntree had 'reluctantly' pared the sum for rural workers to the bone by excluding, for example, any allowance for holidays. In relation to infrastructure, the supply of electricity (which so improved the quality of urban housing) was generally unavailable in the countryside. Largely absent too were the specialist secondary schools, which meant that the majority of children received their whole education in the same 'all age' school. The result was that IQ tests showed rural children to be on average one year behind their urban counterparts—a fact which led to a subsequent outcry when the latter were evacuated during the Second World War. Some relief was brought by the introduction of rural bus services and the building (by voluntary provision) of libraries and village halls in which, amongst others, the escalating number of Women's Institutes could meet. Nevertheless there was rapid rural depopulation. An estimated 17% of the workforce migrated in the 1930s and the figure was greater near prosperous towns or in the remotest areas such as the Hebrides, which lost almost a third of its population between 1901 and 1951.

Perceptions based on the interwar period, however, can be misleading. They overlook the fact that the 'outer' regions enjoyed an exceptional, if somewhat precarious, prosperity before and during the First World War. South Wales, for example, was one of the most buoyant growth centres in the world, drawing immigrants from the depressed south-west of England; and Clydeside was one of the highest wage regions in Britain. Moreover, their fortunes revived with rearmament in the later 1930s and were sustained after the war, in part by the government's active regional policy. Rural Britain may not have shared the earlier prosperity but, as a result of extensive subsidies, it too enjoyed a boom in the 1940s, with land values trebling from their low in 1929 and real wages for agricultural workers increasing by 43%.

Such perceptions also overlook the fact that regional differences were far smaller than in many continental European countries, such as Italy, and that the redistribution of resources through welfare policy helped to minimize them. This was particularly true of Northern Ireland, where two agreements were reached in 1936 and 1941. The first established that, despite a considerably lower standard of living, social benefits should be of equal value to those in the rest of Britain, and the second that resources should be set aside to bring other services up to mainland standards. Historic inequalities elsewhere also started to be addressed. Housing, for example, was notoriously poor in Scotland and in the north-east of England. By 1911, average occupancy in England had fallen below one person per room (a contemporary definition of 'slum' overcrowding) but such a level— for reasons of habit, cost, and geography—had not been attained in Scotland by 1950. In the north-east, where overcrowding was three times above the English average in the 1920s, sanitation was also notorious, with over half the houses in Middlesbrough lacking access to flushing lavatories before 1914 and to indoor lavatories after 1945. Electrification together with programmes of slum clearance and council house building, however, started to raise standards. In relation to health, an 'inverse care' law was widely believed to exist: where need was greatest, provision was least. This may have had some validity in relation to general practitioners and hospital staff, but the latest research shows it was decreasingly valid for hospital provision. Voluntary hospitals, supported by patient payment schemes, remained remarkably resilient, with the spread of cottage hospitals extending their geographical coverage. Where there were gaps, they were increasingly filled by local government in the 1930s and central government during the war.

Gender inequality

Health also lay at the heart of gender inequality. Women's life expectancy may typically have been higher than that for men, but their general health was poorer. A wide-ranging Women's Health Enquiry in the 1930s, for example, established that only one-third of married working-class women were in good health; and, in contrast to other countries, maternal mortality actually increased between the wars, peaking in 1934 at almost 5 per 1,000 births. There were two basic causes. Lack of income both resulted in women putting the nutritional needs of their family before their own and meant that medical care (to which only insured workers were entitled free of charge) frequently could not be afforded. The rise in unskilled wages, abetted after 1948 by fuller employment and the guarantee of a minimum subsistence income, alleviated the first problem. The right under the NHS to health care, free at the point of access, helped to resolve the second.

The creation of the Welfare State, however, by no means met the broader needs of women and in certain ways exacerbated them. This was because it endorsed, and thereby reinforced, the 'male breadwinner' model of welfare, with its underlying assumption that marriage was a partnership between two 'equal but different' people. The male role was to earn both a family wage and, through insurance contributions, the right to social security. The wife, having typically worked before marriage, was to stay at home to care for her husband and children. Inequality of income, however, frequently jeopardized genuine equality within marriage; and the position of a wife was made more vulnerable by her lack of independent access to automatic (as opposed to stigmatized means-tested) benefit. There was, moreover, no effective escape, as equal access to work was impaired by career breaks for childbirth and the 'double burden' imposed by housework and child care. In short, even in the 1940s, a combination of public legislation and private behaviour qualified any *formal* economic and social gains women achieved after 1900.

Formal economic gains accrued largely from occupational change and war. Increasing mechanization and bureaucracy disproportionately benefited women, decreasing the number of sweated trades which had so disfigured Edwardian England and increasing the number of female clerks sixfold to 1.5 million by 1951 (one-fifth of the female workforce). Upward occupational mobility was thus more readily available to women. The two wars also exploded many myths about respective gender capabilities; and the second greatly reduced one of the most exploitative areas of employment, domestic service (which had accounted for one-third of female employment and in which, incidentally, the exploitation was typically of women by women). The beneficial effect of both wars, however, should not be exaggerated. Neither witnessed a breakthrough of women into management or even skilled work; and the First World War resulted in a backlash which was intensified by the interwar Depression. The marriage bar was extended; pay rates remained typically half those of men; jobs continued to be concentrated in occupations dominated by women; and the participation of married women in formal work remained at only about 10%. Women, however, were not simply passive victims. Many, for example, defined liberation as freedom *from* work and naturally resented the loss of their husbands' jobs, and thus their family wage, to other women. Within the professions, the predominantly female membership of the National Union of Teachers also acquiesced, through elected male officials, in differential rates of pay.

Formal social advances included the granting in the 1920s of equal rights with regard to property, divorce, and guardianship in addition to equal enfranchisement. The full exercise of legal rights was constrained, however, by lack of income (which was only remedied by legal aid after 1950); and equal enfranchisement did not lead to equal participation in, let alone the intended 'purification' of, national politics. Inequality similarly lay behind the formal equality of the social services. At all levels within the education system, for example, there were differing gender expectations about the desirable nature and level of qualifications. Equal pension rights, which married women acquired under the 1908 tax-financed scheme, were also quickly qualified when pensions were placed on an insurance basis in 1925 and thus made subject to their husbands' contribution records.

Women's principal welfare interests were defined throughout the period as control over their own bodies and an independent income for mothers; and here the record was equally chequered. Private clinics provided contraceptive advice after 1918 and public ones were permitted to do so after 1930. However, advice to unmarried women, free appliances, and the right to abortion had to await the 1960s. With regard to income, mothers received maternity benefit after 1913, separation allowances during the wars, and family allowances after 1946. The latter, however, was essentially a token payment and fell far short of the initial objective of providing mothers with financial autonomy.

Envious eyes were sometimes cast abroad to interwar France or even fascist countries. There, payments were larger: but they were typically paid to the husband and overtly designed not to reduce but reinforce women's dependency. That at least was never true of British policy.

Both the market and legislation, therefore, offered formal opportunities for greater equality; but its actual realization depended upon the attitudes of both men and women, as expressed by their public and private behaviour. In public, male attitudes within trade unions and the professions alike remained deeply antithetical to economic equality. In private, the number of 'companionate' marriages was believed to have grown, with a relaxation of Victorian discipline and a greater willingness to discuss and respect differing interests. This was particularly true of the middle class, although McKibbin has noted a 'segregated sociability', symbolized by the competing attractions of the Masons and the Women's Institute—and much resented by women. Within working-class households, oral testimony suggests that in the depressed regions deference to men on public issues and silence on personal issues, such as sex, prevailed. In more prosperous areas, this may have changed—but not necessarily to women's advantage. Isolated on new housing estates many developed a 'suburban neurosis'; and, as Elizabeth Roberts has noted, their confidence and status could be undermined by the loss both of traditional support networks and of the need for their specialist skills to balance poverty budgets. Whatever the true extent of companionate marriages, therefore, acceptance of distinctive gender roles remained widespread, and this seriously hampered the translation of formal equality into what a later generation would term 'real' equality.

Racial inequality

Contemporary evidence of racial inequality is particularly sparse. In contrast to the USA or the British Dominions, there was little formal discrimination towards the Irish, Jewish, and black populations. The 1948 British Nationality Act, for instance, reaffirmed the equal rights of all born within the Empire; and even after Eire had gained independence and then left the Commonwealth in 1949 these rights continued to be enjoyed by its citizens. The racial segregation of black troops by the US army in Britain during the Second World War was also disavowed by government. Racial bias, underpinned by eugenicist theories of racial superiority, nevertheless permeated opinion at both a political and public level. The Aliens Act of 1905, implicitly designed to deter Jewish immigration, was the first such restrictive legislation in Britain; and the interwar implementation of successive Alien Acts and Orders deliberately disadvantaged black seamen. Anti-semitism was pervasive, as was anti-Irish feeling, with J. B. Priestley casually reflecting what 'a fine exit of ignorance and dirt and drunkenness and disease' repatriation to Eire would represent. Popular resentment over competition for jobs and housing as well as mixed marriages also flared up into open rioting in ports such as Liverpool and Cardiff in 1919 and 1935. Behind a veil of tolerance, it was such deep-seated antagonism with which—as the vanguard of black immigrants settling in postwar Britain—embarkees from the *Empire Windrush* were immediately confronted in 1948.

The welfare role of government

Individual welfare, as has been seen, was increasingly influenced by the expanding role of government, be it through the redistribution of resources between classes or between regions. This expansion culminated in the establishment of the Welfare State after the Second World War, with its attack on Beveridge's five giants of 'want, disease, ignorance, squalor and idleness'. Want and disease were countered in 1948 by the inauguration of national insurance, national assistance, and the National Health Service; ignorance and idleness by the Butler Education Act and the all-party commitment to maintain employment in 1944; and squalor by a major housebuilding programme after 1945. The comprehensive coverage of both people and need by these reforms, which seemingly delivered the twin postwar ideals of 'social solidarity' and 'social security', established Britain's reputation as a pioneering welfare state. The individual parts, however, had been steadily evolving since 1900 and were common to other European countries.

Government growth is conventionally measured by the proportion of GDP or of the workforce consumed, or by the 'tax take' (tax revenue expressed as a percentage of GDP). By these measures, as

Table 7.4 The growth of government, 1900–1951

	Government expenditure as % of GDP	Tax revenue as % of GDP	Social services expenditure		Public employment as % of workforce
			% of GDP	% of government expenditure	
1900	13.3	8.6	2.3	18	5
1951	37.5	33.5	14.1	46.1	25

Note: Government = central and local government.

illustrated by Table 7.4, the size of British government more than trebled in Britain between 1900 and 1950, with welfare expenditure as the principal engine of growth. In 1900 the cost of the social services was a quarter of that for the other three main categories of government expenditure: defence, law and order, and debt repayment. By 1939 it was equivalent to, and by 1951 it exceeded, their combined cost. Inevitably, such figures can be misleading. Most significantly, they can underestimate the growth of government because much of its power is exercised through regulation (such as rent control) which involves little expenditure or manpower. On the other hand, they can exaggerate its growth because the most dynamic form of expenditure throughout the period was transfer payments (such as pensions). This is money which government merely transfers, through compulsory national insurance, over people's lifetimes from when they are at work to when they are in need. Government, therefore, determines the timing of expenditure but not how it is spent— as it does with its own current expenditure (on, for example, teachers' pay) or capital expenditure (such as school buildings). Because their nature and economic impact is so different, transfer payments are often excluded from estimates of government expenditure. If they are, then the growth of government expenditure after 1900 was more modest, doubling from 11% to only 24% of GDP by 1950.

Such qualifications are important because, in the continuing controversy over the adverse effect of state welfare on economic growth and individual initiative, statistics have been used uncritically. Opponents of state welfare have also typically overlooked the fact that Britain's record was far from unique. In the 1930s, it is true, the number of people covered by unemployment insurance was exceptional; and the coverage of both pensions and health insurance was unmatched outside Scandinavia. This helps to substantiate the claim in the Beveridge Report that provision against want was 'on a scale unsurpassed and hardly rivalled in any other country in the world'. Germany, however, was the pioneer of social insurance under Bismarck, of social rights under the Weimar Republic, and of occupational welfare (such as holidays with pay) under the Nazis. Sweden had also effectively introduced a universal pension and Keynesian demand management in the 1930s. In many areas, such as working conditions and practices, Britain was in fact a laggard; and although aggregate welfare expenditure in 1950 was marginally higher than elsewhere this was only a temporary phenomenon.

What *was* exceptional about Britain's welfare system was its centralization. There are two possible explanations for this unexpected development: a failure of traditional support networks and the capacity of government to intervene. In the nineteenth century, the deliberate purpose of public policy had been to minimize government and to foster self-help and voluntarism through either mutual associations (such as friendly societies) or philanthropy. Many of the functions conventionally performed by government abroad were consequently discharged, in the words of Jose Harris, by 'coteries of citizens governing themselves'. After 1900, friendly societies declined because local loyalty and resources proved unable to satisfy the needs of an increasingly mobile, ageing, and affluent population. The 1911 National Insurance Act, by enabling them to become 'approved societies' for the payment of state benefits, was designed to subsidize their core functions and thereby revitalize them; but they were outmanoeuvred by commercial insurance companies, like the Prudential, whose greater professionalism and marketing skills enabled them to recruit the majority of new contributors.

Philanthropy, on the other hand, did respond to changing circumstances. It maintained its presence in traditional areas such as education (where church schools still catered for one-third of children in 1939) and health (where two-thirds of hospitals remained voluntary). It also advanced, as has been seen, into new areas such as regional adoption schemes or the building of libraries and village halls, financed by the Carnegie Trust. The key to success was a new accommodation with government, brokered after 1919 by the newly founded National Council of Social Service. Before the First World War, as demonstrated by the Royal Commission on the Poor Law, philanthropists had sought to dictate official policy. Afterwards they aimed more to supplement and complement it. Government, they recognized, alone had the resources to meet basic needs such as a national minimum income. To cede such a responsibility, however, was not to subvert their own principles so long as policy reinforced 'active citizenship' by enriching both the giver and recipient of benefits and, above all, by ensuring the independence of the latter. The 'new philanthropy', in other words, sought to forge an optimum accommodation between the resources of government and the virtues of voluntarism.

Between the wars, therefore, both the market and philanthropy appeared sufficiently resilient to provide—as in other countries—an alternative to state welfare. Their underlying dynamism, however, was in fact impaired by the nature of the tax system, inherited from Gladstone and ironically designed to promote self-help. To prevent unfair class advantage and corruption, there were few of the tax breaks which encouraged philanthropy in the USA. The strict regulation of public subsidies also frustrated approved societies (so that their abolition was not too bitterly contested in 1948) and thwarted the development, as in continental Europe, of non-profit-making bodies such as housing trusts (so that, exceptionally, government owned some 12% of housing stock by 1939). Moreover, its perceived probity permitted government to raise taxes far more easily than in countries such as France, even after the overtly redistributive Lloyd George budget of 1909. Central government in Britain, therefore, had a greater fiscal capacity to act than elsewhere. It also enjoyed a greater constitutional freedom to do so. Unlike Bismarck's Reich, it was not constrained by powerful regional states: Scotland enjoyed only administrative autonomy and Northern Ireland was too poor to exploit its tax-raising powers. Local government, traditionally perceived as an embodiment of local self-sufficiency, also lacked a buoyant source of independent income and was constrained by the convention of *ultra vires*—which restricted its actions solely to those expressly sanctioned by Parliament.

Although, therefore, civil servants even in the 1940s typically did not wish to assume more economic and social responsibilities, fiscal and constitutional reality conspired to concentrate power upon them. This 'reality' could, of course, have been changed; but there were powerful countervailing political interests. Interwar Conservative governments did not wish to devolve power to, and thereby strengthen, mutual associations other than friendly societies (especially trade unions) or local government (just as leading cities were coming under Labour Party control). Hence the reform of local government structure and finance in 1929 and the nationalization of poor relief for the able-bodied in 1934 under the Unemployment Assistance Board. Equally, Labour politicians, who had been converted to central planning in the 1930s, remained resentful in the 1940s about the administration of public money by democratically unaccountable insurance companies or by philanthropic organizations, with their history of class condescension.

The exceptional centralization of welfare policy has made it a particular object of attack, especially because it is perceived, contrary to interwar philanthropists' hopes, to have fostered alienation and a dependency culture as well to have 'crowded out' more profitable industrial investment. Most vividly, Correlli Barnett has attacked it for having created a 'segregated, subliterate, unskilled, unhealthy and institutionalized proletariat hanging on the nipple of state maternalism'. Such attacks, at least for the 1940s, are unbalanced. As has been argued, they typically exaggerate the extent and uniqueness of British welfare expenditure. There is, for example, little evidence that it diverted investment or manpower from industry in the 1940s; benefits were low, being deliberately set at subsistence level to maintain the work ethic; and other countries, such as Germany, were soon to spend far more on welfare without impairing their economic revival. The attacks also ignore the ultimate failure of the market, the voluntary sector, and local government to resolve the overall problem of mass unemployment and deprivation; and the irresistible momentum for centralization this created, even in Scotland where popular and political opinion particularly favoured local democracy and personal responsibility. Finally, they ignore the fact—articulated in the Beveridge Report—that, properly targeted, welfare policy is a precondition for and not an obstacle to economic growth. High productivity, after all, requires an educated, healthy, mobile workforce and thus effective education, health and housing policies. In the 1940s, no agency other than central government had a greater potential to ensure that policy was properly targeted and effective.

Conclusion

Was the first half of the twentieth century then, despite its somewhat tarnished reputation, a period of exceptional social change and achievement? In essence it was. Britain was transformed from a society in which there was opulence for the few to one on the verge of achieving affluence for the many. Fundamental to this transformation was the historic shift towards greater equality of personal income and the rise of average manual wages above subsistence level, occasioned by both occupational change and war. These autonomous changes were reinforced by an increased redistribution of resources between classes and regions by government, which had by the 1940s assumed a dominant role over more traditional agencies of welfare. As a result manual workers and their families enjoyed not only a higher standard of living than would have been thought possible in 1900 but also more social rights and political influence. Great inequalities remained, particularly in relation to the distribution of personal wealth, the social divide between (if not within) classes, gender, and race. There were also serious doubts about whether the continuing cultural and institutional legacy from the nineteenth century (both inside and outside government) would permit these inequalities to be tackled as constructively as they were to be elsewhere. At least, however, the battle after 1950 was largely over the more equitable distribution of increased wealth and not the more desperate one to win public recognition for the existence of, let alone the need to redress, severe deprivation amidst opulence. That was the measure of progress between 1900 and 1950.

Plate 10 Welsh miners lift up their hearts (Festival of Britain Pavilion of Minerals of the Island, 1951).

Conclusion: decline and progress

Keith Robbins

In July 1950 Sir Oliver Franks, British Ambassador in Washington, wrote to the Prime Minister, Clement Attlee, with some encouraging news. Three or even two years ago, he wrote, Britain was 'one of the queue of European countries'. Now, however, Britain was effectively out of the queue, one of two world powers outside Russia. How had this come about? He claimed that Britain gained new strength and vitality in its association with the Commonwealth, its domestic economy was much stronger, and there was great improvement in the overseas payments position. In 1954 he gave the BBC Reith Lectures with the title 'Britain and the Tide of World Affairs' and fell naturally to talking about Great Powers. A nation that was a Great Power could decisively affect the fate of other Great Powers in the world. In this sense Franks assumed that Britain's future would be of one piece with her past and that she would continue as a Great Power. What was noteworthy, he continued, was the way in which this was taken for granted rather than arrived at by conscious decision. It was part of the habit and furniture of British minds. A 14-year-old schoolboy, this author, listening to the thoughts of this distinguished former pupil at the same school, even then wondered whether Britain's Great Power status was at this juncture any more than the confidence trick which, to an extent, Franks admitted it was.

In articulating such assumptions, Franks still spoke for the generation which held high office at the time. His biographer notes how the historian of British atomic energy policy finds the decision in January 1947 to make an atomic bomb to be something which emerged from a body of general assumptions. There was simply a feeling that Britain, as a Great Power, had to acquire all major new weapons, and that atomic weapons were a manifestation of the scientific and technological superiority on which Britain's strength would henceforth have to depend. It would also depend, according to Franks, on whether Britain still possessed what he described as 'the Will to Greatness'. Britain could continue to be a leader among the nations if she made it her 'daily business' by action 'in the workaday world'. There were, of course, tides in world affairs which were beyond the capacity of any nation to control, but there were also real choices, moral choices, which still needed to be made. The choices made at this particular juncture would 'declare what sort of people we are'.

The language Franks used was replicated in many other quarters. Sir Stafford Cripps, Chancellor of the Exchequer, told the General Assembly of the Church of Scotland in May 1948 that democracy needed 'our Christian faith' to provide its spiritual power to control the evil things of the world. Without that religious and moral inspiration British democracy would fail, because it would be too feeble to stand up to the ruthless efficiency of material dictatorships. There was a sense that the British Way and Purpose was indeed at a crossroads. Something needed to be done. The intensity of this conviction stemmed, as it had done at the end of the First World War, from the belief that what gave Britain its place in the world was not that intelligence beloved of intellectuals but 'character'. 'Britain is the Mother of Nations', overflowing audiences at King's College, London were told in the autumn of 1915 as they were asked to consider *The Empire and the Future* (1916). Every emigrant ship that left her shores carried with it the seed of new nations whose moral, social, and political standards would be raised or lowered according to the tested quality of that seed. A mere thirty years later, were these moral visions obsolete and merely dying rhetorical flourishes of an exhausted tradition? If so, what might replace them? Perhaps the 'will to greatness' no longer existed?

All of this elevated discourse might simply be taken to illustrate that neither government nor people were prepared to confront directly the fact that the war had bankrupted Britain. A nation which believed itself to have emerged victorious in a great struggle declined to recognize its incompetence in those industrial and technological spheres which would in fact determine its future prospects. An 'audit' of this kind was what Correlli Barnett attempted in 1986. In flinching from reality as they took the bunting down from their streets after VE Day, the British had already written what he called 'the broad scenario for Britain's postwar descent'. His relentless exposure of British shortcomings focused on the Second World War, though the criticisms of plant, management, neglect of research and development, poor marketing, restrictive practices, and poorly trained labour force might be claimed to have been the case for decades. It was, allegedly, the pursuit of 'New Jerusalem', with William Beveridge and William Temple to the fore, which produced a massive and destructive misdirection of effort. Here was another facet of *The Collapse of British Power* about which Barnett had written in 1972. In general, however, this simple thesis has not been found convincing.

At bottom, there was no straightforward choice which could have been made between the pursuit of 'New Jerusalem' and a focused concentration upon the creation of a technically and scientifically skilled bureaucracy and a skilled labour force to match. The search for a more acceptable social order had become an integral part of the war effort itself. Even so, there was an increasing recognition that there was an unresolved issue which went to the very heart of British life: what should be the balance between knowledge and skill, between understanding and action? 'In the future,' G. M. Trevelyan had mused in an essay on 'Past and Future' in 1901, 'nothing will take care of itself, and no nation will ever again "muddle through", or succeed in "a fit of absence of mind" either in material things or in things of higher import.' It looked to some minds in 1951 as if, notwithstanding that conviction, that Britain had again 'muddled through' and was again failing to prepare, as only the state could prepare, for the challenges that existed. A plethora of government reports drew attention to these needs. 'The experience of war', declared the Percy Committee Report on Higher Technological Education, 'has shown that the greatest deficiency in British industry is the shortage of scientists and technologists who can also administer and organise, and can apply the results to development.' It was a conclusion which was to be repeated ad nauseam. 'Science', declared the Association of Scientific Workers in *Science and the Nation* (1947), offered 'the means to use unprecedented powers with which a finer, more beautiful and happier world than ever before can be built'. But how? The extent to which science had been given a privileged position in the school curriculum in the Soviet Union and endowed with the authority of a religion seemed to some to point the way forward. Eric Ashby, however, in *Scientist in Russia* (1947), regarded as nonsense the claim that by virtue of their planning and organization Soviet scientists were able to accomplish wonders impossible outside the Soviet Union. So the balance between freedom and planning, direction and initiative, in this as in so many other areas, remained open and had not been resolved. The recent war might have shifted the balance but it had not ended the argument of decades. During the First World War, Sir Alfred Zimmern contributed an essay on 'German Culture and the British Commonwealth' in a volume on *The War and Democracy* (1914) in which he confessed to an admiration for the discipline, efficiency, duty, obedience, and public service to be found in Germany and inculcated through the educational system but found this combination to be fundamentally flawed. It confused external discipline with self-control, it confused regimentation with corporate spirit, and conceived the nation's duty in terms of 'culture' rather than of character. In different words, but with the same underlying sentiment, it was a conviction which still held sway and continued to make Britain the country it was and should remain.

Taken together, such considerations make it difficult to apply one single word to the British experience of the first fifty years of the twentieth century. Various chapters in this volume record significant social progress in terms of health and welfare. Trevelyan in 1901 saw a need to face a world which he thought was growing ever blacker, uglier, noisier, and more meaningless. There could be a new age which would bring greater and more variegated activity, more spheres of life open, more choice of ideal aims, more leisure for the study both of conduct and beauty and of their active realization, whether with or instead of the money-making business of life'. While it was not altogether clear to the historian himself, half a century later, that this new age had in fact arrived, it had done so for a significant proportion of the population. If that was indeed the case, granted that 'social progress' means different things to different people, it also seemed to be in a context, perhaps paradoxically, of national decline. Whether this was indeed the case is not a straightforward matter to determine. Elsewhere, this author has preferred the word 'eclipse', admittedly taking a longer time-span, as an indication that whatever indices are thought relevant to the assessment of this matter must be considered internationally. That eclipse was most conspicuous in relation to the United States, which had clearly come to succeed John Bull—although, as has been pointed out, the decline of Britain and the ascent of the United States, though linked in time and geographically, were not processes of simple cause and effect, though neither were they wholly independent. The possession of power, however, must be linked to purpose as must prestige be linked to performance—but in neither case is the relationship straightforward. Some may consider the decline of British power, the decline of British industry, and the decline of the British economy to hang together as all of a piece. Taken in the round, however, consideration of the first fifty years in the history of the British Isles in the twentieth century suggests that they are not self-evidently the same things, and that it would be a mistake to reach such a comprehensively gloomy conclusion.

Further reading

Introduction

Keith Robbins, *Bibliography of British History 1914–1989* (1996) is a major guide, and *The Eclipse of a Great Power: Modern Britain 1870–1992* (1994) is a general overview. Other general histories which include coverage of the first half of the twentieth century are C. L. Mowat, *Britain between the Wars, 1918–1940* (1955), Peter Clarke, *Hope and Glory: Britain 1900–1990* (1996), Arthur Marwick, *A History of the Modern British Isles 1914–1999* (2000), and John Davis, *A History of Britain 1885–1939* (1999). Political and constitutional issues receive particular attention in Bernard Porter, *Britannia's Burden: The Political Evolution of Modern Britain 1851–1990* (1994) and Brian Harrison, *The Transformation of British Politics 1860–1995* (1996).

Geoffrey Best's *Winston Churchill: A Study in Greatness* (2001) is also a meditation on the greatness of Britain.

Chapter 1

The best general source for the British Empire and Britain's imperial relationships is Judith M. Brown and Wm. Roger Louis (eds.), *The Oxford History of the British Empire*, vol iv: *The Twentieth Century* (1999). Other useful broad surveys of empire/commonwealth history include T. O. Lloyd, *The British Empire 1558–1995* (2nd edn., 1996), Bernard Porter, *The Lion's Share: A Short History of British Imperialism, 1850–1995* (3rd edn., 1996), D. George Boyce, *Decolonisation and the British Empire, 1775–1997* (1999), and Nicholas Mansergh, *The Commonwealth Experience* (2nd edn., 1982), which is especially sound on constitutional matters.

The global situation of the British imperial system during the first half of the twentieth century is brilliantly sketched in John Gallagher's indispensable and idiosyncratic 1974 Ford Lectures, published in *The Decline, Revival and Fall of the British Empire* (1982), while in the 1970 Ford Lectures, *The Continental Commitment* (1972), Michael Howard lucidly analysed 'the dilemma of British defence policy in the era of two World Wars'. Imperial wars and defence matters generally are covered in an enormous range of works, of very varying quality. The centenary of the Boer War has prompted two good collections: Donal Lowry (ed.), *The South African War Reappraised* (2000) and John Gooch (ed.), *The Boer War: Direction, Experience and Image* (2000). Chapters on the First World War (Robert Holland), imperial defence and security (Anthony Clayton), and the Second World War (Keith Jeffery) are included in the *Oxford History of the British Empire* volume noted above. Some of the difficulties of imperial defence after 1918 are discussed in Keith Jeffery, *The British Army and the Crisis of Empire, 1918–22* (1984), while W. David McIntyre, *The Rise and Fall of the Singapore Naval Base* (1979) details the troubled history of that project.

The wider economic and diplomatic circumstances of Britain and the Empire are explored by Paul Kennedy in two important books: *The Realities behind Diplomacy: Background Influences on British External Policy, 1865–1980* (1981) and *The Rise and Fall of the Great Powers: Economic Change and Military Conflict from 1500 to 2000* (1988). Economic aspects of the British Empire are extensively treated in P. J. Cain and A. G. Hopkins, *British Imperialism* (2 vols., 1993), while specific interwar matters are covered in Ian M. Drummond, *British Economic Policy and the Empire, 1919–39* (1972).

There is a growing literature on social and cultural aspects of the British imperial experience, much of it published in John M. MacKenzie's excellent Studies in Imperialism series for Manchester University Press. Two especially stimulating books are John M. MacKenzie, *Propaganda and Empire* (1986), which has a valuable chapter on imperial exhibitions, and John M. MacKenzie (ed.), *Imperialism and Popular Culture*, which includes studies of the BBC, youth organizations and the Empire Marketing Board, whose publicity is well illustrated in David Meredith, 'Imperial images: the Empire Marketing Board, 1926–32', *History Today* (Jan. 1987), pp. 30–36. Insights into the heraldic and ceremonial aspects of the Empire will be found in Peter Galloway, *The Order of the British Empire* (1996) and T. G. Fraser, 'Delhi Durbar', *Majestas* 2 (1994), pp. 75–91. Finally, the single most rewarding socio-cultural survey of the twentieth-century British Empire is James Morris, *Farewell the Trumpets: An Imperial Retreat* (1978).

Chapter 2

There is a vast literature on British and imperial politics. There is a much smaller literature on democratization and the management of democratic change, and almost nothing on the connections between the process of change in Britain, Ireland, and the Empire.

For an overview of changes in the British political system, see Martin Pugh's *State and Society: A Social and Political History of Britain* (1999). For electoral changes, there are some sharply revisionist essays in Jon Lawrence and Miles Taylor (eds.), *Party, State and Society: Electoral Behaviour in Britain since 1820* (1997).

For doubts about the onset of democracy in Britain before 1914, and for the Empire as a means of preserving aristocratic life, see David Cannadine's entertaining book, *The Decline and Fall of the British Aristocracy* (1990). The Conservatives' fear of the people in the period 1918–22 is detailed in Chris Wrigley, *Lloyd George and the Challenge of Labour* (1990) and K. O. Morgan,

Consensus and Disunity: The Lloyd George Coalition Government 1918–1922 (1979). See also David Close, 'The collapse of resistance to democracy: Conservatives, adult suffrage and Second Chamber reform, 1911–1928', *Historical Journal* 20 (4) (1977), pp. 893–918. For subsequent events, including the importance of imperial concerns in reinforcing desires to construct a national government, see Philip Williamson, *National Crisis and National Government* (1992).

The development of a political class determined to manage and control the democratic process is less adequately covered. For theories and ideas see W. L. Guttsman, *The British Political Elite* (1963) and Harold Perkin, *The Rise of Professional Society* (1989). However, neither work explains the development of the professional politician or examines their attitude to the electorate. For Labour attitudes see Steven Fielding, Peter Thompson, and Nick Tiratsoo, *'England Arise': The Labour Party and Popular Politics in 1940s Britain* (1995). John Ramsden provides a more formal description of a changing Conservative Party in *The Age of Balfour and Baldwin 1902–40* (1978). Biographies are especially useful for examining the professional politician—and the significance of their imperial interests. Good examples are Peter T. Marsh, *Joseph Chamberlain* (1994), Philip Williamson, *Stanley Baldwin* (1999), and Keith Robbins, *Churchill* (1992).

Two excellent overviews of imperial politics are especially helpful. P. J. Cain and A. G. Hopkins, *British Imperialism: Crisis and Disintegration 1914–90* (1993) is strongest on economic aspects. For politics and policies see the authoritative essays in Judith M. Brown and Wm. Roger Louis (eds.), *The Oxford History of the British Empire*, vol. iv: *The Twentieth Century* (1999). For a fuller case study of India's civil servants, see David C. Potter, *India's Political Administrators, 1919–1983* (1986). Labour's imperial policies are regularly attacked by scholars, although comparatively little work has been done on the policy groups within or associated with the party that helped develop a more constructive approach in the 1930s. The best books are currently S. Howe, *Anticolonialism in British politics* (1993), R. J. Moore, *Escape from Empire: The Attlee Government and the Indian Problem* (1983), and D. Cannadine, *Ornamentalism* (2001).

The connection between Irish events and Imperial politics is widely recognized but not widely studied. For informed introductions to Ireland's often unfamiliar internal politics, see in particular K. Theodore Hoppen, *Ireland since 1800* (1989), R. F. Foster, *Modern Ireland 1600–1972* (1988), and J. J. Lee, *Ireland 1912–1985* (1989).

Chapter 3

Two books by Norman Davies, *Europe: A History* (1996) and *The Isles: A History* (1999) offer stimulating and contentious ways of 'placing' the British

Isles. What might have been is suggested in Roy Denman, *Missed Chances: Britain and Europe in the Twentieth Century* (1996).

Particular relationships are pursued in P. M. H. Bell, *France and Britain 1900–1940: Entente and Estrangement* (1996), A. M. Birke, *Britain and Germany: Historical Relations and Comparisons* (1999), Keith Robbins, *Present and Past: British Images of Germany in the First Half of the Twentieth century and their Historical Legacy* (1999), Benedikt Stuchtey and Peter Wende (eds.), *British and German Historiography 1750–1950* (2000), and Anne Orde, *The Eclipse of Great Britain: The United States and British Imperial Decline, 1895–1956* (1996)

Insular components can be unpacked in the following particular histories: T. M. Devine, *The Scottish Nation 1700–2000* (1999), K. O. Morgan, *Modern Wales: Politics, Places and People* (1995), J. J. Lee, *Ireland 1912–1985: Politics and Society* (1989), James Loughlin, *Ulster Unionism and British National Identity since 1885* (1995), J. Belchem, *Merseypride: Essays in Liverpool Exceptionalism* (2000). People becoming British can be followed in G. Hirschfeld (ed.), *Exile in Great Britain* (1984) and Marion Berghahn, *Continental Britons: German-Jewish Refugees from Nazi Germany* (1988). Patriotisms that might have to be acquired are identified in J. H. Grainger, *Patriotisms: Britain 1900–1939* (1986) and Keith Robbins, *History, Religion and Identity in Modern Britain* (1993) and *Great Britain: Identities, Institutions and the Idea of Britishness* (1998).

Imperial dimensions are assessed in D. A. Low, *Eclipse of Empire* (1991), P. J. Cain and A. G. Hopkins, *British Imperialism: Crisis and Deconstruction 1914–1990* (1993), and Judith M. Brown and Wm. Roger Louis, *The Oxford History of the British Empire: The Twentieth Century* (1999).

Carriers and interpreters of the British way can themselves be studied in the following: David Cannadine, *G. M. Trevelyan: A Life in History* (1992), Roland Hill, *Lord Acton* (2000), Victor Eske, *From Belloc to Churchill: Private Scholars, Public Culture and the Crisis of British Liberalism 1900–1939* (1996), and Frank Eyck, *G. P. Gooch: A Study in History and Politics* (1982).

Chapter 4

A solid and informative, if Anglocentric, introduction to British cultural attitudes and behaviour in this period is Ross McKibbin, *Classes and Cultures: England 1918–1951* (1998). For high culture in particular, see Noel Annan's personal reflections in *Our Age: Portrait of a Generation* (1990) or Valentine Cunningham, *British Writers of the Thirties* (1988). Joseph McAleer, *Popular Publishing and Publishing in Britain, 1914–50* (1992) provides a good account of popular reading patterns. D. L. LeMahieu offers an interesting exploration of the development of a middlebrow culture in his *A Culture for Democracy: Mass Communication and the Cultured Mind in Britain Between the Wars* (1988), while Alison Light, *Forever England: Femininity, Literature and*

Conservatism Between the Wars (1991) is an indispensable discussion of the 'feminization' of interwar culture.

Broadcasting has been well served by, for instance, Asa Briggs's multivolume *History of Broadcasting in the United Kingdom* (1961–79) and by Paddy Scannell and David Cardiff, *Serving the Nation: a Social History of British Broadcasting 1922–39* (1991), though John Davies, *Broadcasting and the BBC in Wales* (1994), W. H. McDowell, *The History of BBC Broadcasting in Scotland 1923–1983* (1992), and Rex Cathcart, *The Most Contrary Region: The BBC in Northern Ireland 1924–1984* (1984) offer important sub-national perspectives. For cinema, see Jeffrey Richards, *Age of the Dream Palace: Cinema and Society in Britain 1930–39* (1984) and his edited collection *The Unknown 1930s: an Alternative History of the British Cinema, 1929–39* (1998). Individual sports histories are many and varied, but the collection of chapters in Tony Mason (ed.), *Sport in Britain: A Social History* (1989) offers a good overview. For religion, see especially John Wolffe, *God and Greater Britain: Religion and National Life in Britain and Ireland 1843–1945* (1994).

British wartime culture is comprehensively addressed in Angus Calder's classic *The People's War* (1969), though see too his more recent *The Myth of the Blitz* (1991) or Nick Hayes and Jeff Hill (eds.), *Millions Like Us? British Culture in the Second World War* (1999). Finally, Robert Graves and Alan Hodge, *The Long Weekend: A Social History of Great Britain 1918–1939* (1940) offers a vivid if anecdotal contemporary window onto the attitudes, preoccupations, and personalities of the times.

Chapter 5

Henry Pelling, *Britain and the Second World War* (1970) remains a useful starting point for the impact of the war on British government and society, while Mark Donnelly, *Britain in the Second World War* (1999) summarizes recent historical debates in this area. Brian Brivati and Helen Jones (eds.), *What Difference Did the War Make?* (1993) contains an interesting collection of essays. John W. Young, *Britain and the World in the Twentieth Century* (1997) serves as an antidote to those who have been too obsessed with the notion of Britain's decline, while Sean Greenwood, *Britain and the Cold War* (2000) emphasizes the important role which the country continued to play in world affairs in the immediate postwar period. Alan Bullock, *Ernest Bevin: Foreign Secretary* (1983) considers Britain's postwar inheritance through the eyes of Labour's masterful foreign minister.

Correlli Barnett's works are fundamental to the debate on the cost of Britain's victory and the use or misuse to which that victory was put. But his thesis is controversial and has sometimes been used for political rather than historical purposes. *The Audit of War* (1986) and *The Lost Victory* (1995) may be read with interest but warrant a sceptical eye. Alec Cairncross, *The Price of*

War (1986), Alan Sked, *Britain's Decline: Problems and Perspectives* (1987), and Alan Milward, *The Economic Effects of Two World Wars on Britain* (1970) offer useful material in a less tendentious manner. Sean Greenwood, *Britain and European Cooperation since 1945* (1992) is among many works which consider the beginnings of Britain's troubled relationship with the processes of European integration, while John Kent, *British Imperial Strategy and the Origins of the Cold War* (1993) emphasizes the continuing importance of the imperial dimension.

The debate on the existence and significance of a political consensus has spawned a vast literature in its own right. Paul Addison, *The Road to 1945* (1975) remains fundamental and, in the present writer's view at least, essentially correct. Kevin Jefferys, *The Churchill Coalition and Wartime Politics* (1991) offers a reasoned critique. David Dutton, *British Politics since 1945: The Rise, Fall and Rebirth of Consensus* (1997) reviews the debate while coming down firmly in favour of the reality of a consensus. The postwar Labour government has been well served by its historians, with the majority of the literature (*pace* Barnett) adopting a positive approach to the achievements of Attlee's administration. Kenneth Morgan, *Labour in Power 1945–51* (1984) offers the best introduction. The same author's *The People's Peace: British History 1945–1990* (1990) sets the importance of this period in a broader chronological framework, while Peter Hennessy, *Never Again: Britain 1945–51* (1992) and Alec Cairncross, *Years of Recovery* (1985) both emphasize the scale of Labour's achievement. Steven Fielding, Peter Thompson, and Nick Tiratsoo, *England Arise!* (1995) contains important revisionist essays.

Chapter 6

Readers seeking an overview of economic policy and performance over the course of the twentieth century can find very readable and informed accounts in M. Dintenfass, *The Decline of Industrial Britain, 1870–1980* (1992), B. W. E. Alford, *Britain in the World Economy since 1880* (1996), P. Johnson (ed.), *Twentieth Century Britain* (1994), and A. Booth, *The British Economy in the Twentieth Century* (2001). Britain's relative economic performance before 1914 is detailed in S. Pollard, *Britain's Prime and Britain's Decline* (1989) and in J. Dormois and M. Dintenfass (eds.), The *British Industrial Decline* (1999). The period from 1914 is adequately covered in P. Dewey, *War and Progress: Britain 1914–1945* (1997) and S. Glynn and A Booth, *Modern Britain* (1996).

More specialized treatment of some of the principal themes in this chapter can be found in the essays contained in B. Elbaum and W. Lazonick (eds.), The *Decline of the British Economy* (1986) and P. Clarke and C. Trebilcock (eds.), *Understanding Decline: Perceptions and Realities of British Economic Performance* (1997). The 'political economy' of Britain's relative performance since the turn of the century is addressed in A. Gamble, *Britain in Decline*

(4th edn., 1994). Advanced treatment of economic performance and policy outcomes in Britain over most of the period currently under review can be found in R. Floud and D. McCloskey (eds.), *The Economic History of Britain since 1700* (2nd edn., 1994), vol. ii: *1860–1939*.

Chapter 7

The three best introductions to the subject are Jose Harris, *Private Lives, Public Spirit: A Social History of Britain, 1870–1914* (1993), Ross McKibbin, *Classes and Cultures: England 1918–1951* (1998), and John Stevenson, *British Society 1914–45*, (1984). Their analysis may be illuminated by contemporary evidence in the books cited in this chapter, in J. B. Priestley, *English Journey* (1934), and in John Stevenson (ed.), *Social Conditions in Britain between the Wars* (1977). A broad range of statistical material and analysis is provided by A. H. Halsey and J. Webb (eds.), *Twentieth-Century British Social Trends* (2000). More detailed analysis is available in A. B. Atkinson and A. J. Harrison, *Distribution of Personal Wealth in Britain* (1978) and W. D. Rubinstein, *Wealth and Inequality in Britain* (1986). In relation to poverty, Bernard Harris, *The Health of the Schoolchild* (1995) and Paul Johnson, *Saving and Spending: The Working-Class Economy in Britain, 1870–1939* (1985) provide equally valuable statistical evidence combined with the analysis, respectively, of government policy and poverty culture.

Individual chapters on regional variation are included in F. M. L. Thompson (ed.), *The Cambridge Social History of Britain 1750–1950* (3 vols., 1990). They may be supplemented by three national studies: Derek Birrell and Alan Murie, *Policy and Government in Northern Ireland: Lessons of Devolution* (1980), Kenneth O. Morgan, *Rebirth of a Nation: Wales 1880–1980* (1981), and Ian Levitt, *Poverty and Welfare in Scotland, 1890–1948* (1988). The considerable literature on gender inequality is well summarized in Sue Bruley, *Women in Britain* (1999), whilst a valuable collection of contemporary evidence is Elizabeth Roberts, *A Woman's Place: An Oral History of Working Class Women, 1890–1940* (1984). The fiscal and intellectual bases for government growth are expertly examined in M. J. Daunton, 'Payment and participation: welfare and state-formation in Britain, 1900–1951', *Past and Present* 150 (1996), pp. 169–216 and Jose Harris, 'Political thought and the welfare state, 1870–1940', *Past and Present* 135 (1992), pp. 116–41. The evolution of welfare policy itself is covered in John Macnicol, *The Politics of Retirement in Britain, 1878–1948* (1998) and Rodney Lowe, *The Welfare State in Britain Since 1945* (1993; 2nd edn., 1999), whilst a magisterial biography of one of the leading participants is Jose Harris, *William Beveridge: A Biography* (1977; rev. edn., 1997). Powerful reminders of the relative resilience of the voluntary sector are provided by Martin Gorsky, John Mohan, and Martin Powell, 'British voluntary hospitals, 1871–1938: the geography of provision and utilization', *Journal of*

Historical Geography 25 (1999), pp. 463–82 and by D. Gladstone (ed.), *Before Beveridge: Welfare before the Welfare State* (1999). The ahistorical assumptions underlying more polemic attacks on state welfare, however, are effectively exposed in Jose Harris, 'Enterprise and welfare states: a comparative perspective', *Transactions of the Royal Historical Society* (1990) and Jim Tomlinson, 'Welfare and the economy: the economic impact of the welfare state, 1945–1951', *Twentieth Century British History* 6 (1995), pp. 194–219.

Chronology

1907   Anglo-Russian agreement
Rudyard Kipling wins Nobel prize for literature

1908   Asquith becomes Prime Minister
Old Age Pensions Act
London hosts Olympic Games
Baden-Powell forms Boy Scouts

1909   Lloyd George's 'People's Budget' introduces redistributory
graduated and land taxes
Morley–Minto reforms on Indian governance

1910   Liberal government dependent on Labour and Irish support
constitutional crisis concerning the powers of the House of Lords
death of Edward VII/accession of George V
Roger Fry's post-Impressionist exhibition at the Royal Academy

1911   Parliament Act restricts Lords' power of veto
National Insurance Act introduces health and
unemployment insurance
Daily Mirror is first national daily to reach one million
circulation
Delhi 'durbar'

1912   *Daily Herald* launched

1913   Irish Home Rule Bill twice passed by Commons and twice
rejected by Lords
maternity benefit introduced

1914   war declared on Germany, then on Austria-Hungary
British Expeditionary Force departs for France

1915   British troops land at Gallipoli
rent control introduced
formation of Coalition government

1916   Battle of Jutland
Battle of the Somme
Easter Rising in Dublin proclaims Irish Republic

Lloyd George becomes Prime Minister in new Coalition government

Home Rule Leagues established in India

1917   United States enters the war

1918   Ottoman Empire, Austria-Hungary, and Germany sign armistices

Victory for Lloyd George Coalition in general election

Representation of the People Act enfranchises all men over 21 and most women over 30

Maternity and Child Welfare Act

Sinn Fein victorious in Ireland but boycott Westminster

Montagu–Chelmsford report on Indian governance

1919   Peace settlement: Versailles, St Germain, and Neuilly treaties signed

National Council of Social Service established

Housing and Town Planning Act

Government of India Act establishes principle of dyarchy

war in Ireland

1920   Unemployment Insurance Act greatly extends coverage

disestablishment of the Church of England in Wales

1921   Irish Free State secures independence

T. S. Eliot, *The Waste Land*

James Joyce, *Ulysses*, published in Paris (first UK edition 1936)

Richmal Crompton, *Just William*

British Broadcasting Company begins broadcasting from London; John Reith appointed first Managing Director

1922   fall of Lloyd George Coalition government

1923   Baldwin forms Conservative government

first Wembley FA Cup Final

1924   MacDonald forms first Labour (minority) government

Baldwin forms Conservative government after general election revival of Tailteann Games in Irish Free State

British Empire Exhibition at Wembley

Lee Commission on the role of the Indian Civil Service

1925 Widows', Orphans', and Old Age Contributory Pensions Act

BBC's Daventry long-wave transmitter opens

1926 Imperial Conference considers Balfour Report on inter-imperial relations

General Strike

1927 BBC incorporated as the British Broadcasting Corporation; Sir John Reith appointed Director-General; BBC broadcasts first live sports outside broadcasts

'Abide with Me' first sung at the FA Cup Final

Distribution Act institutes film 'quota quickies'

1928 Representation of the People Act extends vote to all women

House of Commons rejects Church of England's Revised Prayer Book

Construction of Singapore naval base (continues until 1938)

1929 Ramsay MacDonald forms minority Labour government

Local Government Act abolishes poor law guardians

Simon Commission to review constitutional position in India

Blackmail (Alfred Hitchcock) released

1930 inaugural British Empire Games held in Canada

BBC Regional Programme launched

Simon Commission on India reports

1931 Gold Standard suspended

National government formed under MacDonald

general election gives government large majority

Round Table conferences on India

Statute of Westminster defines inter-imperial relationships, confirming autonomy for Dominions

1932 Ottawa conference establishes system of imperial preference

election of Fianna Fáil in Irish Free State

MCC cricket 'Bodyline' tour of Australia (and 1933)

George V broadcasts his first Christmas speech to Britain and the Empire

Shakespeare Memorial Theatre opens at Stratford-upon-Avon

Mosley founds British Union of Fascists

Rutherford, Cockcroft, and Chadwick split the atom

1933 Radio Luxembourg begins broadcasts to Britain

Daily Herald hits two million circulation

The Private Life of Henry VIII (Alexander Korda) released

1934 Unemployment Act nationalizes poor relief for the able-bodied

Special Areas (Development and Improvement) Act

New Survey of London Life and Labour

J. B. Priestley, *English Journey*

1935 National government returned under Baldwin

Government of India Act

1936 death of George V

abdication of Edward VIII and succession of George VI

John Boyd Orr, *Food, Health and Income*

Left Book Club launched by Victor Gollancz

Penguin Books launched by Allen Lane

BBC Television Service launched (London area only)

J. M. Keynes, *General Theory of Employment, Interest and Money*

A. J. Ayer, *Language, Truth and Logic*

1937 Chamberlain succeeds Baldwin as Prime Minister

Irish Free State constitution removes oath of allegiance to the Crown

B. Seebohm Rowntree, *Human Needs of Labour* (in revised form)

George Orwell, *The Road to Wigan Pier*

Mass Observation founded by Madge, Harrisson, and Jennings

1938   Munich Agreement

Picture Post launched by Edward Hulton

Empire Exhibition in Glasgow

1939   Britain declares war on Germany

It's That Man Again (ITMA) first broadcast

BBC television suspended on outbreak of war; BBC Home Service replaces National and Regional Programmes

White Paper on Palestine limits Jewish immigration

1940   Churchill succeeds Chamberlain as Prime Minister; formation of wartime coalition

Dunkirk evacuation

Battle of Britain

Golden Treasury of Scottish Verse, ed. Hugh MacDiarmid

Gone With the Wind opens in London

BBC launches Forces Programme

Colonial Welfare and Development Act

1941   British forces active in North Africa

British/US 'Atlantic Charter'

Britain declares war on Japan

B. Seebohm Rowntree, *Poverty and Progress*

Determination of Needs Act abolishes household means test

Purchase Tax introduced

1942   Surrender of Singapore

British–Soviet Treaty of Friendship

William Temple, *Christianity and Social Order*

Beveridge Report published

Cripps mission to India; Quit India movement

1943   Battle of the Atlantic
PAYE introduced as income tax greatly extended
Daily Express hits three million circulation

1944   White Paper on postwar employment policy
Butler's Education Act
first edition of BBC's *War Report*
F. von Hayek, *The Road to Serfdom*
John Hilton, *Rich Man, Poor Man*

1945   German surrender
Labour government under Attlee returned with large majority

1946   BBC radio reorganized: Home Service, Light Programme, and
Third Programme
BBC Television Service restarts
Family Allowances introduced
New constitution for Nigeria, Gold Coast, and Gambia

1947   partition and independence for India and Pakistan, which
remain in the Commonwealth

1948   British Nationality Act
Marshall Aid agreement
The 'Appointed Day' on which the NHS, national insurance,
and national assistance were introduced; formal abolition
of the Poor Law
Empire Windrush docks, carrying first wave of
Jamaican immigrants
Representation of the People Act
London hosts the first postwar Olympic Games
Burma, on independence, leaves the Commonwealth
Ceylon (Sri Lanka), on independence, remains
in Commonwealth
British withdrawal from Palestine mandate

1949   Formation of North Atlantic Treaty Organization
promulgation of Republic of Ireland and departure from the
Commonwealth
George Orwell, *1984*

1950 Attlee forms Labour government with slim majority
Schuman Plan—Britain keeps its distance
Britain recognizes Communist China
first postwar British Empire Games
outbreak of Korean War

1951 Churchill forms Conservative government after election victory
Festival of Britain opens
B. Seebohm Rowntree, *Poverty and the Welfare State*

Maps

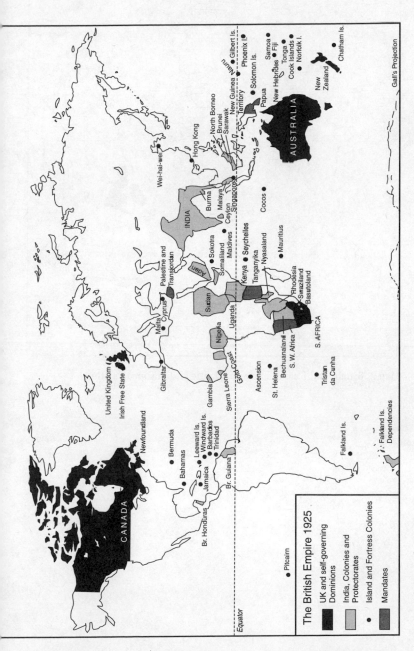

The British Empire 1925

- **UK and self-governing Dominions**
- **India, Colonies and Protectorates**
- Island and Fortress Colonies
- **Mandates**

Equator

Gall's Projection

United Kingdom
Irish Free State
Newfoundland
CANADA
Bermuda
Bahamas
Leeward Is.
Windward Is.
Barbados
Trinidad
Jamaica
Br. Honduras
Br. Guiana
Falkland Is.
Falkland Is. Dependencies
Pitcairn

Gibraltar
Malta
Cyprus
Palestine and Transjordan
Aden
Sudan
Nigeria
Gold Coast
Gambia
Sierra Leone
Ascension
St. Helena
Tristan da Cunha
Sokotra
Somaliland
Maldives
Seychelles
Uganda
Kenya
Tanganyika
Nyasaland
Mauritius
Rhodesia
Swaziland
Basutoland
S. AFRICA
Bechuanaland
S. W. Africa

INDIA
Burma
Ceylon
Malaya
Singapore
Cocos
Hong Kong
Wei-hai-wei
North Borneo
Brunei
Sarawak
New Guinea Territory
Papua
AUSTRALIA
Nauru
Gilbert Is.
Phoenix Is.
Solomon Is.
New Hebrides
Samoa
Fiji
Tonga
Cook Islands
Norfolk I.
New Zealand
Chatham Is.

Map 1 The British Empire in 1925.

Map 2 Britain and Ireland in their Atlantic and European setting.

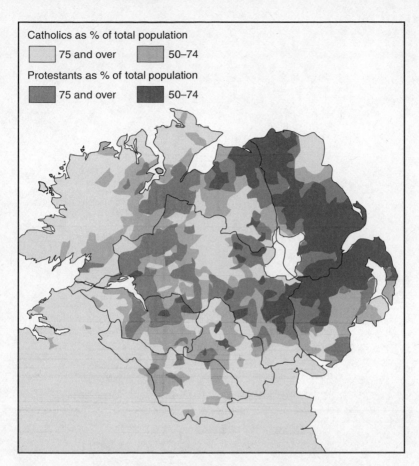

Map 3 Distribution of Catholics and Protestants in Ulster by electoral divisions (1911).

Source: T. W. Moody, F. X. Martin, and F. J. Byrne eds., *A New History of Ireland*, vol. IX, Part II (Oxford, 1984)

Index

British Empire (*cont'd.*)
  pattern of democratic change
    within 55
  restored to full territorial extent 138
  Scotland's patriotism 78–9
British Guiana 14
British Nationality Act (1948) 148, 220
British Union of Fascists 66, 150
British Way and Purpose, The 36,
  73–102, 230
British Workers' League 50
Britishness 78, 83, 84, 91, 103, 124, 126,
  128, 150
  clichés of 133
  defined in terms of self-governing
    Dominions 148
  inward-looking interwar
    formulations of 129
  wartime 131
Britten, Benjamin, Lord 105
broadcasts 28, 33, 66, 119
  outside 116, 126–7
  populist 132
  religious 112, 124
broadsheets 110–11
Brockway, Fenner (Baron) 69
Brooke, Rupert 106
Bryant, Arthur 122
Bryce, James 88–9
Brynmawr 215
'Bulldog Drummond' 119, 121
Bullock, Alan 140
bureaucracy 192–3, 218
Burma 14, 37, 39
Burroughs, Edgar Rice 108
Burton, Nat 133
Butler, R. A. 221
by-elections 150
Byelorussia 147
Byzantine emperors 41

Caernarfon 80
Cairncross, Alec 142
Cambridge University 2, 60, 73, 87, 127
  Boat Race 116, 126
  King's College Chapel 118

Campbell, R. J. 3
Canada 17, 26, 32, 40, 176
  emigration to 38
  Empire Day 25
  first reigning British monarch to
    visit 28
  GDP per capita 160
  Royal Canadian Navy 21
  troops from 16
  see also Hamilton; Laurier;
    Newfoundland; Ottawa
Canterbury, archbishop of, *see*
  Davidson
capacity 180, 186
  adaptive 193
  excess 175, 187
  inefficient 187
Cape Colony 14, 15
capital 172, 175, 180, 186
  cultural 183
  external and internal loss 188
  industrial, political subordination
    of 168
  redistribution of 153–4
  shake-out of 187
  social 183
capitalism 169, 171
Cardiff 80, 221
Cardus, Neville 116
Caribbean 14, 39, 40
  immigrants from 134
Carnegie Trust 223
cartelization 181, 185, 187
cartoons 126
Catholicism/Catholics 65, 77, 83, 115,
  117
  clergy 123
  converts to 86
  treatment of 54
Cecil, Robert, 1st Viscount Cecil of
  Chelwood 44
celebrity 111, 113, 119
'Celtic fringe' 70
Celts 96, 123
CEMA (Committee for Education in
  Music and the Arts) 130, 134

Lloyd George, David (1st Earl) 24, 44,
    45, 48, 50, 57, 79, 82, 95, 203, 204,
    224
    reputation in Wales tarnished 80
loans 143, 174
local government 53, 217, 225
    restoration of powers to 68
London 52, 112, 114, 125, 131, 207
    Blitz 67, 132, 151, 152
    Cenotaph 80
    Charing Cross Road 128
    Earl's Court 29
    East End 118
    Guildhall 26
    lousy with parasites 5
    Millennium Dome 159
    Muslim communities 118
    National Gallery 130
    Olympia 29
    Palladium 135
    poverty 210
    schooling 214
    Underground 130
    Whitehall 80
    see also City of London; Wembley
London County Council 66, 68
London Exhibitions Limited 29
London School of Economics 60, 62
Londonderry, Marquis of 58
Lords, House of 45, 46, 149
    strengthening 50
Low, David 126
Low, Sidney 92
lowbrow tastes 110
lower classes 134
loyalty 20, 85
    local 223
Luftwaffe 151
Lynn, Vera 121, 132

McCormick, John 123
MacDiarmid, Hugh 122
MacDonald, Ramsay 47, 49, 53, 62–3,
    95–6, 147
Macdonell, A. G. 122
McKibbin, R. 204, 206, 207

Mackinder, Sir Halford 3
Maclean, John 78
McMahon Act (US 1946) 144
MacNeice, Louis 106, 130
Mafeking, relief of (1900) 16
magazines:
    family- and juvenile-oriented 107
    literary 106
    serial 108
    women's 111
Magnet 119
Maitland, F. W. 87
Malawi 14
Malaya 39, 40
    Japanese invasion (1941) 21
Malaysia 14
Malta 26
Manchester 115, 124
Manchester Guardian 116
mandarins 43–4
mandates 92, 146
Mannheim, Karl 96
manual workers 154, 202, 203, 206,
    226
    antagonism towards 205
    mortality rate for 214
manufacturing sector 33, 177, 204
markets 177
    financial 182
    fluctuating 181–2
    foreign 34
    imperial 34
    international 193
    invasion of 176
    low income 165
    mass 107, 108, 124
    proximity 180
    world 194
Marlborough, Dukes of 143, 153
marriage(s) 65, 218, 219
    'companionate' 220
    mixed 221
Marryat, Captain (Frederick) 119
Marshall, T. H. 198
Marshall Aid (1947) 144
Marwick, Arthur 6, 7